Quick Creative Quilting™

Edited by Jeanne Stauffer
and Sandra Hatch

HOUSE of
WHITE
BIRCHES
PUBLISHERS
SINCE 1947

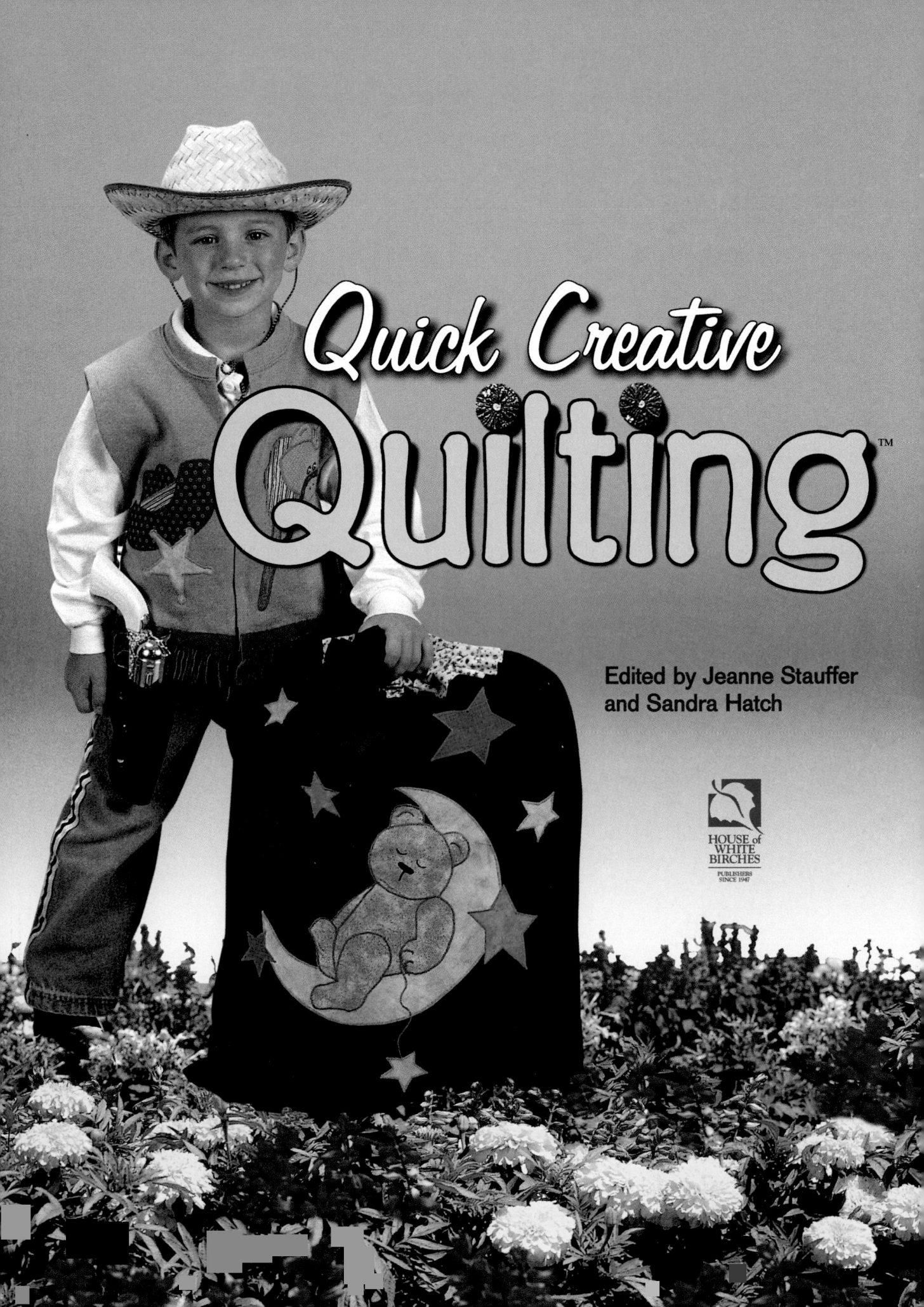

Contents

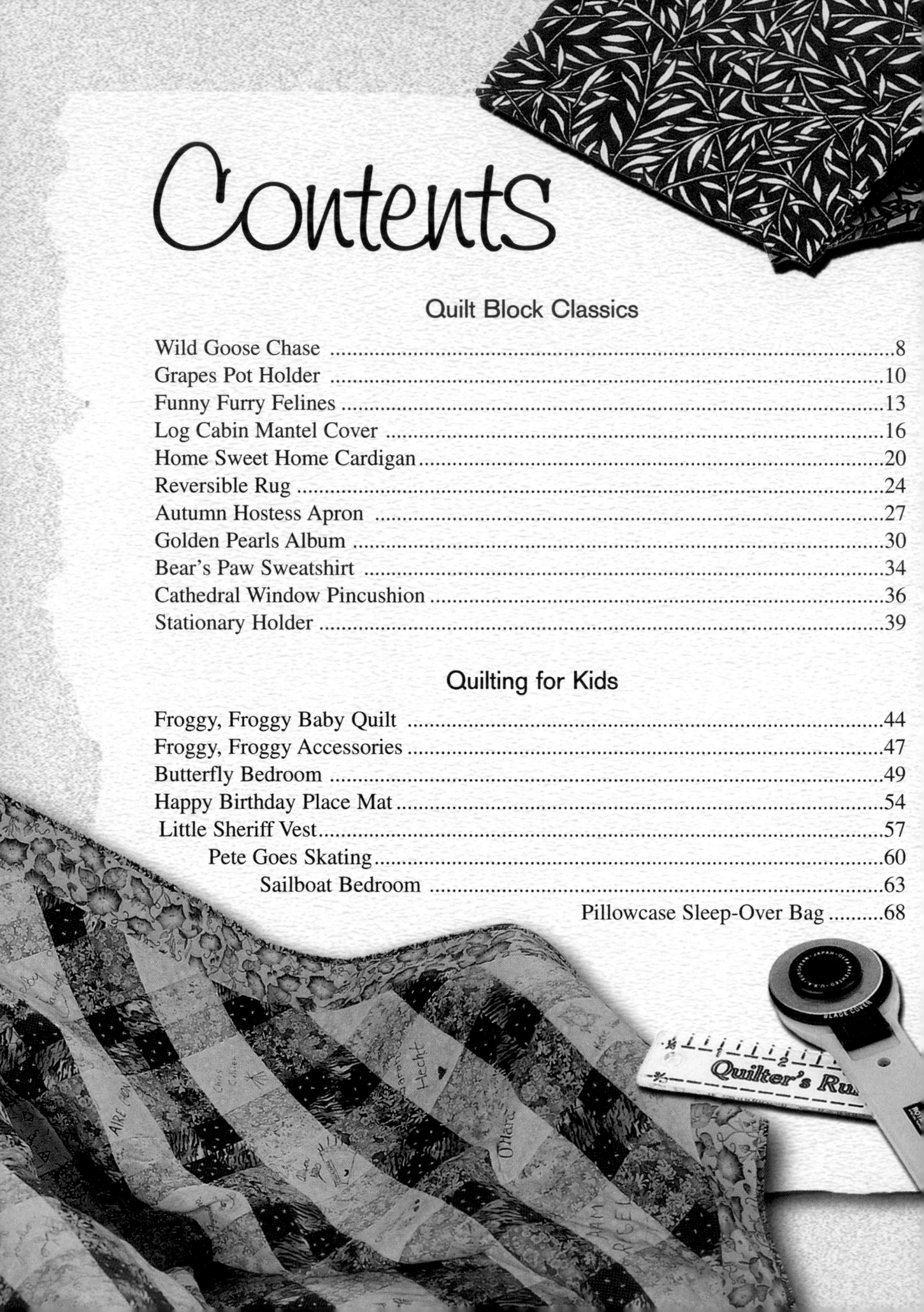

Quilt Block Classics

Quilting for Kids

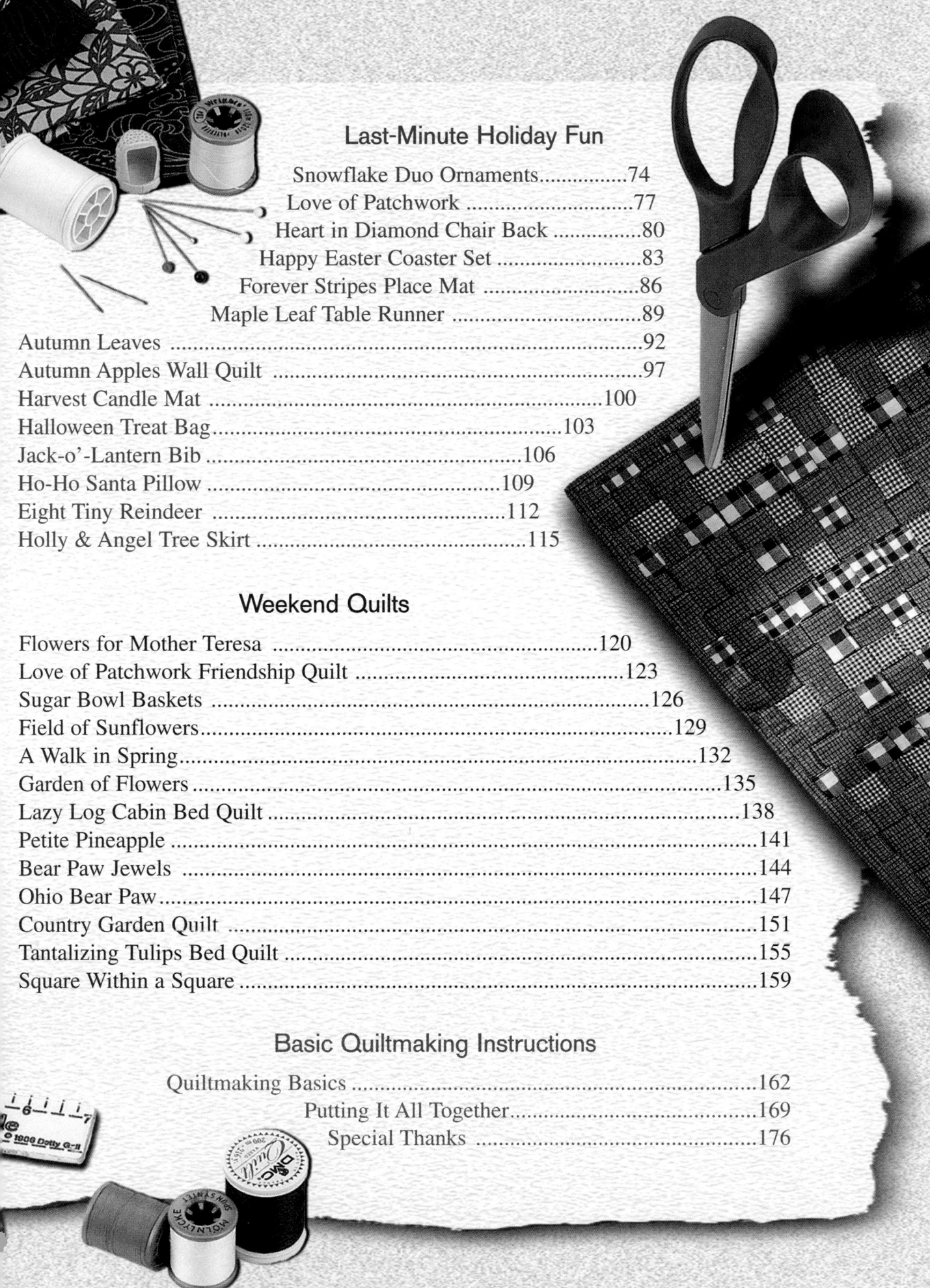

Last-Minute Holiday Fun

Weekend Quilts

Basic Quiltmaking Instructions

Editors: Sandra L. Hatch, Jeanne Stauffer
Associate Editor: Barb Sprunger
Copy Editor: Mary Nowak
Editorial Coordinator: Tanya Turner

Photography: Tammy Christian, Jennifer Fourman, Jeff Chilcote
Photography Stylist: Arlou Wittwer
Photography Assistant: Linda Quinlan

Production Coordinator: Brenda Gallmeyer
Book Design: Sandy Bauman
Technical Artist: Connie Rand
Production Artist: Ronda Bollenbacher
Production Assistants: Shirley Blalock, Dana Brotherton, Carol Dailey
Traffic Coordinator: Sandra Beres

Publishers: Carl H. Muselman, Arthur K. Muselman
Chief Executive Officer: John Robinson
Marketing Director: Scott Moss
Product Development Director: Vivian Rothe
Publishing Services Manager: Brenda R. Wendling

Printed in the United States of America
First Printing: 2000
Library of Congress Number: 99-073199
ISBN: 1-882138-51-1

A Quick Note

Some quilters have the mistaken impression that beautiful and creative quilting projects can't be made using quicker methods—that somehow creative does not equal quick. The wonderful projects in this book prove otherwise.

We asked our designers to create a project that could be made in a few hours or a weekend. Of course, a large quilt cannot be constructed and hand-quilted in a weekend, so we recommended machine techniques for all projects. A few hand stitches could be added to smaller projects to add a special touch for those quilters who love handwork.

Our designers challenged themselves to create a variety of projects to appeal to different tastes. When choosing projects for this book we considered young and old, beginner and advanced and a variety of decorating styles.

If you are looking for last-minute holiday decorations, something for a child, traditional patterns used in new ways or a quilt to make in a weekend, you will find just what you are looking for in this inspiring book of brand-new designs.

Much thought and work go into the production of a book such as *Quick Creative Quilting*. The process begins with an idea which is circulated to designers all over the United States and Canada. Their ideas are considered and a team chooses those that most fit the book's theme. From this point instructions and drawings are done, photographs taken and layout begins. It is always a pleasant surprise to me to see what the photos, drawings and instructions look like when they are finally all put together in a book.

I am proud of the team who has worked together to bring you this beautiful book. It is our desire to bring you a wonderful selection of projects with easy-to-follow instructions and drawings to illustrate them. We hope you will agree that our work was worth the effort, and thousands of quilters will spend enjoyable hours recreating our projects in their own creative way.

Sincerely,

Sandra L. Hatch

Sandra L. Hatch

Quilt Block Classics

Start with a traditional quilt block design and turn it into a nap mat, Cathedral Window pincushion, Log Cabin mantel cover, wearables and more. They are quick and easy to make as gifts for your family and friends.

Wild Goose Chase

By Jill Reber

Make a table runner for the holiday season using plaids for a homespun look.

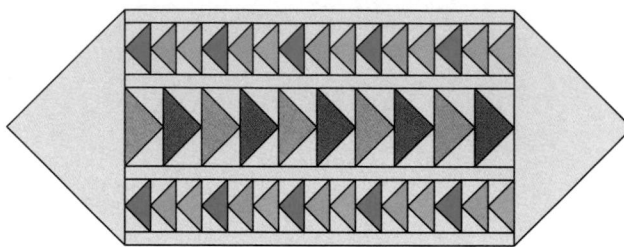

Wild Goose Chase
Placement Diagram
18" x 48"

Instructions

Step 1. Cut one strip tan check 3 7/8" by fabric width; subcut into 3 7/8" squares. Cut each square in half on one diagonal to make A triangles; you will need 20 A triangles.

Step 2. Cut red plaid or red check 7 1/4" x 7 1/4" squares in half on both diagonals to make B triangles; you will need 10 B triangles.

Step 3. Sew an A triangle to each short side of B to make a Flying Geese unit as shown in Figure 1; press seams toward A. Repeat for 10 units.

Figure 1
Sew B to A as shown.

Figure 2
Join 10 units to make a strip.

Step 4. Join the 10 A-B units to make a strip as shown in Figure 2; press seams in one direction.

Step 5. Cut three strips tan check 2 7/8" by fabric width; subcut into 2 7/8" squares. Cut each square in half on one diagonal to make C triangles; you will need 60 C triangles.

Step 6. Subcut each 5 1/4" x 16" strip green plaid or check into 5 1/4" squares. Cut each square in half on both diagonals to make D triangles. You will need 30 D triangles.

Step 7. Sew a C triangle to each short side of D; press seams toward C. Repeat for 30 units.

Project Specifications

Skill Level: Beginner
Project Size: 18" x 48"

Materials

- 3 different 5 1/4" x 16" strips green plaids or checks
- 3 squares red plaids or checks 7 1/4" x 7 1/4"
- 1 yard tan check
- Backing 22" x 52"
- Batting 22" x 52"
- 3 1/2 yards self-made or purchased binding
- Neutral color all-purpose thread
- Basic sewing supplies and tools

Step 8. Join 15 units as shown in Figure 3 to make one strip; press seams in one direction. Repeat for two strips.

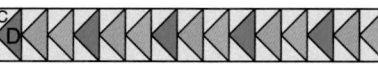

Figure 3
Join 15 units to make a strip.

Step 9. Cut four strips tan check 1 1/2" x 30 1/2". Join the pieced strips with the tan check strips as shown in Figure 4; press seams toward strips.

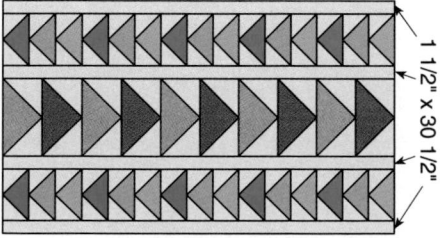

Figure 4
Join strips with 1 1/2" x 30 1/2" strips as shown.

Step 10. Cut one square tan check 13 5/8" x 13 5/8".

Cut in half on one diagonal to make two triangles. Sew a triangle to each end of the pieced unit.

Step 11. Finish referring to General Instructions. *Note: Project shown is machine-quilted in a meandering design on the tan check background and in a curved design and along*

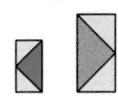

Flying Geese
2" x 4" Unit
3" x 6" Unit

Figure 5
Quilting design stitched on A and D triangles.

longest edge on the A and D triangles as shown in Figure 5. ❖

Grapes Pot Holder

By Barbara A. Clayton

Combine piecing with appliquéd leaves and yo-yos and machine embroidery to make these neat pot holders.

Instructions

Step 1. Prepare templates using pattern pieces given. Cut as directed on each piece for one pot holder; repeat for second pot holder.

Step 2. Sew a green solid B to opposite sides of E; repeat. Sew to opposite sides of D; press. Sew a purple print B to a green solid B to E to green solid B to purple print B; press. Repeat for second unit. Sew to the remaining sides of D to complete block piecing as shown in Figure 1. Repeat for second block.

Step 3. Turn under edge of each A circle 1/4"; hand-stitch in place using long stitches. Pull stitches to gather as shown in Figure 2. Knot and tie off; cut thread. Flatten to make yo-yo.

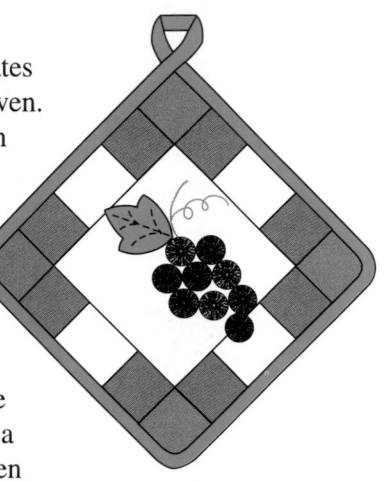

Grapes Pot Holder
Placement Diagram
8 1/2" x 8 1/2"

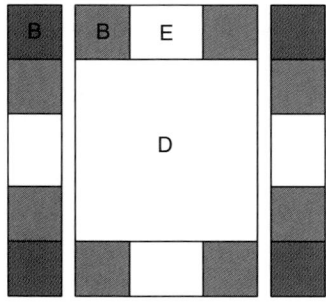

Figure 1
Piece block as shown.

Figure 2
Pull stitches to gather as shown.

Project Specifications

Skill Level: Intermediate
Project Size: 8 1/2" x 8 1/2"
Block Size: 8" x 8"
Number of Blocks: 2

Materials

- 1/8" yard or 6" x 16" scrap purple print
- 1/4 yard off-white solid
- Scraps of fabric in green solid and 2 shades of purple solid
- 1/3 yard dark green print
- 2 squares batting 8 1/2" x 8 1/2"
- 1 spool each white and dark green all-purpose and quilting thread
- Green rayon thread
- Clear nylon monofilament
- 6" x 6" piece fusible interfacing
- Basic sewing supplies and tools, white typing paper, black marker and water-erasable marker

Step 4. Pin leaf shapes to fusible interfacing pieces with glue side and right side together. Sew around each leaf. Clip curves and points and trim seams. Make a cut through the center back of the interfacing and turn each leaf right side out. Smooth points using pencil with broken lead or other pointed object.

Step 5. Referring to the Placement Diagram and photo of project, position yo-yo grapes and leaf

Figure 3
Reverse designs on 1 block.

on one pieced block. Fuse leaf in place. *Note: Reverse design on one pot holder to make one reversed pot holder as shown in Figure 3.* Machine-stitch leaf and yo-yo grape edges using clear nylon monofilament in the top of the machine and matching all-purpose thread in the bobbin. Repeat for second block.

Step 6. Trace pattern given for stem onto white typing paper with black marker. Pin the paper under appliquéd pot holder top to use as a sewing guide referring to the Placement Diagram for positioning.

Step 7. Using green rayon thread in the top of the machine and matching all-purpose thread in the bobbin, machine zigzag-stitch on marked lines. Repeat on leaf vein lines. Tear off paper when stitching is complete. Repeat for second pot holder.

Step 8. Cut two squares off-white solid 8 1/2" x 8 1/2"

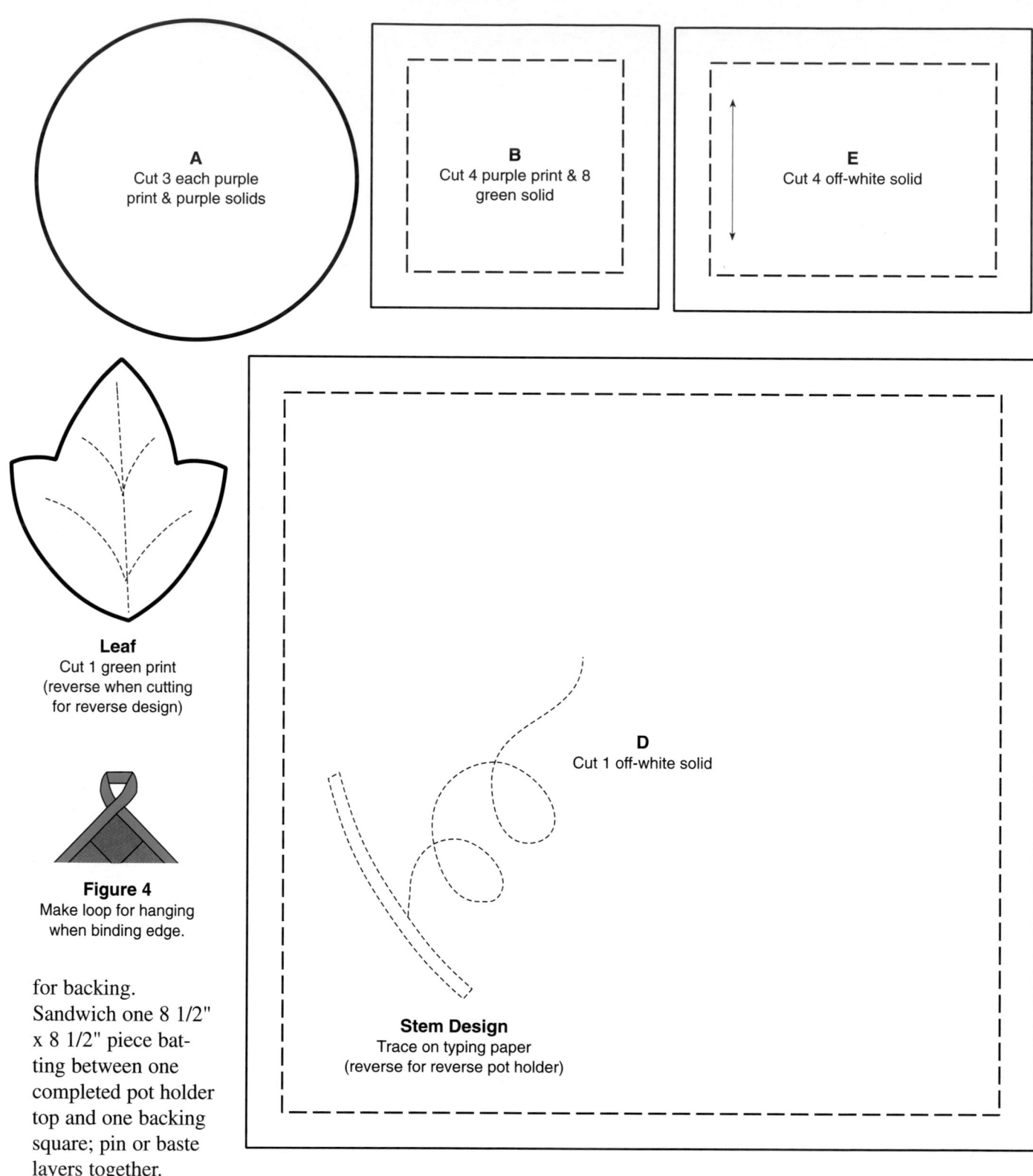

A
Cut 3 each purple
print & purple solids

B
Cut 4 purple print & 8
green solid

E
Cut 4 off-white solid

Leaf
Cut 1 green print
(reverse when cutting
for reverse design)

Figure 4
Make loop for hanging
when binding edge.

D
Cut 1 off-white solid

Stem Design
Trace on typing paper
(reverse for reverse pot holder)

for backing. Sandwich one 8 1/2" x 8 1/2" piece batting between one completed pot holder top and one backing square; pin or baste layers together.

Step 9. Hand-quilt in the ditch of block seams using white quilting thread. Hand-quilt 1/4" from appliquéd design edge using dark green quilting thread. Remove pins or basting.

Step 10. Round three corners on each pot holder

referring to the Placement Diagram for positioning.

Step 11. Prepare 2 1/2 yards self-made green print binding referring to the General Instructions.

Step 12. Bind the edges of each pot holder, making a loop for hanging on one corner referring to Figure 4. ❖

Funny Furry Felines

By Carla Schwab

Make this cat-lover's wall or lap quilt using soft and cuddly flannel.

Project Specifications

Skill Level: Beginner
Project Size: 47" x 47"
Block Size: 4" x 4"
Number of Blocks: 20

Materials

- 1/8 yard heavy black satin
- 1/3 yard gray flannel
- 1/2 yard white flannel
- 5/8 yard black flannel
- 1 yard blue plaid flannel
- Backing 51" x 51"
- Batting 51" x 51"
- 6 yards self-made or purchased binding
- Black and white all-purpose thread
- Black cotton yarn or floss
- 1/8 yard fusible transfer web
- Basic sewing supplies and tools and large-eye needle

Instructions

Step 1. Prepare template for A triangle using pattern piece given; cut as directed on the piece.

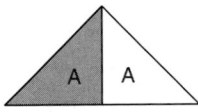

Figure 1
Join 2 A pieces as shown.

Step 2. Cut 20 squares white flannel 4 1/2" x 4 1/2" for B.

Step 3. Sew a gray flannel A to a white flannel A as shown in Figure 1; repeat for 40 units.

Step 4. Join two A units as shown in Figure 2; repeat for 20 blocks.

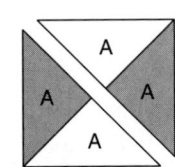

Figure 2
Join 2 A units as shown.

Step 5. Bond fusible transfer web to the wrong side of the black satin. Prepare templates for eye and nose. Trace shapes on paper side of fusible transfer web as directed on each piece for number to cut.

Step 6. Cut out shapes on traced lines; remove paper backing.

Step 7. Position two eyes and a nose on one pieced A unit referring to A template for placement; fuse in place. Repeat for all A units.

Step 8. Using black all-purpose thread, satin-stitch around each shape and from nose to bottom of triangle again referring to A template for placement.

Step 9. Join five blocks with four B squares to make a strip as shown in Figure 3; repeat for four strips.

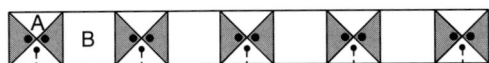

Figure 3
Join 5 pieced blocks with 4 B squares to make a strip.

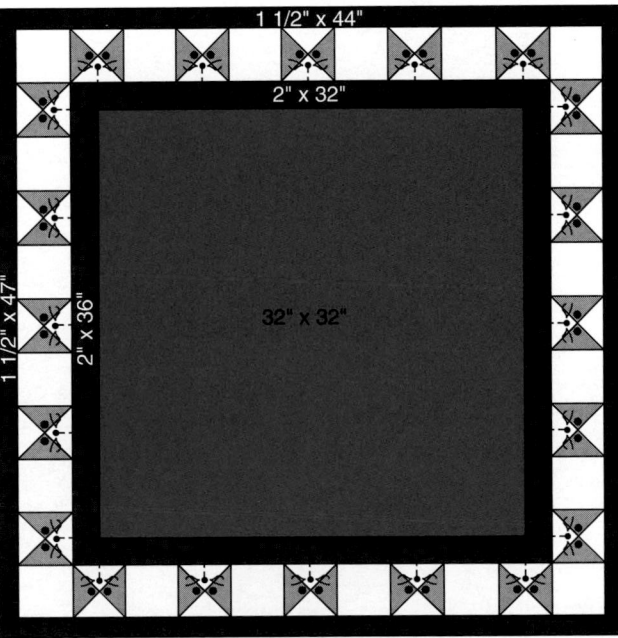

Funny Furry Felines
Placement Diagram
47" x 47"

Step 10. Cut a piece of blue plaid flannel 32 1/2" x 32 1/2".

Step 11. Cut two strips each black flannel 2 1/2" x 32 1/2" and 2 1/2" x 36 1/2". Sew the shorter strips to two opposite sides and the longer strips to remaining sides of the blue plaid flannel square; press seams toward strips.

Step 12. Sew a pieced strip to two opposite sides of the pieced center; press seams away from strip.

Step 13. Sew a B square to each end of the remaining two pieced strips referring to Figure 4. Sew a strip to the two remaining sides of the pieced center; press seams away from strips.

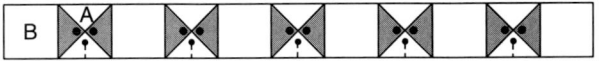

Figure 4
Sew a B square to each end of a pieced strip.

Step 14. Cut and piece two strips each black flannel 2" x 44 1/2" and 2" x 47 1/2". Sew the shorter strips to two opposite sides and the longer strips to the remaining sides; press seams toward strips.

Step 15. Prepare quilt for quilting, quilt and bind as desired referring to the General Instructions. *Note: The quilt shown was machine-quilted in the ditch of seams in white areas with white all-purpose thread and 1/4" from seams on black strips using black all-purpose thread.*

Step 16. Thread black cotton yarn or floss into large-eye needle. Poke needle through A pieces as marked with X on A template leaving a 2" tail; bring needle back to top side. Cut yarn or floss leaving a 2" tail. Tie a square knot on each side to secure. Repeat on all blocks to make whiskers. ❖

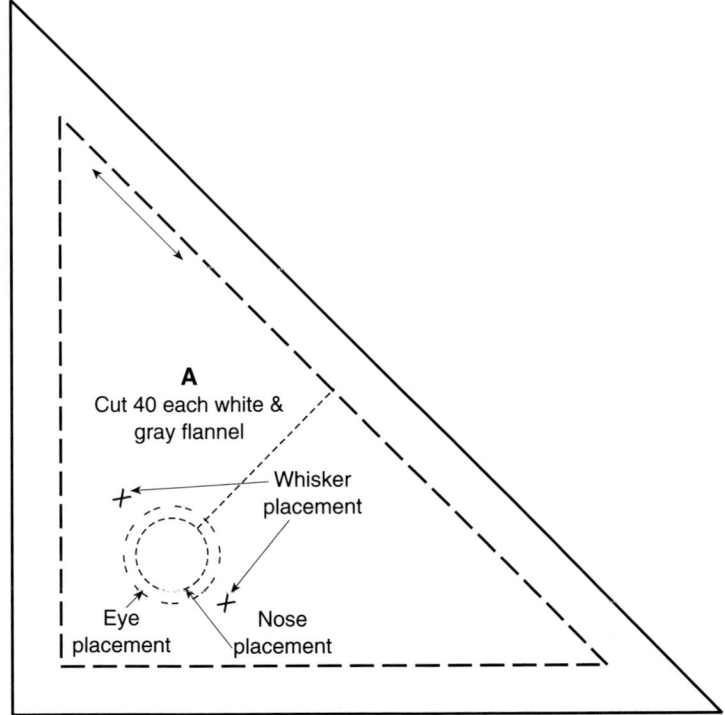

A
Cut 40 each white & gray flannel

Whisker placement

Eye placement

Nose placement

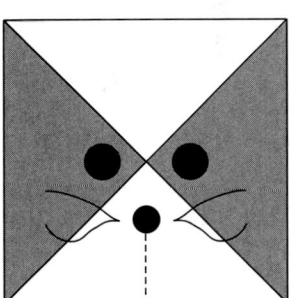

Funny Furry Felines
4" x 4" Block

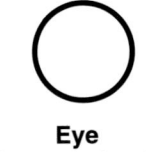

Eye
Cut 40 black satin

Nose
Cut 20 black satin

Log Cabin Mantel Cover

By Phyllis Dobbs

Give your mantel a country look with this simple Log Cabin-design cover.

Project Specifications

Skill Level: Beginner
Project Size: 17 1/2" x 47" (includes binding)
Block Size: 10 1/4" x 10 1/4" x 14 1/2"
Number of Blocks: 3

Materials

- 1/4 yard 8 different plaids and/or stripes
- 1 piece each backing 18" x 32" and 11" x 49"
- 1 piece each batting 18" x 32" and 11" x 49"
- 4 yards self-made or purchased binding
- Neutral color all-purpose thread
- Clear nylon monofilament
- Basic sewing supplies and tools

Instructions

Step 1. Prepare templates using pattern pieces given. Cut as directed on each piece.

Step 2. To piece one triangle block, sew one of each piece together in alphabetical order as shown in Figure 1; press seams away from center. Repeat for three triangle blocks.

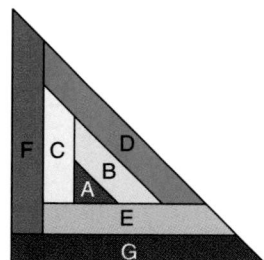

Figure 1
Join pieces in alphabetical order as shown.

Step 3. Cut and piece eight different fabric strips 1 3/4" x 47". *Note: If making project from fabrics on hand, cut strips along length of yardage so they won't need to be pieced. If using pieced strips, stagger the seams on the strips so they don't all end up in the*

same place when strips are stitched together. Sew strips together along length as shown in Figure 2.

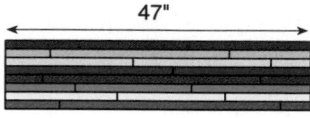

47"

Figure 2
Sew strips together along length.

Step 4. Lay pieced triangle blocks on 18" x 32" piece batting; cut out. Repeat with 18" x 32" backing piece. Sandwich batting pieces between pieced triangle blocks and backing pieces; pin or baste layers together to hold.

Step 5. Using clear nylon monofilament in the top of the machine and neutral color all-purpose thread in the bobbin, machine-quilt in the ditch of seams on each triangle block.

Step 6. Bind the F and G edges of each triangle block using self-made or purchased binding referring to General Instructions.

Step 7. Lay triangles right sides together along one long edge of pieced strip referring to Figure 3; pin in place. Place 11" x 49" piece backing fabric right sides together with pinned unit; pin layers together. Place on top of 11" x 49" piece of batting; pin.

Figure 3
Lay triangles on pieced strip as shown.

Step 8. Trim backing and batting layers 1" larger all around except on pinned triangle edge; trim that edge even. Machine-stitch along pinned triangle edge.

Step 9. Flip fabrics right side out with batting sandwiched between backing and pieced top and triangles hanging down; press. Pin layers together. Machine-quilt in the ditch of seams on pieced strip section referring to Step 5.

Step 10. When quilting is complete, remove pins; trim batting and backing even with top. Bind the three

straight sides of the mantel cover using self-made or purchased binding referring to the General Instructions. ❖

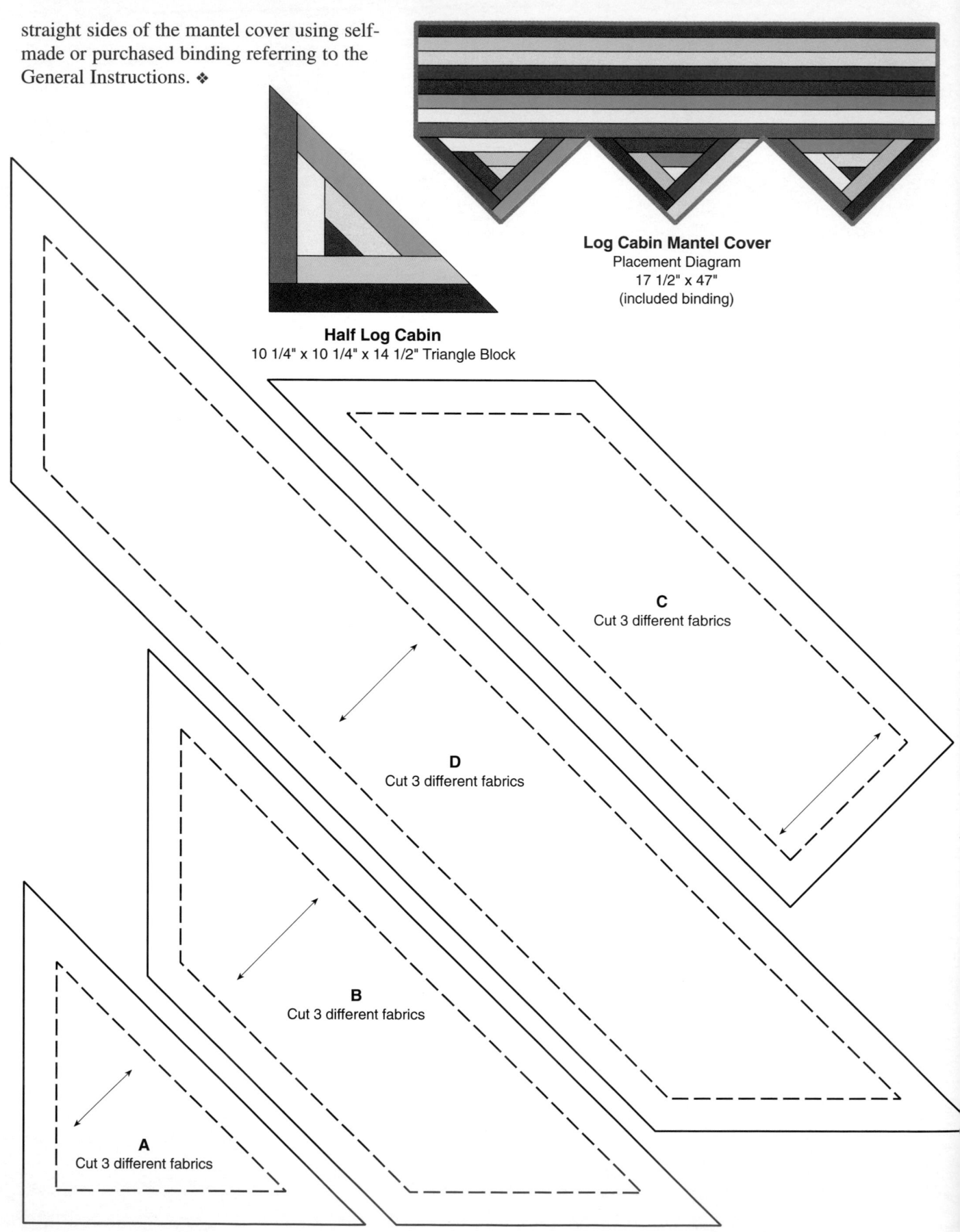

Log Cabin Mantel Cover
Placement Diagram
17 1/2" x 47"
(included binding)

Half Log Cabin
10 1/4" x 10 1/4" x 14 1/2" Triangle Block

C
Cut 3 different fabrics

D
Cut 3 different fabrics

B
Cut 3 different fabrics

A
Cut 3 different fabrics

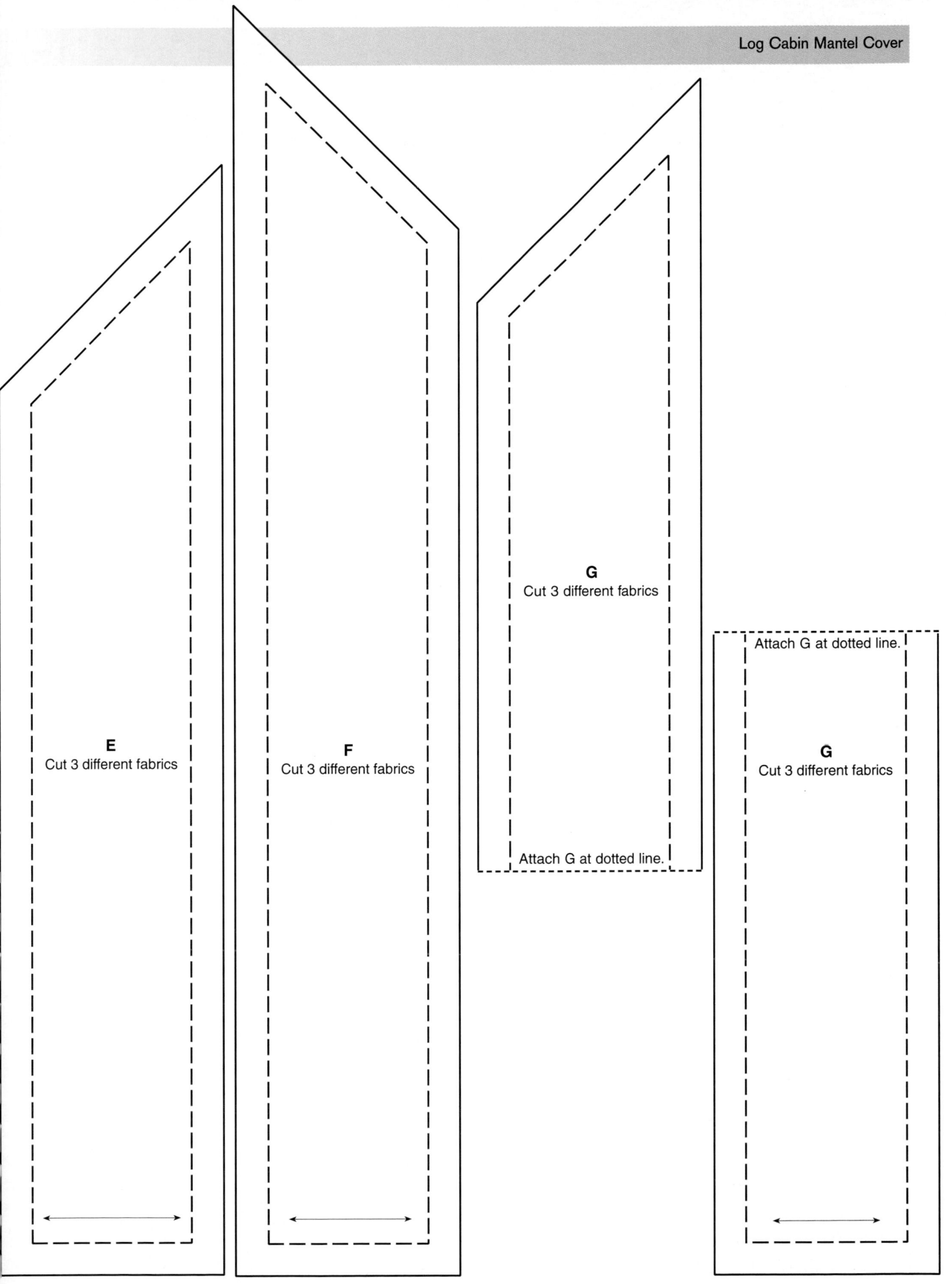

E
Cut 3 different fabrics

F
Cut 3 different fabrics

G
Cut 3 different fabrics

Attach G at dotted line.

Attach G at dotted line.

G
Cut 3 different fabrics

Home Sweet Home Cardigan

By Ann Boyce

Turn an ordinary sweatshirt into a creative wearable using machine-appliqué and some simple designs.

Project Specifications

Skill Level: Beginner
Project Size: Adult
Block Size: 4 1/2" x 4 1/2"
Number of Blocks: 10

Materials

- Adult-size plum sweatshirt
- Scraps green, tan and plum checks and plaids
- Scraps tan print
- 2 squares green/tan plaid 4 1/2" x 4 1/2"
- 2 squares blue plaid 4 1/2" x 4 1/2"
- 3 squares blue sky print 4 1/2" x 4 1/2"
- 3 squares dark tan check 4 1/2" x 4 1/2"
- 1/2 yard plum plaid
- Plum all-purpose thread
- 1 yard fusible transfer web
- Basic sewing supplies and tools and water-erasable fabric pen

Instructions

Step 1. Prepare templates for star, tree and house shapes using full-size patterns given.

Step 2. Trace shapes onto paper side of fusible transfer web referring to patterns for number to cut.

Step 3. Cut out shapes leaving a margin all around.

Step 4. Fuse shapes to wrong side of fabrics referring to patterns for color. Cut out shapes on traced lines; remove paper backing.

Step 5. Arrange and fuse stars on 4 1/2" x 4 1/2" green/tan plaid squares, trees on 4 1/2" x 4 1/2" blue plaid squares and house shapes on 4 1/2" x 4 1/2" blue sky print squares referring to the Placement Diagram for positioning of pieces.

Step 6. Make templates for Log Cabin block using full-size pattern given. Prepare pieces as in Steps 2–4.

Step 7. Arrange and fuse Log Cabin pieces on 4 1/2" x 4 1/2" dark tan check squares referring to full-size pattern and Placement Diagram for positioning of pieces.

Step 8. Lay out one each Tree, House and Star blocks and two Log Cabin blocks to make one block strip as shown in Figure 1. Lay out one each Tree, Star and Log Cabin blocks with two House blocks to make a strip again referring to Figure 1.

Step 9. Carefully cut ribbing off bottom and neck edges of sweatshirt. Fold and mark center front; cut along marked line to make a cardigan.

Figure 1
Lay out blocks to make block strips.

Step 10. Measure in 4 1/2" from each center front edge of sweatshirt; draw a line from bottom to shoulder edge using water-erasable fabric pen. Measure the length of this line referring to Figure 2.

Step 11. Measure block strip. Cut a piece of green check large enough to make the block strip the same length as the measurement taken in Step 10. ***Note: Don't worry about the shape of the piece of green check; it will be trimmed to fit later. Place piece of green check at top of each block strip.***

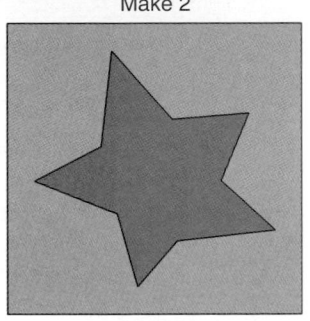

Tree
4 1/2" x 4 1/2" Block

Make 2

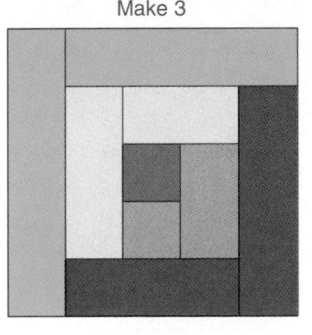

Star
4 1/2" x 4 1/2" Block

Make 2

Log Cabin
4 1/2" x 4 1/2" Block

Make 3

House
4 1/2" x 4 1/2" Block

Make 3

Step 12. Using block strips as patterns, cut a piece of fusible transfer web for each strip. Carefully fuse to wrong side of block strips; remove paper backing.

Step 13. Place a block strip along each cut edge of sweatshirt, matching bottom and center front edges and referring to the Placement Diagram for positioning of strips; fuse in place. Trim excess green check piece and top block even with sweatshirt neck edge.

Step 14. Measure inside edge of fused block strip. Cut two strips plum plaid 1" by this measurement plus 1". Fold under one long edge of each strip 1/4"; press.

Step 15. With raw edges even and right sides together, stitch one strip to the inside edge of each block strip as shown in Figure 3.

Step 16. Press stitched strip flat. Trim bottom edge even with sweatshirt; trim top edge even with neck edge of sweatshirt. Topstitch close to seam and folded edges as shown in Figure 4.

Step 17. Buttonhole-stitch around appliquéd shapes, along edges of Log Cabin block pieces and between each block.

Step 18. Prepare 4 yards single-fold, plum plaid bias binding referring to the General Instructions.

Step 19. Fold over 1/4" along one long raw edge of binding; press. Stitch binding strip right side together with wrong side of sweatshirt around bottom, neck and center front edges.

Step 20. Fold binding to right side of sweatshirt; topstitch in place along folded and pressed edge to finish. ❖

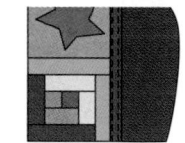

Figure 4
Topstitch along seam and folded edges as shown.

Home Sweet Home Cardigan
Placement Diagram
Adult Size

Star
Cut 2 tan print scraps
(reverse 1)

Figure 2
Measure along marked
line from top to bottom.

Figure 3
Sew a plum plaid strip to 1 inside
edge of each block strip as shown.

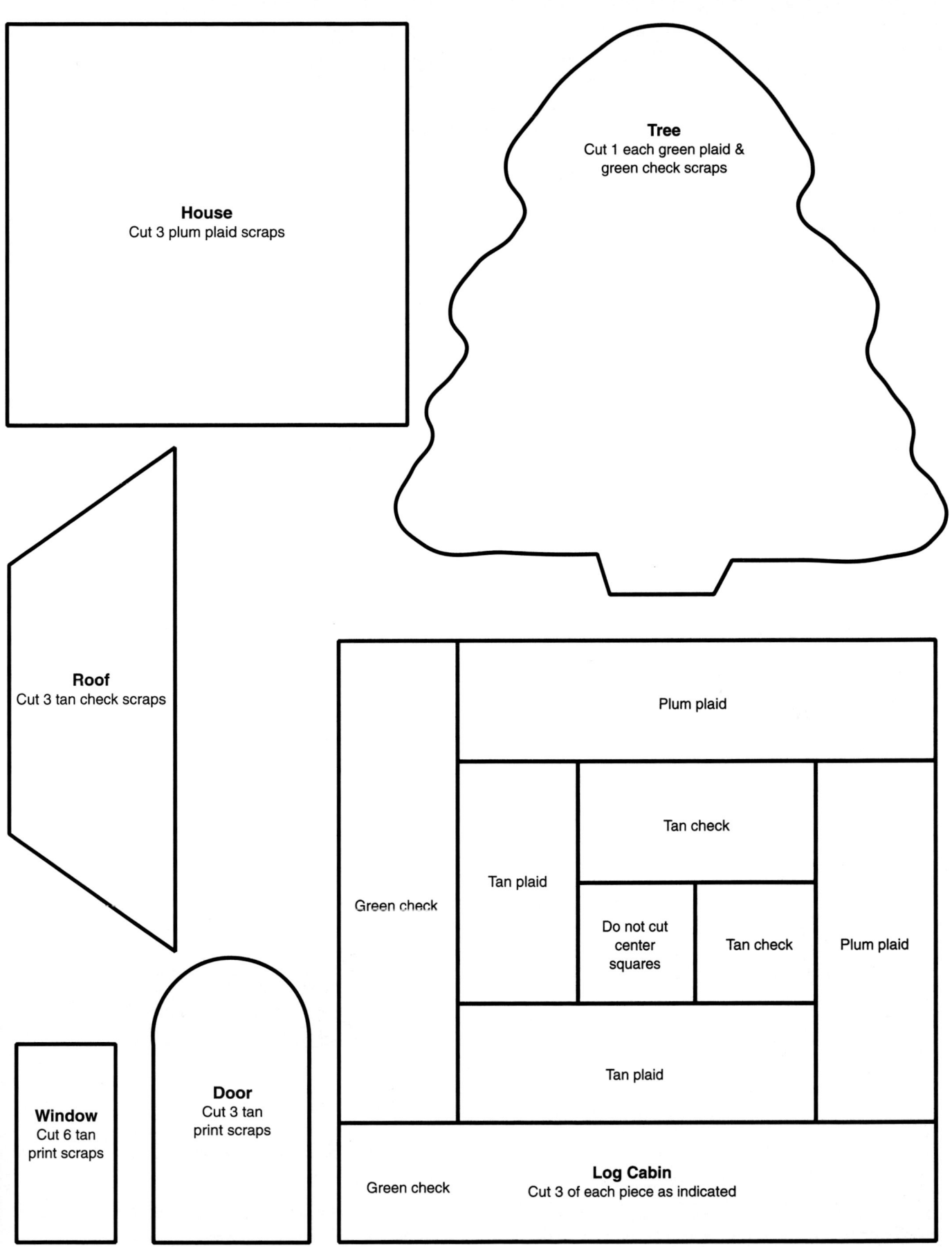

House
Cut 3 plum plaid scraps

Tree
Cut 1 each green plaid &
green check scraps

Roof
Cut 3 tan check scraps

Window
Cut 6 tan
print scraps

Door
Cut 3 tan
print scraps

Plum plaid

Tan check

Green check

Tan plaid

Do not cut
center
squares

Tan check

Plum plaid

Tan plaid

Green check

Log Cabin
Cut 3 of each piece as indicated

Reversible Rug

By Ann Boyce

Weave strips of homespun plaid to make a reversible fabric rug to match your quilt.

Instructions

Step 1. Cut a total of 24 strips 3 3/4" x 58" from red, blue and green plaids or checks.

Step 2. Prepare 3 1/4 yards blue check self-made binding referring to General Instructions.

Figure 1
Prepare strips using bias tape maker.

Step 3. Using bias tape maker and iron, prepare each fabric strip as shown in Figure 1. Fold prepared strips in half along length to make 1" double-thickness strips as shown in Figure 2.

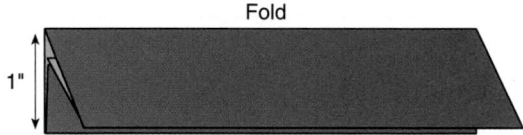

Figure 2
Fold prepared strips as shown.

Step 4. Topstitch along open edge of each strip 1/8" from open edges as shown in Figure 3. Cut each strip in half to make forty-eight 1" x 29" strips.

Figure 3
Topstitch along open edges of strips.

Step 5. Lay out 24 strips on cardboard or foam board in random color order. Stick a pin in each edge of each strip, butting strips against one another as shown in Figure 4.

Step 6. Pin first weaving strip at one end of cardboard or foam board and weave under and over pinned strips as shown in Figure 5; pin at the end. Pin second

Project Note

The reversible rug uses 58"-wide plaid fabrics.

Project Specifications

Skill Level: Beginner

Project Size: Approximately 28" x 28"

Materials

- 1/4 yard blue check
- 1/2 yard each of 6 different red, blue and green plaids or checks
- White all-purpose thread
- No. 50 Clover bias tape maker
- 34" x 34" piece cardboard or foam board
- Basic sewing supplies and tools and straight pins

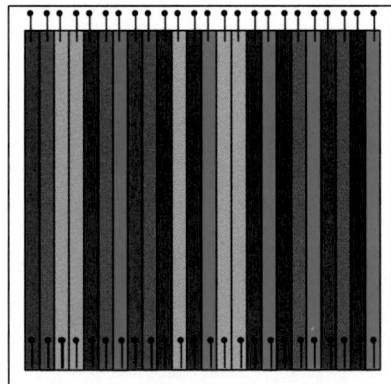

Figure 4
Pin strips butting edges as shown.

weaving strip below the first one and weave over and under strips as shown in Figure 6.

Step 7. Continue weaving strips in this basket-weave pattern until all strips are used.

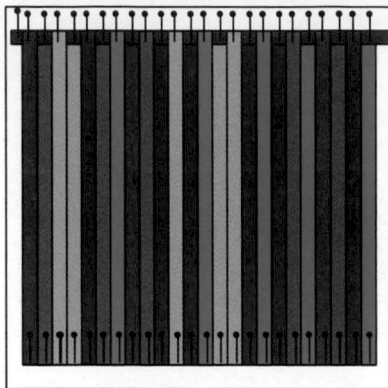

Figure 5
Weave first strip under and over as shown.

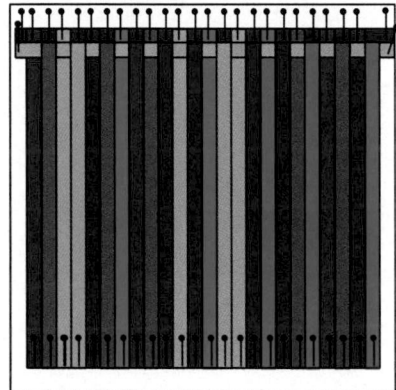

Figure 6
Weave second strip over and under as shown.

Reversible Rug
Placement Diagram
Approximately 28" x 28"

Step 8. Pin all strips at edges and remove from cardboard or foam board. Topstitch around outside edges to hold pieces together.

Step 9. Bind edges with blue check binding referring to the General Instructions. ❖

Autumn Hostess Apron

By Eileen Westfall

The Maple Leaf block works perfectly as the bodice and pocket of this pretty apron.

Project Specifications

Skill Level: Intermediate
Project Size: Adult Size
Block Size: 8 1/2" x 8 1/2" and
  11 3/4" x 11 3/4"
Number of Blocks: 1 each size

Materials

- 1/4 yard green print
- 1/2 yard rust print
- 1 1/4 yards white solid
- 3/8 yard lightweight batting
- Neutral color all-purpose thread
- Clear nylon monofilament
- Basic sewing supplies and tools

Instructions

Step 1. To make the 11 3/4" x 11 3/4" block, cut two 3 5/8" x 3 5/8" squares each white solid and rust print. Cut each square in half on one diagonal to make A triangles. You will need four A triangles in each color.

Step 2. Sew a white solid A to a rust print A as shown in Figure 1; repeat for four units.

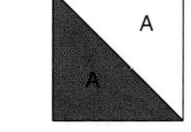

Figure 1
Join A triangles as shown.

Step 3. Cut two squares white solid and three squares rust print 3 1/4" x 3 1/4" for B.

Step 4. Cut one piece green print 1 1/2" x 4 1/2" for D.

Step 5. Turn under 1/4" along each 4 1/2" edge on piece D; press. Place the D piece on one white solid B square

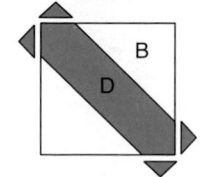

Figure 2
Stitch D on 1 diagonal of B; trim excess at corners.

along one diagonal as shown in Figure 2; appliqué in place by hand or machine. Trim excess D even with B.

Step 6. Arrange two pieced A units with one white solid B square to make a row as shown in Figure 3; stitch and press seams in one direction.

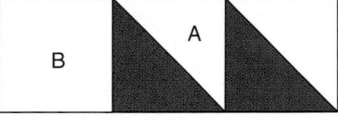

Figure 3
Join 2 A units with 1 white solid B square.

Step 7. Arrange two rust print B squares with one A unit to make a row as shown in Figure 4; stitch and press seams in opposite direction from previously stitched unit.

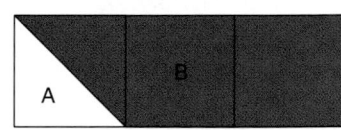

Figure 4
Join 2 rust print B squares with 1 A unit.

Step 8. Join the B-D square with one rust print B square and one A unit to make a row as shown in Figure 5; press seams in the same direction as the unit stitched in Step 6.

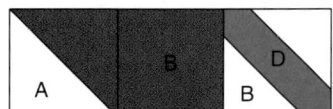

Figure 5
Join the B-D unit with 1 rust print B square and 1 A unit.

Step 9. Join rows as shown in Figure 6; press seam in one direction.

Autumn Hostess Apron
Placement Diagram
Adult Size

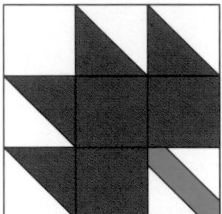

Figure 6
Join rows as shown.

Step 10. Cut two squares green print 6 3/4" x 6 3/4"; cut each square in half on one diagonal to make C triangles.

Step 11. Sew a C triangle to each side of the pieced unit to complete one block as shown in Figure 7; press seams toward C.

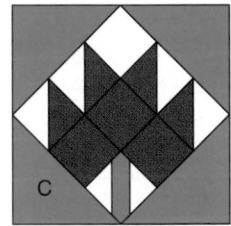

Figure 7
Add C to each side
to complete 1 block.

Step 12. To make 8 1/2" x 8 1/2" block, cut two 2 7/8" x 2 7/8" squares each white solid and rust print for A; cut each square in half on one diagonal to make A triangles. Cut two squares white solid and three squares rust print 2 1/2" x 2 1/2" for B. Cut two squares 5 1/8" x 5 1/8" green print; cut in half on one diagonal to make C triangles. Cut one piece green 1 1/4" x 4" for D.

Maple Leaf
8 1/2" x 8 1/2" and 11 3/4" x 11 3/4" Blocks

Step 13. Complete one 8 1/2" x 8 1/2" block referring to Steps 1–11.

Apron

Step 1. Cut the following from rust print: two strips 2" x 15" for bib ties; two strips 3" x 18" for waist ties; two strips 1 3/4" x 20 1/2" for waistband; one strip 1 1/2" x 39 1/2" for bib binding; one strip 1" x 44" for strip on skirt; and one strip 1 1/2" x 34" for pocket binding.

Step 2. Cut a 19 1/2" x 44" white solid rectangle for skirt bottom.

Step 3. Cut one piece batting and white solid using large block as a pattern. Sandwich batting between finished block and backing piece; pin or baste layers together.

Step 4. Quilt as desired by hand or machine. Trim edges even. Bind around side edges and across top edge using 1 1/2" x 39 1/2" rust print strip cut in Step 1 and referring to the General Instructions.

Step 5. Center one 1 3/4" x 20 1/2" waistband strip wrong side up on front bottom of bib; Place the second 1 3/4" x 20 1/2" waistband strip right side facing the bib back bottom edge; pin in place. Stitch along edges as shown in Figure 8 to enclose bib bottom in waistband.

Figure 8
Stitch as shown to enclose bib in waistband.

Step 6. Press 19 1/2" edges of 19 1/2" x 44" white solid rectangle under 1/4"; turn under again, press and stitch in place.

Step 7. Gather one 44" edge of 19 1/2" x 44" white solid rectangle.

Step 8. Place bib/waistband unit right side down on the gathered rectangle as shown in Figure 9; readjust gathers to fit; stitch.

Step 9. On wrong side of apron, turn waistband bottom edge under 1/4". Cover previously stitched seam; stitch in place using clear nylon monofilament in the top of the machine and neutral color all-purpose thread in the bobbin, leaving ends open to insert ties.

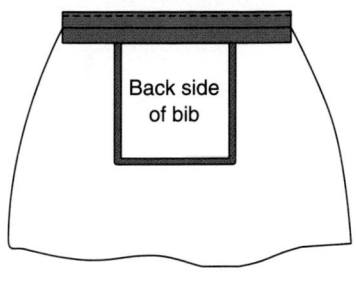

Figure 9
Sew skirt piece to bottom of front waistband.

Step 10. To make bib ties, fold both long edges of each 2" x 15" rust strip in 1/4"; press. Fold each strip in half wrong sides together along length; fold ends in 1/4"; press. Topstitch close to open edge as shown in Figure 10. Repeat with both 3" x 18" strips for waistband ties, folding in only one end, again referring to Figure 10.

Figure 10
Topstitch ties as shown.

Step 11. Insert waistband ties at ends of waistband; topstitch in place to secure. Pin one end of each bib tie at top edge of bib; topstitch in place to secure.

Step 12. Press under 1/4" on bottom edge of apron skirt; press under 3 1/2" to make hem. Pin in place; stitch to hold.

Step 13. Press under 1/4" along long edges of 1" x 44" strip rust print. Pin in place along hem seam; topstitch in place along both edges.

Step 14. Prepare 8 1/2" x 8 1/2" block to make a pocket referring to Steps 3 and 4 except use 1 1/2" x 34" rust print strip and bind around all sides.

Step 15. Position pocket 8" from one side and 7" from bottom edge; pin in place. Topstitch in place along inside seam of pocket binding around both sides and across bottom, leaving top edge open. ❖

Golden Pearls Album

By Barbara A. Clayton

*Give this special photo album to the bride and groom
as a gift to preserve photos of that memorable day.*

Project Specifications

Skill Level: Intermediate
Project Size: Approximately 11" x
    12" x 3"

Materials

- 1/2 yard white taffeta
- 1 yard white satin
- 10" x 16" piece gold lamé
- Batting 14" x 38"
- White all-purpose thread
- Gold metallic thread
- 3" binder
- 4 yards gold cording with bound edge
- About 210 (3mm) and 18 (5mm) pearls
- 1/3 yard 3/8"-wide gold metallic ribbon
- Hot-glue gun
- 4" x 6" piece fusible transfer web
- 4" x 6" piece tear-off stabilizer
- 22" x 20" piece lightweight cardboard or white poster board
- 8" x 10" piece medium-weight cardboard
- 6" x 8" piece clear, thin plastic
- Basic sewing supplies and tools, water-erasable marker, pencil, yardstick or ruler, utility knife or paper scissors and metallic sewing machine needle

Instructions

Step 1. Cut a rectangle from the white taffeta 2" longer and wider than the binder (about 14" x 27").

Using ruler or yard stick and pencil, draw diagonal lines 1" apart in both directions to make a grid as shown in Figure 1. *Note: The taffeta is the cover backing so all pencil lines will be hidden later.*

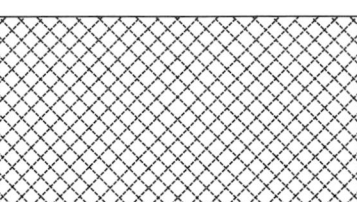

Figure 1
Draw a 1" diagonal grid as shown.

Step 2. Cut a matching piece of white satin and batting to match the piece of white taffeta; pin the three thicknesses together all around the edges and at several points inside to keep it from slipping. *Note: Be careful when using pins on satin and taffeta as large pins leave holes which do not go away.*

Step 3. Using metallic sewing machine needle and gold metallic thread in the top of the machine and in the bobbin and a long machine running stitch, stitch on all drawn lines, being careful at intersections to avoid puckers.

Step 4. Trace the frame pattern given onto the medium-weight cardboard; cut out using a utility knife or scissors.

Step 5. Lay the quilted cover over the binder, positioning equally on all sides. Lay the cardboard frame on the center front of the binder cover as shown in Figure 2. Mark its outside edge with pins.

Figure 2
Mark the frame area as shown.

Step 6. Hand-sew or glue the 3mm pearls at each intersection point of the gold metallic stitching; do not place pearls in the frame area.

Step 7. Cut two strips white satin 2" x 11"; glue to the inside of the binder, slipping one edge under each side of the ring mechanism as shown in Figure 3. *Note: All raw edges will be covered later.*

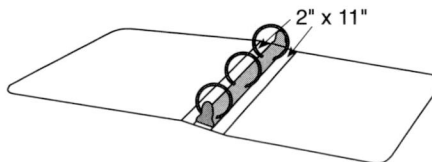

Figure 3
Glue 2" x 11" strips under each side of the binder rings.

Step 8. Lay the finished cover wrong side up on a work surface. Center the open binder on top. Fold the cover to the inside over one end as shown in Figure 4; hot-glue in place, stopping about 1/2" from curved corners.

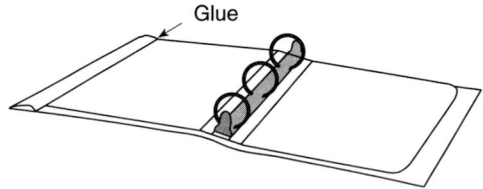

Figure 4
Fold cover to inside over one end only; glue in place.

Step 9. Close the binder; wrap the cover over it tightly, folding excess to inside at remaining end. Hot-glue to inside edge, stopping 1/2" from each curved corner.

Step 10. Open binder again. Fold bottom and top excess to inside; hot-glue to inside of binder.

Step 11. Cut the center of top and bottom to fit around ring mechanism; hot-glue. Fold corners over and gather slightly with your fingers as you glue them down. Cut off any excess fabric beyond the glue about 1" from edges.

Step 12. Hot-glue the bound edge of the gold cording around outside edge of binder as shown in Figure 5. To start and stop, measure, cut exactly and hot glue by butting ends together. Trim bound edge as necessary to fit around ring mechanism.

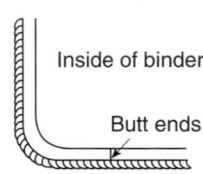

Figure 5
Glue gold cording around outside edge; butt ends to finish.

Step 13. Cut two pieces lightweight cardboard to fit the inside covers of the binder, from the fold of the binder to the outer end (about 11" x 11 1/2" each).

Step 14. Using binder corners as a guide, round off the two corners on both squares of cardboard. Cut a piece of white satin about 1" larger on all four sides than each cardboard piece; fold edges over and hot-glue in place.

Step 15. Lay each covered piece on the inside of the binder; hot-glue in place to enclose all raw edges.

Frame

Step 1. Trace frame onto medium-weight cardboard; cut out. Trace frame onto poster board; cut out leaving center area intact. Cover with gold lamé as for binder cover and inside covered cardboard pieces.

Step 2. Hot-glue the gold-lamé covered piece to the front of the binder on previously marked frame lines.

Step 3. Trace six heart shapes onto paper side of fusible transfer webbing. Cut out leaving a margin all around. Fuse to wrong side of remaining gold lamé; cut out shapes on traced lines. Remove paper backing.

Step 4. Cut a piece of white satin 1" larger all around than the medium-weight cardboard frame. Referring to the frame pattern given, position gold lamé hearts; fuse in place. Pin a piece of tear-off stabilizer under satin for stability. Using metallic sewing machine needle and gold metallic thread in the top of the machine and in the bobbin, satin-stitch around each heart shape. Remove stabilizer.

Golden Pearls Album
Placement Diagram
Approximately 11" x 12" x 3"

Step 5. Using frame pattern and water-erasable marker, mark quilting lines on satin.

Step 6. Cut a matching piece of white taffeta and batting for the frame top; pin the three layers together. Hand-quilt around heart shapes and a little less than 1/4" around heart shapes again and over all eight feather designs with gold metallic thread doubled in the needle. Sew three 5mm pearls in the center of each heart shape.

Step 7. Center the frame top over the cardboard frame; fold edge over and hot-glue in place. Make an X cut through the center of the frame cover; cut on the diagonal to within 1/4" of inside frame corners as shown in Figure 6. Fold over edges; hot-glue, cutting off excess fabric.

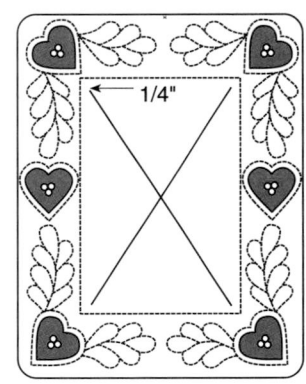

Figure 6
Make an X cut through frame cover; cut diagonally to within 1/4" of each corner.

Step 8. Hot-glue remaining gold cording around inside and outside edges of frame as for binder. Hot-glue the plastic to the inside back of the frame.

Step 9. Hot-glue the frame to the binder, covering the gold lamé fabric. Glue only on the outside near the cording on the two sides and bottom of the frame, leaving the top edge open to insert photo.

Step 10. Tie a bow with 3/8"-wide gold metallic ribbon; cut ends diagonally and hot-glue to top of frame to finish. ❖

×
Bow placement

Heart
Cut 6 gold lamé

Frame Pattern

------- Quilting lines

- -- -- Placement lines

Bear's Paw Sweatshirt

By Kathy Brown

Decorate the front of a sweatshirt with a Bear's Paw block to make the perfect warm-up for camping or other outdoor activities.

Project Specifications

Skill Level: Beginner
Project Size: Adult

Materials

- Adult-size tan sweatshirt
- Fat quarter brown/tan plaid flannel
- Fat quarter brown print
- Brown all-purpose thread
- 3/4 yard fusible transfer web
- Basic sewing supplies and tools

Instructions

Step 1. Cut one each 9" x 9" square brown print and fusible transfer web. Fuse transfer web to wrong side of brown print square.

Step 2. Prepare templates using pattern pieces given for bear and bear's paw (page 38).

Step 3. Trace shapes onto paper side of fusible transfer web referring to patterns for number to cut.

Step 4. Cut out shapes leaving a margin all around.

Step 5. Fuse shapes to wrong side of fabrics referring to patterns for color. Cut out shapes on traced lines; remove paper backing.

Step 6. Center and fuse brown print square on sweatshirt front referring to Figure 1.

Step 7. Fuse a bear's paw shape on fused square referring to Figure 2; repeat with remaining bear's paw pieces.

Step 8. Fuse the bear shape in the center of the fused design.

Step 9. Machine satin-stitch across all raw edges, across bottom of each bear's paw point and around bear shape. ❖

Templates on page 38

Bear's Paw Sweatshirt
Placement Diagram
Adult Size

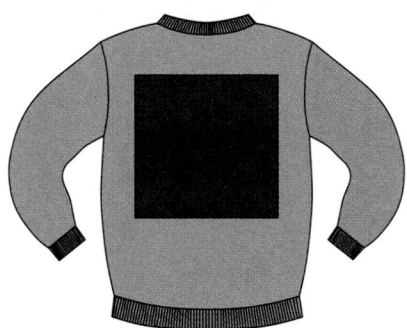

Figure 1
Fuse square to sweatshirt front as shown.

Figure 2
Place 1 bear paw motif on fused square as shown.

Cathedral Window Pincushion

By Norma Storm

This elegant little pincushion makes a wonderful gift for any quilter or seamstress. It only takes a couple of hours to make one.

Project Specifications

Skill Level: Beginner
Project Size: 3" x 3" x 3"
Block Size: 3" x 3"
Number of Blocks: 1

Materials

- 8 1/2" x 8 1/2" square 1 fabric
- 2" x 15" strip same fabric
- 3 1/2" x 3 1/2" square same fabric
- 2 1/2" x 2 1/2" square contrasting fabric
- All-purpose thread to match fabrics
- 15" contrasting 1/8" piping
- 2/3–3/4 cup uncooked rice
- Basic sewing supplies and tools and zipper foot

Instructions

Step 1. Fold the 8 1/2" x 8 1/2" fabric square in half right sides together; sew across both ends as shown in Figure 1.

 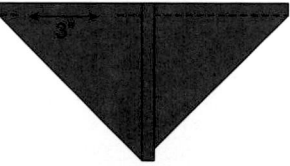

Figure 1
Stitch across both ends.

Figure 2
Fold with seams together; stitch as shown.

Step 2. Reposition so the seams come together as shown in Figure 2; pin. Stitch across raw edge from one side to the center; skip about 3"; sew to the other side referring again to Figure 2. Turn right side out through opening; smooth out and press if needed.

Step 3. Fold two opposite corners to the center as

shown in Figure 3; mark the folds. Open flat; fold unit in half, seam side out and stitch the two marked folds together as shown in Figure 4. Cut unit in half along center fold, again referring to Figure 4.

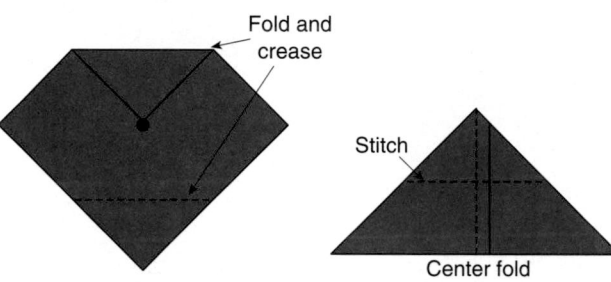

Figure 3
Fold 2 opposite corners to the center; mark folds.

Figure 4
Stitch the 2 marked folds together. Cut apart along center fold.

Step 4. Open and press; center the 2 1/2" x 2 1/2" contrasting fabric square in the center of the stitched unit; pin in place.

Step 5. Roll the bias fold over the edge of one side of the contrasting fabric square as shown in Figure 5; hand-appliqué in place with matching thread, making a smooth curve. Repeat with remaining three sides.

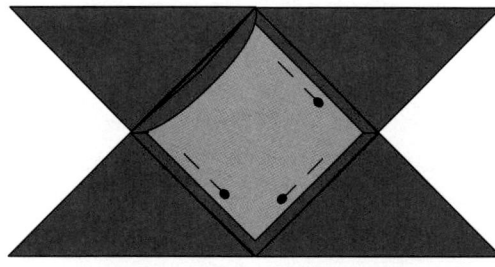

Figure 5
Roll the bias-fold edge over square as shown.

Step 6. Place one end of 1/8"-wide contrasting piping 1/4" from one outside corner of the window area with raw edges away from window area and straight across one side to the opposite corner. Continue around window area, making a square with the piping; pin to hold. End by crossing the piping end over the beginning end. Measure to check that sides are equal. Readjust piping if necessary.

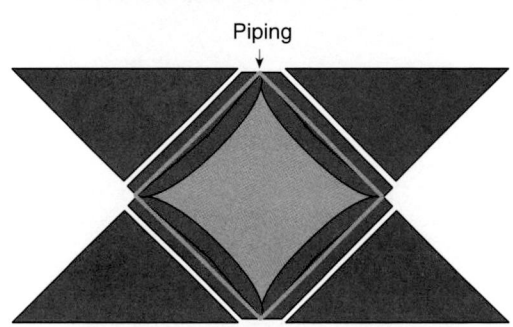

Step 7. Using a zipper foot, stitch piping in place. Clip piping seam allowance at corners. Trim excess fabric as shown in Figure 6, leaving 1/4" seam allowance around the block.

Step 8. Trim the 3 1/2" x 3 1/2" same fabric square to the same size as the window block. Set aside.

Step 9. Beginning at a corner, place the 2" x 15" fabric strip right sides together and raw edges on top of the piping with raw edges aligned; pin. Using the zipper foot, stitch all round, clip seam allowance at

Piping

Figure 6
Trim excess, leaving 1/4" seam allowance.

corners as needed. Stitch strip ends together at the corner; trim excess strip to form pincushion sides.

Step 10. Sew the trimmed square right sides together on the bottom edge of the pincushion sides, leaving one side open. Turn right side out. Fill with rice through opening; slipstitch opening closed to finish. ❖

Cathedral Window Pincushion
Placement Diagram
3" x 3" x 3"

Cathedral Window
3" x 3" Block

Bear's Paw Sweatshirt

Continued from page 34

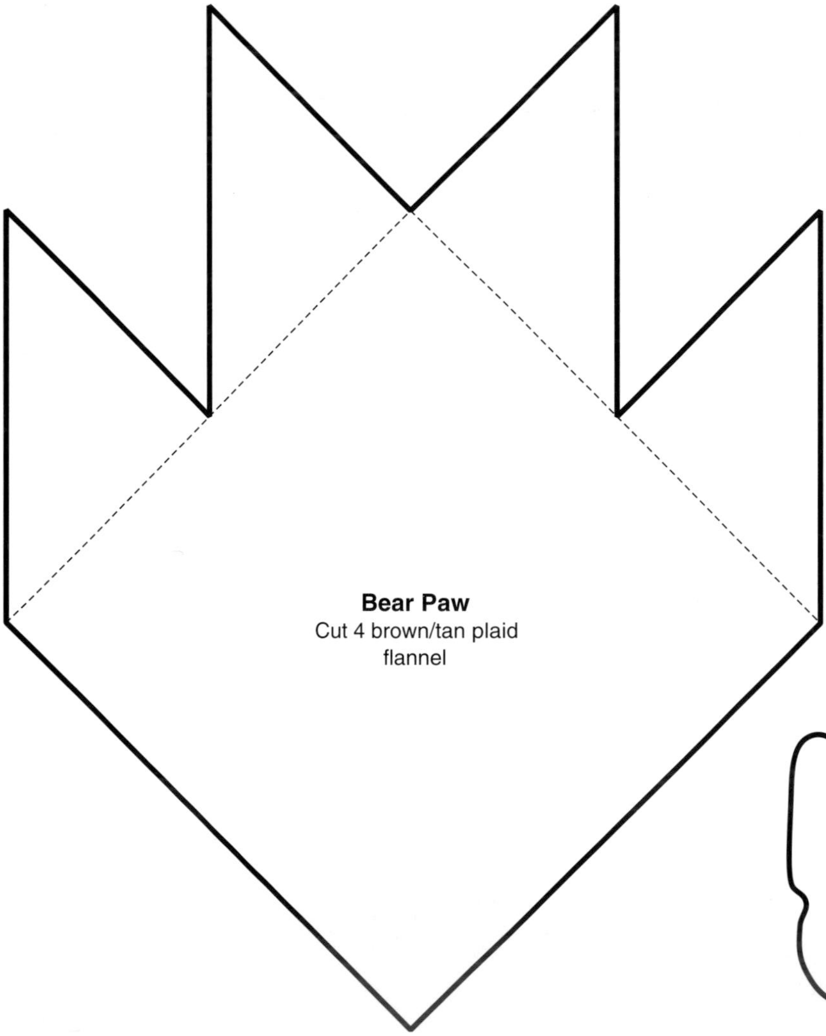

Bear Paw
Cut 4 brown/tan plaid
flannel

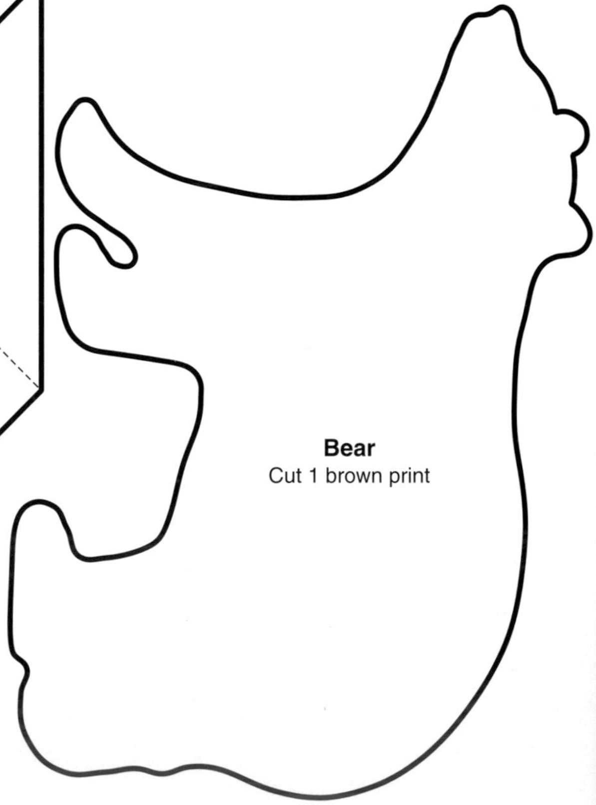

Bear
Cut 1 brown print

Stationery Holder

By Holly Daniels

Make a gift of note cards extra special by sewing up a matching stationery holder.

Instructions

Step 1. Cut the following from dark blue print: 7 1/2" x 13" rectangle (lining); 6 3/4" x 7 1/2" rectangle (outside back); four 1" x 8" strips (trim on front cover); and 3" x 3" square (inside stamp pocket).

Step 2. Cut four 1" x 8" strips red print 2 (block trim).

Step 3. Prepare templates for A and B; cut as directed on each piece.

Step 4. Sew four B triangles to one A diamond as shown in Figure 1 to complete one block; Press seams toward B. Repeat for four blocks.

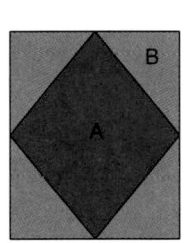 

Figure 1
Sew 4 B triangles to A to complete 1 block.

Figure 2
Join 4 blocks as shown.

Step 5. Join the four blocks to complete front panel as shown in Figure 2; press.

Step 6. Sew a 1" x 8" red print 2 strip to each opposite long side of pieced center; press seams toward strips. Trim excess strip even as shown in Figure 3. Repeat on the top and bottom.

Step 7. Sew a 1" x 8" dark blue print strip to each opposite long side of pieced center; press seams toward strips. Trim excess strip even as for red strips as shown in Figure 3. Repeat on the top and bottom.

Step 8. Trim pieced panel to measure 6 3/4" x 7 1/2".

Step 9. Sew a button at a butting

Figure 3
Add strips to opposite long sides; trim excess even as shown.

Project Notes

This stationery holder has two pockets for cards, envelopes and stickers and extra pockets for stamps and a pen.

Project Specifications

Skill Level: Beginner
Project Size: 6 1/4" x 7" (when folded)
Block Size: 2 1/4" x 2 3/4"
Number of Blocks: 4

Materials

- 4" x 13" piece red print 1
- 5" x 10" piece red print 2
- 8" x 8" square gold print
- Scraps of 4 red prints
- 1/4 yard dark blue print
- Neutral color all-purpose thread
- 4 assorted 5/8" buttons
- 1/2 yard 3/8"-wide navy grosgrain ribbon
- Heavy cardboard or plastic canvas
- Basic sewing supplies and tools

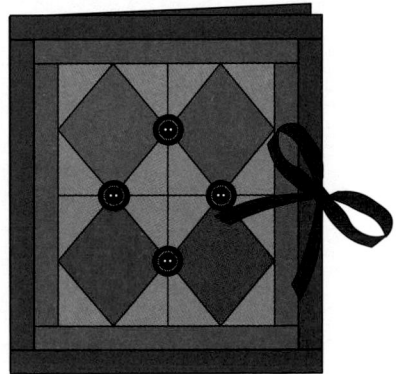

Stationery Holder
Placement Diagram
6 1/4" x 7" (when folded)

seams of red diamonds as shown in Figure 4.

Step 10. Sew the 6 3/4" x 7 1/2" dark blue print rectangle to the pieced panel as shown in Figure 5; press seams toward rectangle.

Step 11. Press one long edge of the 4" x 13" red print 1 inner pocket piece under 1/4"; stitch to hold. Press all edges

Figure 4
Sew a button at block seam joints.

of the 3" x 3" stamp pocket under 1/4"; stitch across top edge only.

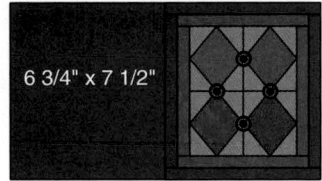

Figure 5
Sew the 6 3/4" x 7 1/2" dark blue print rectangle to the pieced panel.

Step 12. Pin stamp pocket to the inner pocket piece as shown in Figure 6; stitch around unstitched sides, leaving stitched top edge open.

 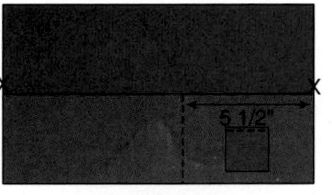

Figure 6
Pin the stamp pocket to the inner pocket.

Figure 7
Stitch in 5 1/2" from 1 short end as shown.

Step 13. Lay the inner pocket right side up on the 7 1/2" x 13" dark blue lining piece raw edges even. Stitch on ends and across bottom edge. Measure in 5 1/2" from one short end; mark. Stitch a line to make one edge of pen pocket as shown in Figure 7.

Step 14. Cut 3/8"-wide navy grosgrain ribbon into two 9" lengths. Pin a piece on each end of the stitched pocket/lining piece as marked with an X on Figure 7 with loose ends toward pen pocket.

Step 15. Layer pocket/lining piece and front panel with right sides together. Pin together along top and side edges; stitch along pinned edges. Trim corners; turn right side out. Press bottom edges up 1/4".

Step 16. Stitch in the ditch of the seam joining front and back panels as shown in Figure 8.

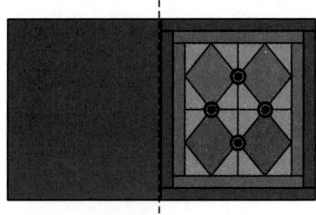 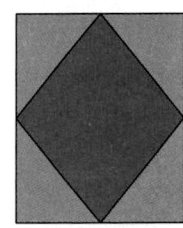

Figure 8
Stitch in the ditch of the seam between front and back panels.

Diamond Square
2 1/4" x 2 3/4" Block

Step 17. Cut two pieces of heavy cardboard or plastic canvas to fit inside front and back panels (about 6 1/4" x 7"). Slip inside through open bottom. Slipstitch bottom opening closed to finish. ❖

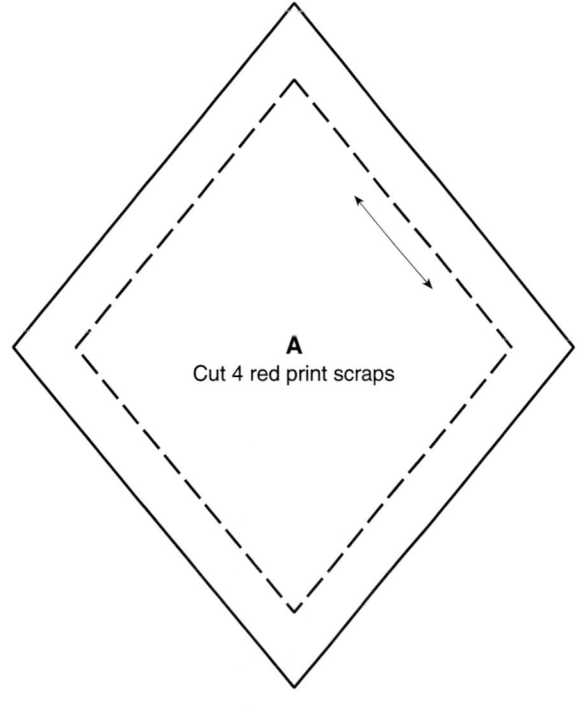

A
Cut 4 red print scraps

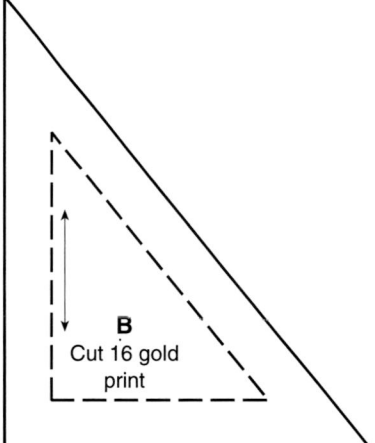

B
Cut 16 gold print

Quilting for Kids

For a weekend of fun quilting, make one of these quick-to-stitch projects for your children. They'll love the bedroom sets, Little Sheriff vest, pillowcase sleep-over bag or Happy Birthday place mat.

Froggy, Froggy Baby Quilt

By Jill Reber

Kids will love the frog-print fabric and bright-colored coordinates used to make this simple block quilt.

Instructions

Step 1. Cut four 2 1/2" x 4 1/2" rectangles from each of the 12 bright-colored print strips for A.

Step 2. Trim remainder of each strip to 2 7/8" x 22". Subcut into 2 7/8" squares. Cut each square in half on one diagonal to make B triangles. You will need 12 B triangles of each color.

Step 3. Cut two strips white-on-white print 2 7/8" x 42"; subcut strips into 2 7/8" squares. Cut each square in half on one diagonal to make B triangles. You will need 48 B white-on-white print triangles.

Step 4. Cut three strips white-on-white print 4 7/8" x 42"; subcut into 4 7/8" squares. Cut each square in half on one diagonal to make C triangles. You will need 48 C triangles.

Step 5. Cut one strip white-on-white print 2 1/2" x 42"; subcut strip into 2 1/2" squares for D. You will need 12 D squares.

Step 6. Sew a bright-colored print B triangle to a white-on-white print B triangle as shown in Figure 1; repeat for four units of the same bright-colored fabric.

Step 7. Sew a same-color bright-colored B triangle to each white-on-white print side of the pieced unit as shown in Figure 2; repeat for four units.

Step 8. Sew a C triangle to each pieced B unit as shown in Figure 3.

Project Specifications

Skill Level: Beginner
Project Size: 42" x 52"
Block Size: 10" x 10"
Number of Blocks: 12

Materials

- 12 different 4 1/2" x 32" bright-colored fabric strips
- 1 yard frog print for borders
- 1 yard white-on-white print
- Backing 46" x 56"
- Batting 46" x 56"
- 5 1/2 yards self-made or purchased binding
- Neutral color all-purpose thread
- Basic sewing supplies and tools

Step 9. Sew a D square between two same-color A rectangles as shown in Figure 4.

Figure 4
Sew A to opposite sides of D.

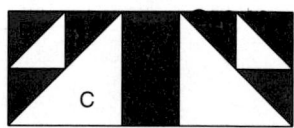

Figure 5
Join 2 B-C units with A.

Step 10. Join two B-C units with A as shown in Figure 5; repeat.

Step 11. Join the pieced units to complete one block as shown in Figure 6; press. Repeat for 12 blocks.

Step 12. Join blocks in four rows of three blocks

Figure 1
Join B triangles.

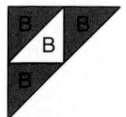

Figure 2
Sew 2 B triangles to the pieced B unit.

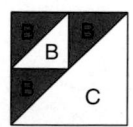

Figure 3
Sew C to B unit.

each; press seams in one direction. Join rows to complete pieced center; press seams in one direction.

Step 13. Cut two strips each white-on-white print 2 1/2" x 40 1/2" and 2 1/2" x 34 1/2". Sew the longer strips to opposite long sides and shorter strips to top and bottom; press seams toward strips.

Step 14. Cut and piece two strips each frog print 4 1/2" x 34 1/2" and 4 1/2" x 52 1/2". Sew the shorter strips to the top and bottom and the longer strips to opposite long sides; press seams toward strips.

Step 15. Finish quilt referring to the General Instructions. ❖

Figure 6
Join pieced units to complete 1 block.

Froggy, Froggy
10" x 10" Block

Froggy, Froggy Baby Quilt
Placement Diagram
42" x 52"

Froggy, Froggy Accessories

By Jill Reber

*Make a pillowcase and pocket organizer to match the Froggy, Froggy Quilt.
The pocket organizer is great for storing baby stuffed animals.*

Pockets Organizer

Project Specifications
Skill Level: Beginner
Project Size: 16" x 23"

Materials
- 1/8 yard pink accent fabric
- 1/4 yard frog print
- 5/8 yard green print
- Backing 20" x 27"
- Batting 20" x 27"
- 2 1/2 yards self-made or purchased binding
- Neutral color all-purpose thread
- 1 1/2 yards 1"-wide white grosgrain ribbon
- Basic sewing supplies and tools

Instructions

Step 1. Cut a 10 1/2" x 23 1/2" rectangle green print for background and two strips 3 1/2" x 23 1/2" green print for borders.

Step 2. Cut three 5 1/2" x 10 1/2" rectangles frog print for pockets. Fold up 1/2" on one 10 1/2" edge of each pocket piece; press.

Step 3. Cut three strips 2 1/2" x 10 1/2" pink accent fabric for pocket finish. Fold each strip along length with wrong sides together; press.

Step 4. Pin one folded pink accent strip along unpressed 10 1/2" edge of one pocket piece.

Sew or serge pieces together; press seam toward frog print. Repeat for three pockets.

Step 5. Pin pockets to background piece referring to Figure 1 for placement. Stitch in place along folded and pressed 10 1/2" bottom edge on each pocket again referring to Figure 1.

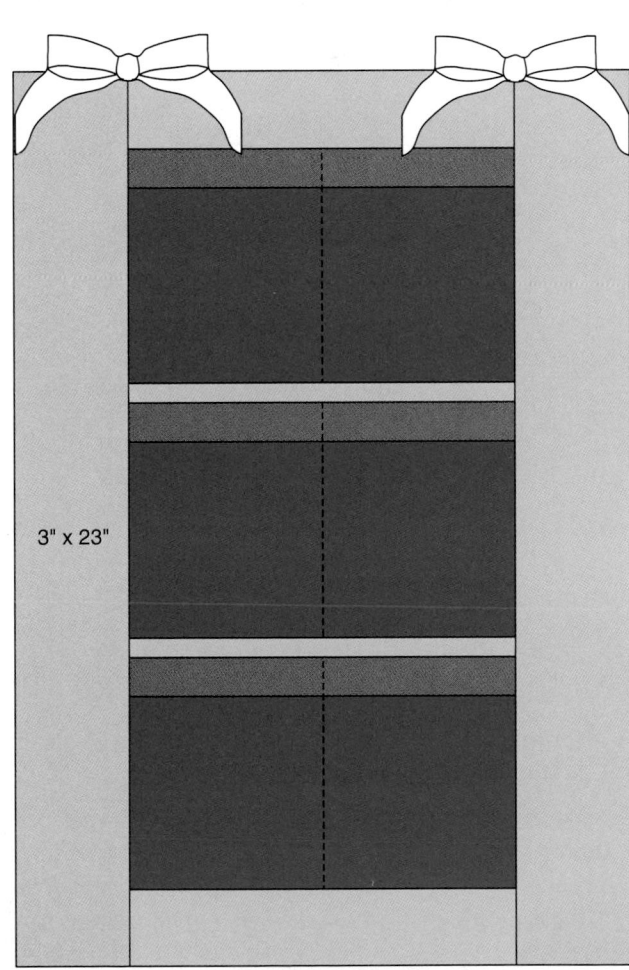

3" x 23"

Froggy Pockets Organizer
Placement Diagram
16" x 23"

Step 6. Sew a 3 1/2" x 23 1/2" border strip to opposite long sides of the green print background, including pockets in seam; press seams toward strips.

Step 7. Prepare for quilting and finish referring to General Instructions.

Step 8. Mark the center of each pocket. Stitch on marked lines to make two sections in each pocket.

Step 9. Cut 1"-wide white grosgrain ribbon in half to make two equal lengths. Fold each piece in half and sew to top backside of finished quilt at folded half to make ribbon ties for hanging.

← 2 3/4"

← 1/2"

← 1/2"

← 2 1/2"

Figure 1
Arrange pockets on background as shown. Stitch along bottom folded and pressed edge.

Pillowcase

Project Specifications
Skill Level: Beginner
Project Size: Size varies

Materials
- 1/4 yard white-on-white print
- 1 yard frog print
- Purchased pillow or pillow form of desired size
- Neutral color all-purpose thread
- Basic sewing supplies and tools

Instructions

Step 1. Measure the outside edge of the pillow or pillow form. Use this formula to cut the frog print fabric: width (?? x 2) + 3" and length ?? + 3. *Note: For example, for a 12" x 18" pillow, cut the width 12" x 2 + 3" or 27" and length 18" + 3" or 21". You would need a piece 27" x 21".*

Froggy Pillowcase
Placement Diagram
Size Varies

Step 2. Cut a 6 1/2" x 42" strip white-on-white print for band. Trim to the cut size of the width figured in Step 1.

Step 3. Fold the band in half along length with wrong sides together. Serge or sew to rectangle cut in Step 1 with right sides together as shown in Figure 2; press seam toward frog print.

Figure 2
Sew folded band to frog print rectangle.

Step 4. Fold stitched piece in half along length with right sides together; serge or sew along bottom and side edge using a 1/2" seam allowance; finish seam edge, if desired.

Step 5. Turn right side out; press. ❖

Figure 3
Stitch along bottom and side edge.

Butterfly Bedroom

By Norma Storm

Stitch this pretty butterfly set in your child's favorite colors, as a scrap quilt or in pinks as shown.

Butterfly Lap Quilt

Instructions

Step 1. Cut 12 squares light pink solid 11" x 11" for background.

Step 2. Cut seven squares each 10 7/8" x 10 7/8" light pink solid and pink print. Cut each square in half on one diagonal to make triangles. Sew a light pink solid triangle to a pink print triangle to make triangle/square blocks. You will need 13 of these pieced blocks.

Step 3. Prepare templates for butterfly motifs using patterns given. Trace shapes onto paper side of fusible transfer web as directed for lap quilt on each piece. Cut out shapes leaving a margin all around traced lines.

Step 4. Fuse shapes to fabric scraps as desired to make colorful butterflies. Cut out shapes on traced lines; remove paper backing.

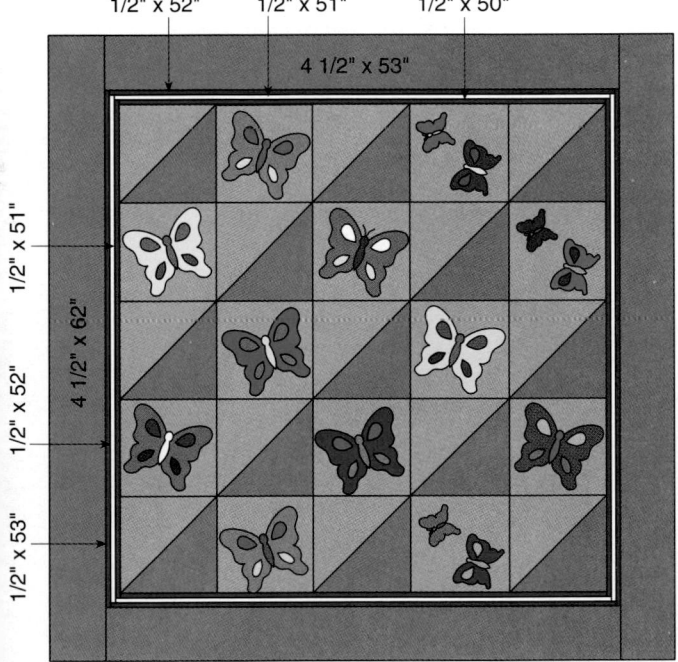

Butterfly Lap Quilt
Placement Diagram
62" x 62"

Project Specifications

Skill Level: Intermediate
Project Size: 62" x 62"
Block Size: 10" x 10"
Number of Appliquéd Blocks: 12
Number of Pieced Blocks: 13

Materials

- Bright-colored scraps for butterflies
- 1/2 yard each white, turquoise and bright pink solids or prints
- 1 3/4 yards light pink solid
- 2 yards pink print
- Backing 66" x 66"
- Batting 66" x 66"
- 2 1/2 yards self-made or purchased binding
- All-purpose thread to match fabrics
- 2 yards fusible transfer web
- 2 yards tear-off fabric stabilizer
- Basic sewing supplies and tools

Step 5. Arrange three Double Butterfly Blocks, 5 Butterfly A Blocks and four Butterfly B Blocks referring to block drawings for positioning of butterflies on blocks. Fuse shapes in place referring to manufacturer's instructions.

Step 6. Pin a piece of tear-off stabilizer behind each butterfly motif. Using thread to match fabrics, machine-appliqué around each shape. When appliqué is complete, remove stabilizer and trim blocks to 10 1/2" x 10 1/2".

Step 7. Arrange appliquéd blocks with pieced blocks in rows referring to Figure 1. Join blocks in rows; join rows to complete quilt center. Press seams in one direction.

Figure 1
Arrange pieced blocks with appliquéd
blocks in rows as shown.

Step 8. Cut and piece two strips each turquoise solid 1" x 50 1/2" and 1" x 51 1/2". Sew the shorter strips to the top and bottom and longer strips to opposite sides; press seams toward strips.

Step 9. Cut and piece two strips each white solid 1" x 51 1/2" and 1" x 52 1/2". Sew the shorter strips to the top and bottom and longer strips to opposite sides; press seams toward strips.

Step 10. Cut and piece two strips each bright pink solid 1" x 52 1/2" x 1" x 53 1/2". Sew the shorter strips to the top and bottom and longer strips to opposite sides; press seams toward strips.

Step 11. Cut two strips each pink print 5" x 53 1/2" and 5" x 62 1/2". Sew the shorter strips to the top and bottom and longer strips to opposite sides; press seams toward strips.

Step 12. Prepare for quilting and finish with self-bound edges referring to the General Instructions. *Note: The project shown was machine-quilted in the ditch of seams and around the appliqué shapes.*

Butterfly Pillow

Instructions

Step 1. Prepare one Double Butterfly Block referring to Steps 3–6 for Butterfly Lap Quilt; machine-stitch antennae on each butterfly referring to the full-size patterns for placement. *Note: Refer to the Placement Diagram for arrangement of butterfly shapes.*

Step 2. Sew a 1" x 13" turquoise solid strip to top and bottom of appliquéd block; press seams toward strips. Trim excess strip even with block edge as shown in Figure 2. Sew remaining strips to opposite sides; press and trim as before.

Step 3. Add the 1"-wide white and bright pink solid strips to the block in that order as for turquoise solid strips.

Step 4. Sew the 3"-wide pink print strips starting with the top and bottom and then sides, trimming and pressing as for other strips.

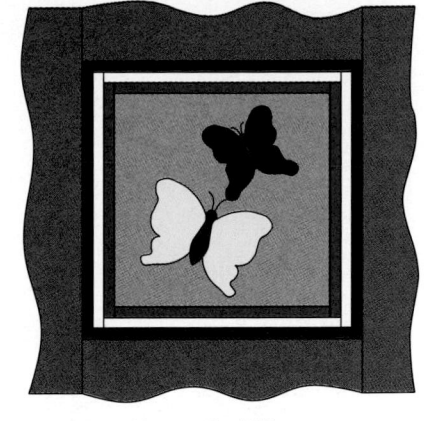

Butterfly Pillow
Placement Diagram
18" x 18" including flange

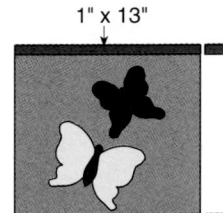

Figure 2
Trim strip even with block.

Project Specifications
Project Size: 18" x 18" including
  flange
Block Size: 10" x 10"
Number of Blocks: 1

Materials
- 11" x 11" square light pink solid
- Scraps for butterfly appliqué
- 4 strips turquoise solid 1" x 13"
- 4 strips white solid 1" x 15"
- 4 strips bright pink solid 1" x 17"
- 4 strips pink print 3" x 20"
- Backing 20" x 20"
- Batting 20" x 20"
- 14" square pillow form
- All-purpose thread to match fabrics
- Basic sewing supplies and tools

Step 5. Place batting under completed pillow top. Machine-quilt in the ditch of seams and around butterfly shapes using white all-purpose thread.

Step 6. Place backing piece right sides together with quilted pillow top; trim edges even. Stitch around sides leaving an 8" opening on one side.

Step 7. Turn pillow right side out; press edges flat.

Step 8. Mark a line 1/2" from seam between dark pink and pink print strips as shown in Figure 3. To make flange, stitch on the marked line all around except between opening left in seams.

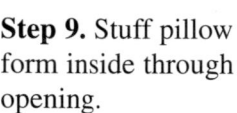 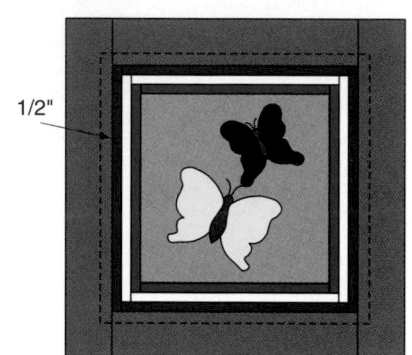

Figure 3
Mark a line 1/2" from seam between dark pink and pink print strips; stitch on line to make flange.

Step 9. Stuff pillow form inside through opening.

Step 10. Stitch on remainder of marked line. Slip-stitch opening closed to finish.

Butterfly Bedroom Mini-Quilt

Instructions

Step 1. Complete one Butterfly B Block as in Steps 3–6 for Butterfly Lap Quilt; machine-stitch antennae referring to the full-size pattern for placement.

Step 2. Sew border strips to appliquéd blocks as in Steps 2–4 for Butterfly Pillow.

Butterfly Mini-Quilt
Placement Diagram
18" x 18"

Step 3. Place appliquéd top on top of the batting square. Place the prepared backing piece right sides together with the appliquéd top. Trim backing and batting even with appliquéd top edges.

Step 4. Stitch all around edges, leaving a 6" opening on one side; turn right side out. Slipstitch opening closed.

Step 5. Machine-quilt in the ditch of seams, around the appliqué shapes and as desired to finish. ❖

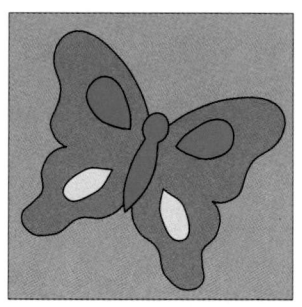

Butterfly A
10" x 10" Block

Butterfly B
10" x 10" Block

Double Butterfly
10" x 10" Block

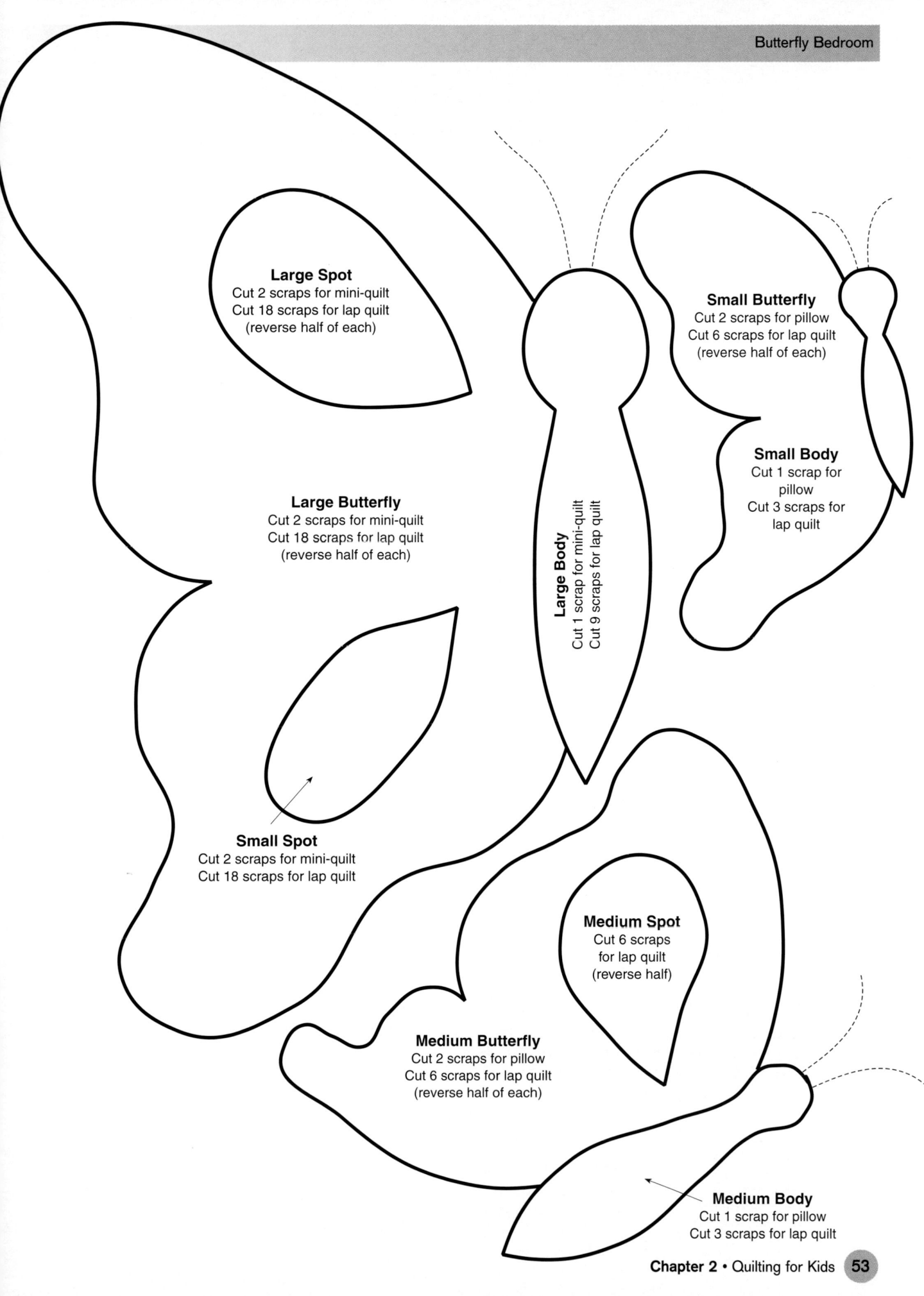

Large Spot
Cut 2 scraps for mini-quilt
Cut 18 scraps for lap quilt
(reverse half of each)

Small Butterfly
Cut 2 scraps for pillow
Cut 6 scraps for lap quilt
(reverse half of each)

Small Body
Cut 1 scrap for
pillow
Cut 3 scraps for
lap quilt

Large Butterfly
Cut 2 scraps for mini-quilt
Cut 18 scraps for lap quilt
(reverse half of each)

Large Body
Cut 1 scrap for mini-quilt
Cut 9 scraps for lap quilt

Small Spot
Cut 2 scraps for mini-quilt
Cut 18 scraps for lap quilt

Medium Spot
Cut 6 scraps
for lap quilt
(reverse half)

Medium Butterfly
Cut 2 scraps for pillow
Cut 6 scraps for lap quilt
(reverse half of each)

Medium Body
Cut 1 scrap for pillow
Cut 3 scraps for lap quilt

Happy Birthday Place Mat

By Janice Loewenthal

Make a place mat for the special birthday person to use on his or her important day.

Instructions

Step 1. Prepare patterns for appliqué pieces using patterns given. Trace shapes on paper side of fusible transfer web; cut out shapes leaving a margin around traced line.

Step 2. Fuse paper shapes onto wrong side of fabric scraps as directed on patterns for color. Cut out shapes on traced lines; remove paper backing.

Step 3. Arrange pieces on 12" x 16" background piece referring to the Placement Diagram and photo of project for positioning of pieces.

Step 4. Fuse shapes in place referring to manufacturer's instructions.

Step 5. Place a piece of tear-off fabric stabilizer behind fused motifs. Using thread to match fabrics in the top of the machine and in the bobbin, machine-appliqué all pieces in place.

Happy Birthday Place Mat
Placement Diagram
12" x 16"

Project Specifications
Skill Level: Beginner
Project Size: 12" x 16"

Materials
- 12" x 16" rectangle blue print for background
- Scraps red, orange, green, peach, white, brown, blue and gold prints or solids
- Backing 14" x 18"
- Batting 14" x 18"
- 2 yards self-made or purchased binding
- Thread to match appliqué fabrics
- 1/3 yard fusible transfer web
- 1/3 yard tear-off fabric stabilizer
- Permanent fabric pen
- Basic sewing supplies and tools

Step 6. Add detail lines for balloon strings, candlewicks and hat top again referring to the Placement Diagram and photo of project for positioning.

Step 7. Add words "It's Your Day" using a permanent fabric pen or machine-embroider using contrasting thread.

Step 8. When appliqué and words are complete prepare place mat for quilting and finish referring to General Instructions. ❖

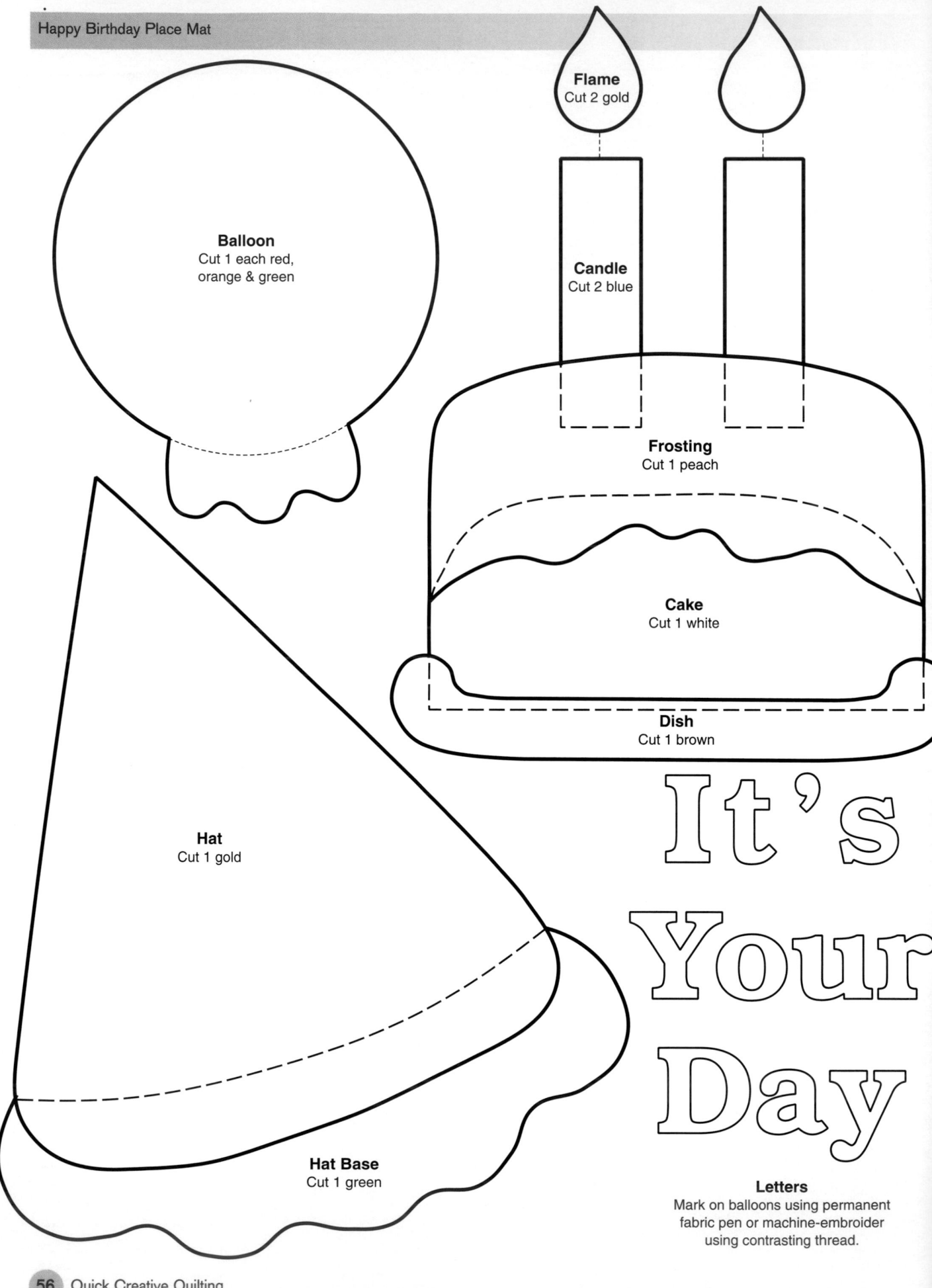

Balloon
Cut 1 each red,
orange & green

Flame
Cut 2 gold

Candle
Cut 2 blue

Frosting
Cut 1 peach

Cake
Cut 1 white

Dish
Cut 1 brown

Hat
Cut 1 gold

Hat Base
Cut 1 green

It's
Your
Day

Letters
Mark on balloons using permanent
fabric pen or machine-embroider
using contrasting thread.

Little Sheriff Vest

By Janice Loewenthal

Your little cowboy can wear this vest as he pretends to be the sheriff.

Instructions

Step 1. Wash sweatshirt and all fabrics; do not use fabric softener.

Step 2. Use a water-erasable marker and straight edge to draw a line down the center front of the sweatshirt; cut open along line.

Step 3. Carefully remove the bottom ribbing and sleeves from the sweatshirt.

Step 4. Unfold one edge of the rust single-fold bias tape; align the outer edge of the tape with the bottom edge of the sweatshirt with right sides together; stitch along the pressed line of the bias tape. Turn to wrong side of sweatshirt; press. Repeat on sleeve openings. Hand-stitch binding in place.

Step 5. Prepare patterns for appliqué pieces using full-size patterns given. Trace shapes on paper side of fusible transfer web; cut out shapes leaving a margin around traced line.

Project Specifications
Skill Level: Beginner
Project Size: Child size

Materials
- Brown child-size sweatshirt with set-in sleeves
- Scraps rust, stripe, gold, tan and brown
- Thread to match appliqué fabrics
- 1/3 yard fusible transfer web
- 1/4 yard tear-off fabric stabilizer
- 1 package rust single-fold bias tape
- 1 yard purchased 2 1/4"-wide rust fringe
- Black and white permanent fabric pens
- Basic sewing supplies and tools and water-erasable marker

Step 6. Fuse paper shapes onto wrong side of fabric scraps as directed on patterns for color. Cut out shapes on traced lines; remove paper backing.

Step 7. Arrange hat motif on one side and pony motif on other side of vest front, layering pieces as necessary and referring to the Placement Diagram and photo of project for positioning of pieces. Fuse pieces in place.

Step 8. Place a piece of tear-off fabric stabilizer behind fused motifs. Using thread to match fabrics in the top of the machine and in the bobbin, machine-appliqué all pieces in place; stitch detail lines.

Step 9. Draw eyes and nostrils referring to marks on pattern for positioning and using black and white permanent fabric pens.

Step 10. Cut the 2 1/4"-wide rust fringe to fit around bottom edge of vest. Topstitch in place to finish. ❖

Little Sheriff Vest
Placement Diagram
Child Size

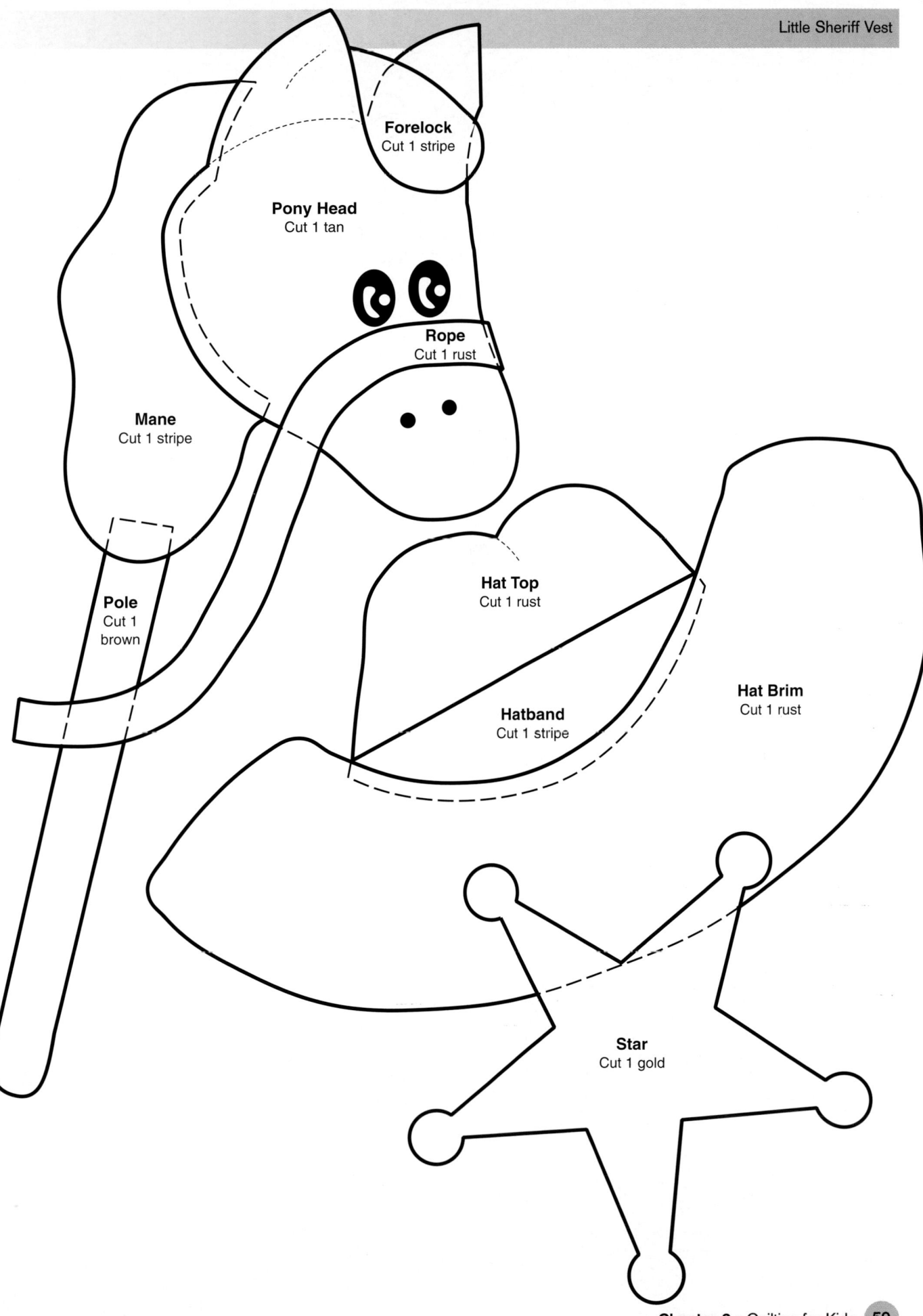

Forelock
Cut 1 stripe

Pony Head
Cut 1 tan

Rope
Cut 1 rust

Mane
Cut 1 stripe

Pole
Cut 1
brown

Hat Top
Cut 1 rust

Hatband
Cut 1 stripe

Hat Brim
Cut 1 rust

Star
Cut 1 gold

Pete Goes Skating

By Sue Kruger

Combine fused fabric with simple painting techniques to decorate a child's sweatshirt.

Instructions

Step 1. Prepare patterns for appliqué motif using full-size pattern given. Trace shapes on paper side of fusible transfer web; cut out shapes leaving a margin around traced line.

Step 2. Fuse paper shapes onto wrong side of fabric scraps as directed on pattern for color. Cut out shapes on traced lines; remove paper backing.

Step 3. Using full-size pattern as a guide, arrange fabric pieces on center front of sweatshirt in numerical order, overlapping pieces as necessary; fuse in place referring to manufacturer's instructions.

Step 4. Using black fine-point permanent fabric pen, add details to hat, skates and beak referring to lines on pattern.

Step 5. Make a milk chocolate wash; shade pompom in various places, along inside edge of chest and face and on top edges of feet.

Step 6. Make a black wash; shade hat under pompom,

Project Specifications

Skill Level: Intermediate
Project Size: Child size

Materials

- Child-size sweatshirt
- Scraps of white, black, blue, gray and orange
- Clear nylon monofilament
- Gray all-purpose thread
- 1/4 yard fusible transfer web
- 1/4 yard tear-off fabric stabilizer
- Black fine-point permanent fabric pen
- White nylon flat brush #8
- Small stencil brush
- White, black, milk chocolate and navy blue acrylic paints
- Fabric medium
- Paprika stencil cream
- Palette paper or waxed paper
- Machine-embroidery needle
- Basic sewing supplies and tools

above brim area, along back edge and between lines on brim. Shade top edges of skate blades.

Step 7. Make a white wash; highlight front edge of hat and top of brim, toe area of feet, penguin body to separate head, arms, legs and tail feathers and around skate blades on ice.

Step 8. Using white, paint snow around ice. Make a navy blue wash; shade snow and ice in various places to make shadows.

Step 9. Use small stencil brush and paprika stencil cream to make cheek.

Pete Goes Skating
Placement Diagram
Child Size

Step 10. Use the end of the flat brush to add a black dot for eye and white dot highlights to the cheek and top of the eye.

Step 11. Position tear-off fabric stabilizer under appliqué motif. Using a darning foot and machine-embroidery needle with clear nylon monofilament in the top of the machine and gray all-purpose thread in the bobbin, lower machine feed dogs and stitch in a back-and-forth motion over all fused pieces covering all pieces with stitches up to edges. Remove fabric stabilizer to finish. ❖

Painting Hints

Put a small amount of acrylic paint on your palette or waxed paper; add fabric medium to about half and half. Stir with a toothpick.

To make a wash of color for shading along one side of the appliqué shape (example: the brown around inside of chest and face), place a small puddle of fabric medium off to one side of the palette. Walk one corner of the flat brush corner into the paint, then walk it back out on the palette. There should only be a small amount of paint on the brush. If you have paint across the brush, clean out the brush in the water and start over. **Note:** *If your paint puddle gets messy, pour another puddle of paint and fabric medium.*

When you have paint only on one side, dip the other side of the brush into the puddle of fabric medium. Work the brush back and forth on the palette; make sure paint is only on one side and that it fades away to nothing. When you are happy with the color, dip the brush back into the fabric medium.

Note: The fabric medium helps the paint adhere to the fabric and also helps the color float.

Highlights are most often added with white on the top side (for example, penguin's hat). Highlights are applied in the same manner as shading except they are applied to the opposite side of the shape.

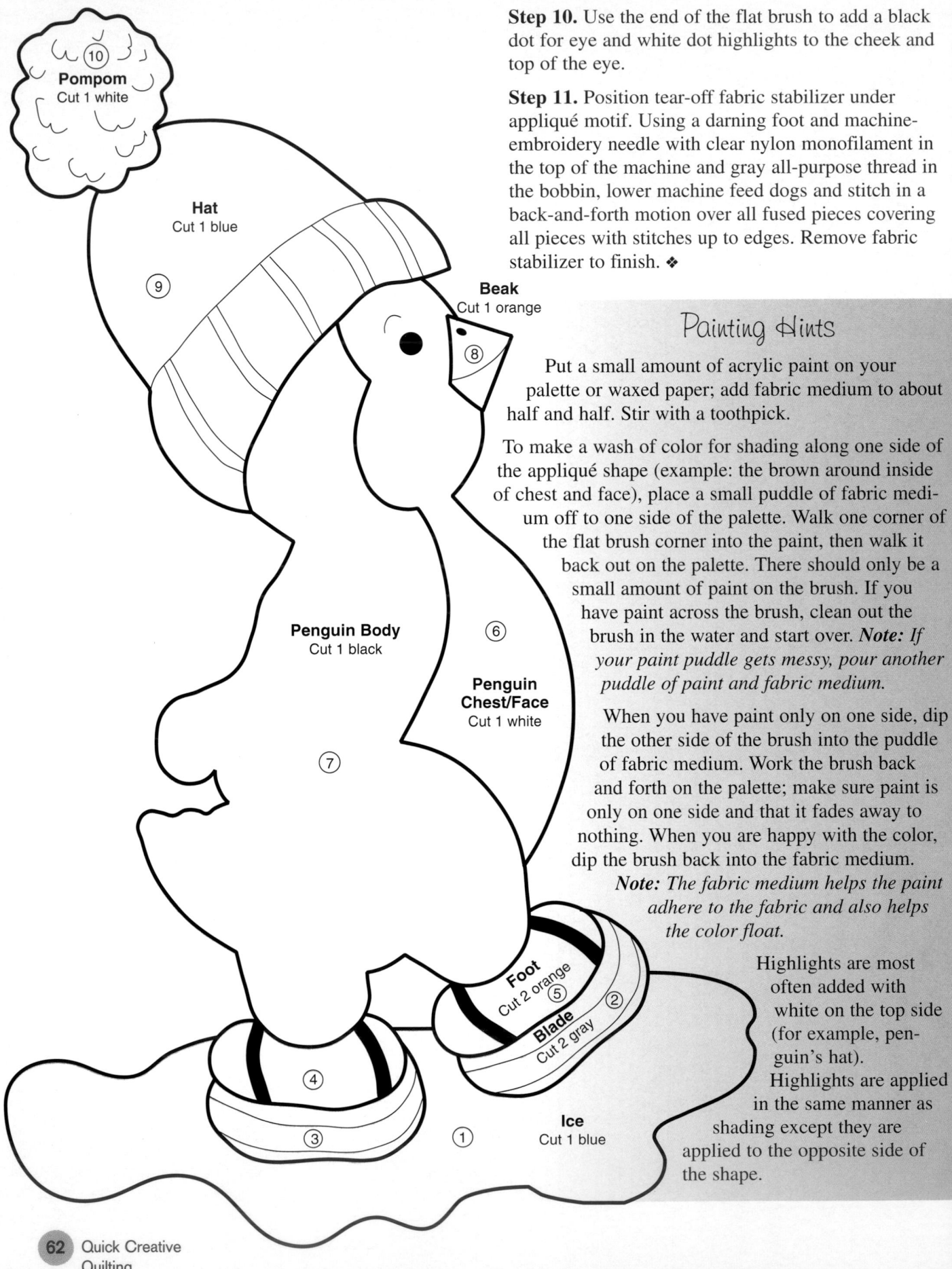

Pompom
Cut 1 white

Hat
Cut 1 blue

Beak
Cut 1 orange

Penguin Body
Cut 1 black

Penguin Chest/Face
Cut 1 white

Foot
Cut 2 orange

Blade
Cut 2 gray

Ice
Cut 1 blue

Sailboat Bedroom

By Norma Storm

Make this sailboat ensemble for your future sailor. It will help him or her sail into dreamland.

Sailboat Lap Quilt

Instructions

Step 1. Cut 12 rectangles light blue print 8 1/2" x 10 1/2" for sky. Cut 12 strips medium blue print 2 1/2" x 10 1/2" for water. Sew medium blue print strip to a light blue print rectangle to complete background as shown in Figure 1; repeat for 12 background blocks.

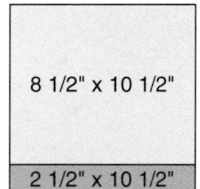

8 1/2" x 10 1/2"

2 1/2" x 10 1/2"

Figure 1
Sew medium blue strip to light blue rectangle to complete background.

Step 2. Cut seven squares each 10 7/8" x 10 7/8" medium blue and navy blue print. Cut each square in half on one diagonal to make triangles. Sew a medium blue print triangle to a navy blue print triangle to make triangle/square alternating blocks. You will need 13 alternating pieced blocks.

Step 3. Prepare templates for sailboat motifs using patterns given. Trace shapes onto paper side of fusible

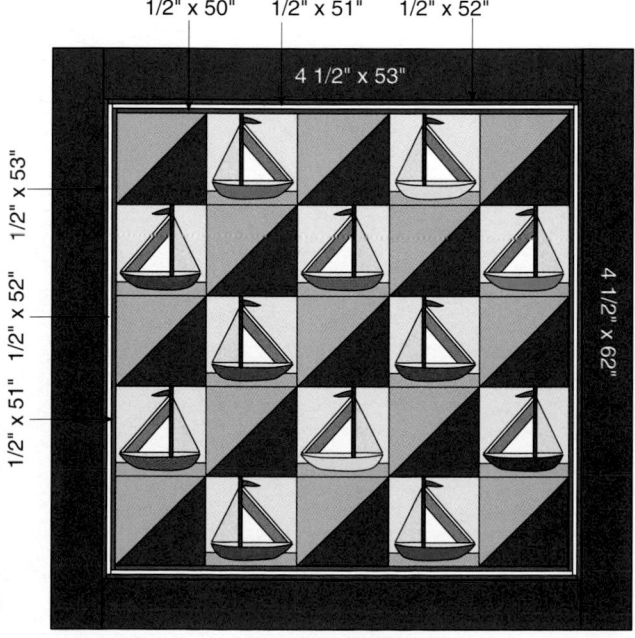

1/2" x 50"   1/2" x 51"   1/2" x 52"

4 1/2" x 53"

1/2" x 53"   1/2" x 52"   1/2" x 51"

4 1/2" x 62"

Sailboat Lap Quilt
Placement Diagram
62" x 62"

Project Specifications

Skill Level: Intermediate
Project Size: 62" x 62"
Block Size: 10" x 10"
Number of Appliquéd Blocks: 12
Number of Pieced Blocks: 13

Materials

- Scraps for boats and flags
- Scraps stripes for sail trim
- 1/4 yard tan print for small sails
- 1/2 yard white solid for large sails and narrow border
- 1/2 yard each bright blue print and red solid for narrow borders
- 3/4 yard light blue for sky
- 1 yard medium blue print for water and alternating blocks
- 2 yards navy blue print for borders and alternating blocks
- Backing 66" x 66"
- Batting 66" x 66"
- All-purpose thread to match fabrics
- 3 yards 1/2"-wide navy blue ribbon
- 2 yards fusible transfer web
- 2 yards tear-off fabric stabilizer
- Basic sewing supplies and tools

transfer web as directed for lap quilt on each piece. Cut out shapes leaving a margin all around traced lines.

Step 4. Fuse shapes to fabric scraps as desired to make colorful boats. Cut out shapes on traced lines; remove paper backing.

Step 5. Arrange sailboats on background blocks referring to the block drawings for positioning to make six Sailboat A blocks and six Sailboat B

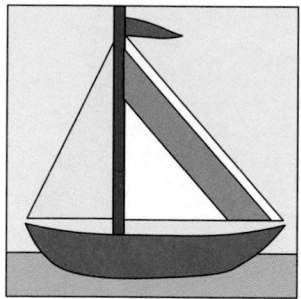

Sailboat A
10" x 10" Block

Sailboat B
10" x 10" Block

blocks. Fuse shapes in place referring to manufacturer's instructions.

Step 6. Cut a piece of navy blue ribbon 9" long. Fold one end under to fit against boat piece. Position on block referring to the block drawings for placement and leaving unfolded end extending on top. Stitch in place on both sides of ribbon and across edge by boat; trim excess even with block edge. Repeat for all blocks.

Step 7. Pin a piece of tear-off stabilizer behind each sailboat motif. Using thread to match fabrics, machine-appliqué around each shape; remove stabilizer.

Figure 2
Join 3 Sailboat B blocks with 2 alternating blocks to make a row.

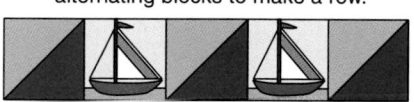

Figure 3
Join 2 Sailboat A blocks with 3 alternating blocks to make a row.

Step 8. Join three Sailboat B blocks with two alternating blocks to make a row referring to Figure 2; press seams in one direction. Repeat for two rows. Join two Sailboat A blocks with three alternating blocks to make a row referring to Figure 3; press seams in one direction. Repeat for three rows.

Step 9. Join rows to complete pieced center beginning and ending with the Sailboat A block rows. Press seams in one direction.

Step 10. Cut and piece two strips each bright blue print 1" x 50 1/2" and 1" x 51 1/2". Sew the shorter strips to the top and bottom and longer strips to opposite sides; press seams toward strips.

Step 11. Cut and piece two strips each white solid 1" x 51 1/2" and 1" x 52 1/2". Sew the shorter strips to the top and bottom and longer strips to opposite sides; press seams toward strips.

Step 12. Cut and piece two strips each red solid 1" x

52 1/2" x 1" x 53 1/2". Sew the shorter strips to the top and bottom and longer strips to opposite sides; press seams toward strips.

Step 13. Cut two strips each navy blue print 5" x 53 1/2" and 5" x 62 1/2". Sew the shorter strips to the top and bottom and longer strips to opposite sides; press seams toward strips.

Step 14. Prepare for quilting and finish referring to the General Instructions for self-bound edges.

Sailboat B Pillow

Project Specifications
Project Size: 18" x 18" including flange
Block Size: 10" x 10"
Number of Blocks: 1

Materials
- 2 1/2" x 10 1/2" rectangle medium blue print
- 8 1/2" x 10 1/2" rectangle light blue print
- Scraps white, tan, blue and stripe for sailboat
- 4 strips bright blue print 1" x 13"
- 4 strips white solid 1" x 15"
- 4 strips bright red solid 1" x 17"
- 4 strips navy blue print 3" x 20"
- Backing 20" x 20"
- Batting 20" x 20"
- 14" square pillow form
- All-purpose thread to match fabrics
- 9" piece 1/2"-wide navy blue ribbon
- Basic sewing supplies and tools

Instructions
Step 1. Sew the medium blue print rectangle to the light blue print rectangle to complete background as shown in Figure 1.

Step 2. Prepare one Sailboat B block referring to Steps 3–7 for Sailboat Lap Quilt.

Step 3. Sew a 1" x 13" bright blue print strip to top and bottom of appliquéd block; press seams toward strips. Trim excess strip even with block edge as shown in Figure 4. Sew remaining strips to opposite sides; press and trim as before.

Step 4. Add the 1"-wide white and red solid strips to the block in the same order as for bright blue print strips.

Step 5. Sew the 3"-wide navy blue print strips starting with the top and bottom and then sides, trimming and pressing as for other strips.

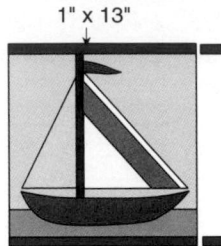

Figure 4
Trim strip even with block.

Step 6. Place batting under completed pillow top. Machine-quilt in the ditch of seams and around sailboat shape using blue all-purpose thread.

Sailboat B Pillow
Placement Diagram
18" x 18" including flange

Step 7. Place backing piece right sides together with quilted pillow top; trim edges even. Stitch around sides leaving an 8" opening on one side.

Step 8. Turn pillow right side out; press edges flat.

Step 9. Mark a line 1/2" from seam between red and navy blue strips as shown in Figure 5. To make flange, stitch on the marked line all around except between opening left in seams.

Figure 5
Mark a line 1/2" from seam between navy blue and red strips; stitch on line to make flange.

Step 10. Stuff pillow form inside through opening.

Step 11. Stitch on remainder of marked line. Slip-stitch opening closed to finish.

Sailboat A Mini-Quilt

Instructions

Step 1. Sew the medium blue print rectangle to the

Project Specifications
Project Size: 18" x 18"
Block Size: 10" x 10"
Number of Blocks: 1

Materials
- 2 1/2" x 10 1/2" rectangle medium blue print
- 8 1/2" x 10 1/2" rectangle light blue print
- Scraps white, tan, red and stripe for sailboat
- 4 strips bright blue print 1" x 13"
- 4 strips white solid 1" x 15"
- 4 strips bright red solid 1" x 17"
- 4 strips navy blue print 3" x 20"
- Backing 20" x 20"
- Batting 20" x 20"
- 2 1/2 yards self-made or purchased binding
- All-purpose thread to match fabrics
- 9" piece 1/2"-wide navy blue ribbon
- Basic sewing supplies and tools

light blue print rectangle to complete background as shown in Figure 1.

Step 2. Complete one Sailboat A block as in Steps 3–7 for Sailboat Lap Quilt. *Note: The flag on the sample project was stitched as a three-dimensional piece. If you prefer to make your project using this method, cut one extra flag piece, layer both pieces right sides together, stitch and turn right side out; press. Insert raw ends of stitched flag under ribbon before stitching.*

Sailboat A Wall Quilt
Placement Diagram
18" x 18"

Step 3. Sew border strips to appliquéd block as in Steps 3–5 for Sailboat B Pillow.

Step 4. Prepare for quilting and finish with bound edges referring to the General Instructions. ***Note:*** *The* *project shown was machine-quilted in the ditch of seams* *and around the appliqué shapes.* ❖

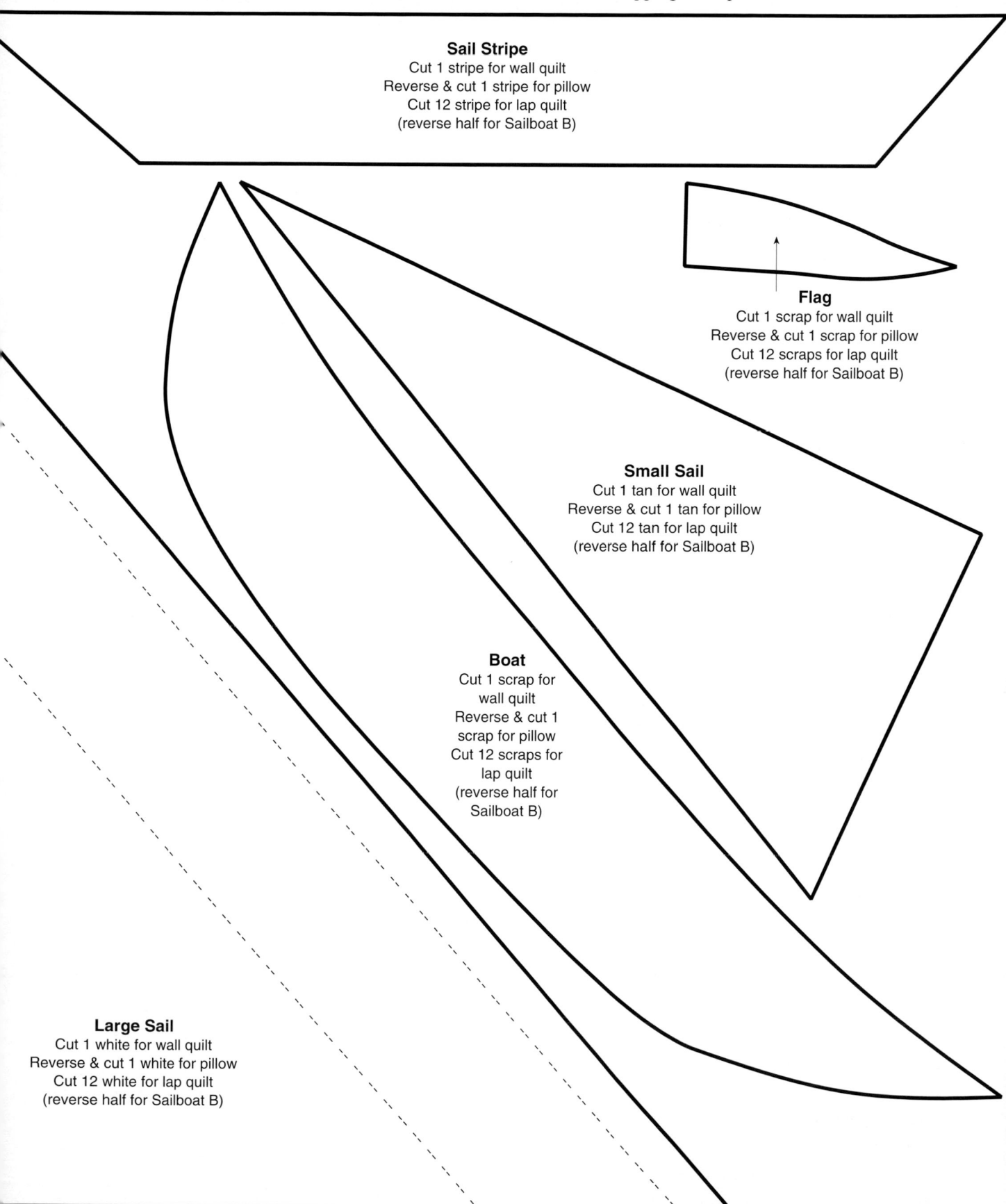

Sail Stripe
Cut 1 stripe for wall quilt
Reverse & cut 1 stripe for pillow
Cut 12 stripe for lap quilt
(reverse half for Sailboat B)

Flag
Cut 1 scrap for wall quilt
Reverse & cut 1 scrap for pillow
Cut 12 scraps for lap quilt
(reverse half for Sailboat B)

Small Sail
Cut 1 tan for wall quilt
Reverse & cut 1 tan for pillow
Cut 12 tan for lap quilt
(reverse half for Sailboat B)

Boat
Cut 1 scrap for
wall quilt
Reverse & cut 1
scrap for pillow
Cut 12 scraps for
lap quilt
(reverse half for
Sailboat B)

Large Sail
Cut 1 white for wall quilt
Reverse & cut 1 white for pillow
Cut 12 white for lap quilt
(reverse half for Sailboat B)

Pillowcase Sleep-Over Bag

By Janice Loewenthal

Use a purchased pillowcase to make this neat drawstring bag to carry a sleeping bag or other sleep-over items.

Instructions

Step 1. Wash pillowcase and all fabrics; do not use fabric softener.

Step 2. Measure distance around top of pillowcase; add 1" for hem on each end. Cut a piece of yellow print 5" wide by this length.

Step 3. Press under 1/2" on each end and along long edges of the yellow print strip.

Step 4. Align top edge of strip with the stitched edge of pillowcase hem, beginning and ending at side seam on pillowcase. Stitch in place along long edges as shown in Figure 1; leave ends open.

Figure 1
Stitch yellow print strip on pillowcase as shown.

Figure 2
Stitch 1" in from each edge to make casing.

Step 5. Stitch a second seam 1" in from each of the edge seams to make casing as shown in Figure 2.

Step 6. Prepare patterns for appliqué pieces using full-size patterns given. Trace shapes on paper side of fusible transfer web; cut out shapes leaving a margin around traced line.

Step 7. Fuse paper shapes onto wrong side of fabric scraps as directed on patterns for color. Cut out shapes on traced lines; remove paper backing.

Step 8. Arrange bear on moon with stars on pillowcase referring to the Placement Diagram and photo

Project Specifications
Skill Level: Beginner
Project Size: 20" x 32"

Materials
- Scraps gold, green, aqua, purple and brown
- 1/6 yard yellow print
- Purchased 20" x 32" pillowcase
- Threads to match appliqué fabrics
- 5/8 yard fusible transfer web
- 5/8 yard tear-off fabric stabilizer
- 1 1/2 yards 1"-wide black cord
- Black permanent fabric pen
- Basic sewing supplies and tools

of project for positioning of pieces. Fuse pieces in place.

Step 9. Place a piece of tear-off fabric stabilizer behind fused motifs. Using thread to match fabrics in the top of the machine and in the bobbin, machine-appliqué all pieces in place. Add detail lines on bear's ears and body referring to pattern for placement. Stitch a line from bear's paw to lower star for string.

Step 10. Make eyes and nose using black permanent fabric pen referring to marks on pattern for positioning.

Step 11. Fold 1"-wide black cord in half along length; slip through casing in top of pillowcase and tie a knot in each end to finish. ❖

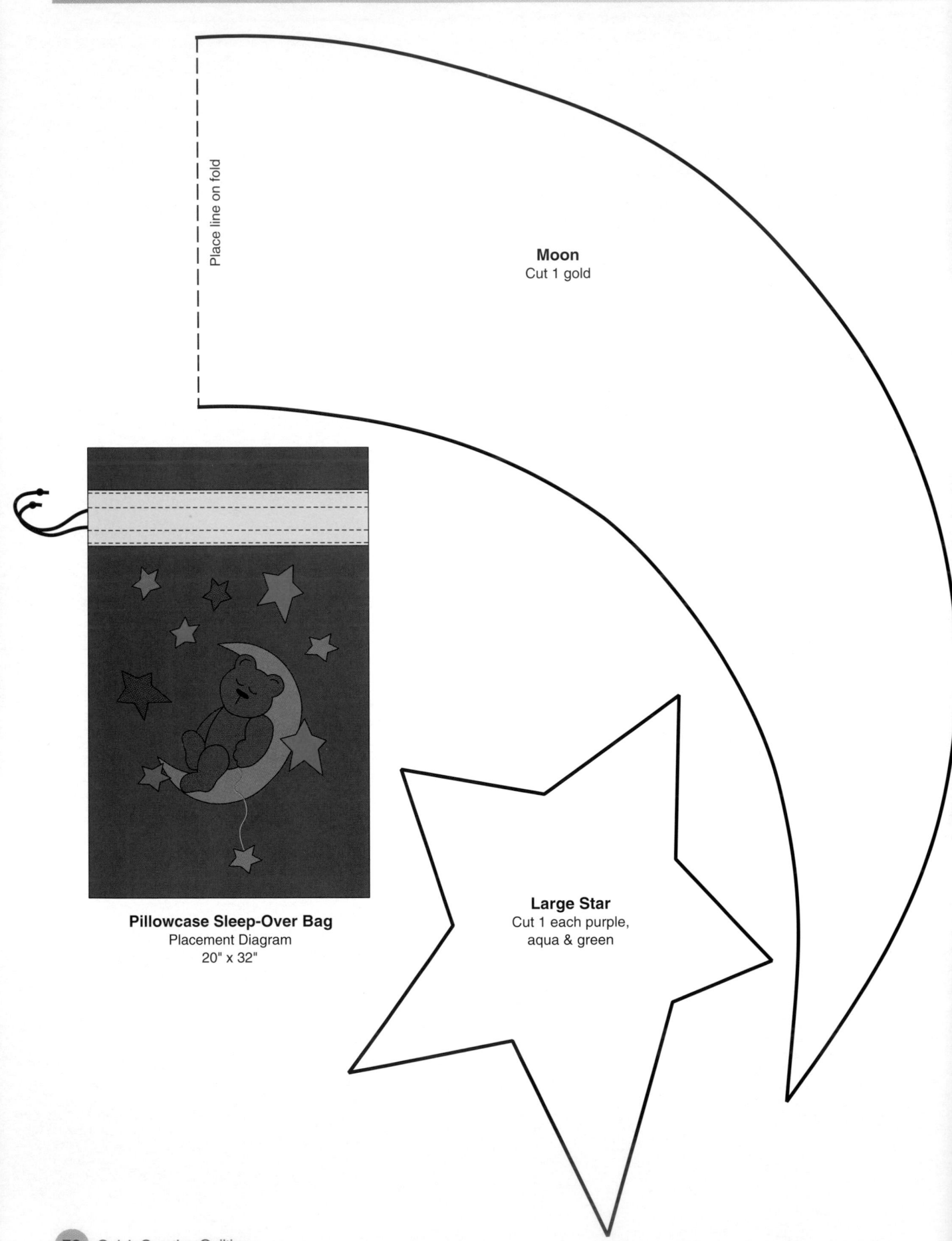

Place line on fold

Moon
Cut 1 gold

Pillowcase Sleep-Over Bag
Placement Diagram
20" x 32"

Large Star
Cut 1 each purple,
aqua & green

Small Star
Cut 1 each aqua,
purple & green & 3
gold

Bear
Cut 1 brown

Last-Minute Holiday Fun

You don't need to wait until the last weekend before a holiday to enjoy stitching a Santa pillow, Jack-o-Lantern bib, harvest candle mat, patriotic place mat, Easter coaster set or angel tree skirt. Begin your holiday fun now!

Snowflake Duo Ornaments

By Charlyne Stewart

Hang these pretty snowflake ornaments in a window or on your tree.

Instructions

Step 1. Cut two 6" x 6" squares from the pattern paper.

Step 2. Fold the paper in half on the diagonal; fold in half again and again as shown in Figure 1 to make an eight-layered piece.

Step 3. Prepare templates for each snowflake using the patterns given. Glue the template to the file folder cardboard using rubber cement; cut out.

Step 4. Place the template on the folds of the pattern paper as shown in Figure 2; pin in place. Trace; remove template and re-pin layers. Cut out on traced lines; open paper to reveal pattern.

Step 5. Cut two squares white, sheer iridescent fabric and one piece fleece 6 1/2" x 6 1/2". Pin or baste the fleece between the fabric layers.

Step 6. Place the pattern on top of the layered fabrics as shown in Figure 3; pin. Trace around shape and in all open areas using the fine-point blue permanent marking pen. Unpin; remove pattern.

Step 7. Using silver metallic thread in the top of the machine and white all-purpose thread in the bobbin, machine-stitch using a medium-width zigzag stitch on all marked lines; repeat using a slightly wider stitch.

Step 8. Using sharp craft scissors, cut close to stitching lines all around outside and inside edges as shown in Figure 4, being careful not to cut through stitches; trim all loose threads.

Project Specifications
Skill Level: Beginner
Project Size: Approximately 6" x 6"

Materials
- 3/8 yard white, sheer iridescent fabric
- 1/2 yard quilter's fleece
- 1 spool white all-purpose thread
- 1 spool silver metallic thread
- 1/4 yard pattern paper
- Fine-point blue permanent marking pen
- 24" (1/8"-wide) white satin ribbon
- Rubber cement
- File folder cardboard, tracing paper and pencil
- Basic sewing supplies and tools and sharp craft scissors

Step 9. Machine-quilt angled straight lines referring to Figure 5 for positioning of lines to simulate ice fractures.

Step 10. Cut the 1/8"-wide white satin ribbon into two 12" lengths. Using a large-eyed needle, thread the ribbon

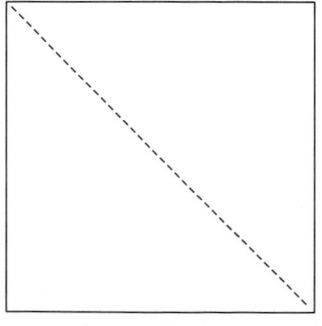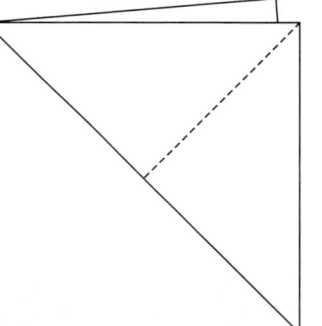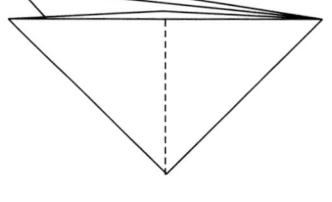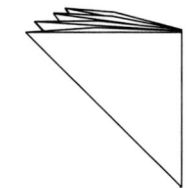

Figure 1
Fold paper as shown.

through one point of the snowflake. Tie ends in a double knot for hanging loop. Repeat for several snowflakes in each design or make up more of your own. ❖

Figure 2
Pin template on folded pattern paper.

Figure 3
Lay open pattern on layered fabric and fleece.

Figure 4
Cut close to stitching.

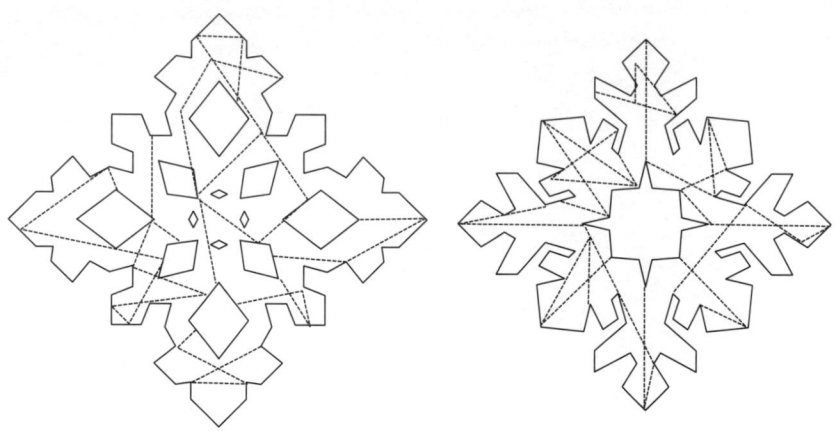

Figure 5
Machine-quilt angled straight lines as shown.

Snowflake 1
Placement Diagram
Approximately 6" x 6"

Snowflake 2
Placement Diagram
Approximately 6" x 6"

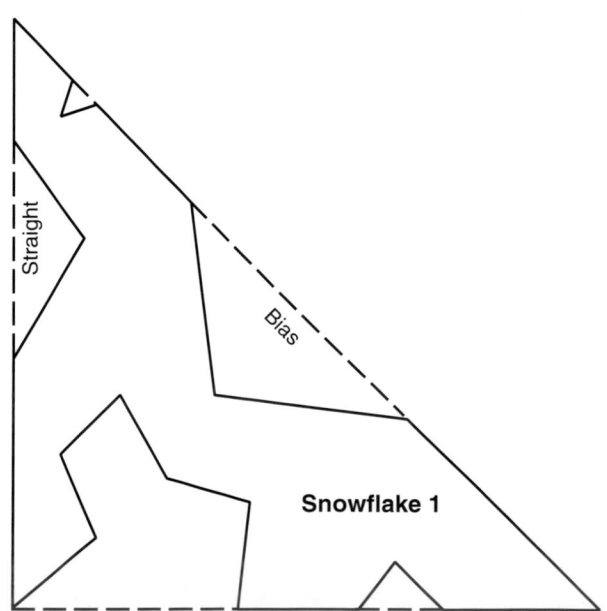

Straight

Bias

Snowflake 1

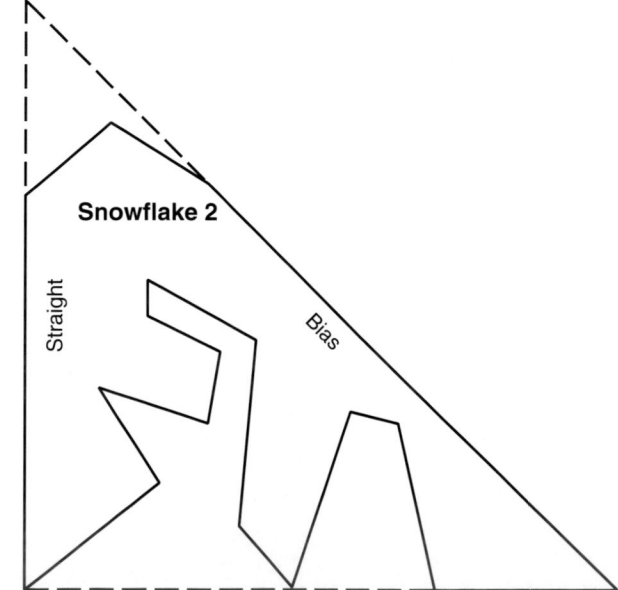

Snowflake 2

Straight

Bias

Love of Patchwork

By Judith Sandstrom

*Choose a border stripe and coordinating fabrics
to make this bright wall quilt with a lot of heart.*

Instructions

Step 1. From tan-on-tan print, cut one 2" by fabric width strip and four 1 1/2" by fabric width strips. Cut the 1 1/2" strips in half to make eight 1 1/2" x 21" strips.

Step 2. From the red print, cut one strip each 2" by fabric width and 3 1/2" by fabric width.

Step 3. From the gold print, cut three 1 1/2" by fabric width strips; cut each strip in half. Set aside one half-strip.

Step 4. From the blue print, cut two 1 1/2" by fabric width strips; cut each strip in half.

Step 5. From the brown print, cut one 1 1/2" by fabric width strip; cut the strip in half. Set aside one half-strip.

Step 6. From the green print, cut eight 3 7/8" x 3 7/8" squares, one 4 1/4" x 4 1/4" square and nine 1" by fabric width strips. Cut each of the 3 7/8" x 3 7/8" squares in half on one diagonal to make A triangles; you will need 16 A triangles. Cut the 4 1/4" x 4 1/4" square in half on both diagonals to make B triangles; you will need four B triangles. Cut two of the 1"

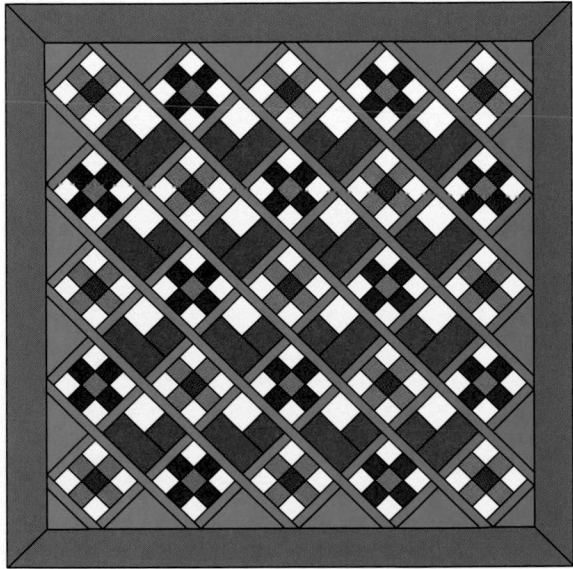

Love of Patchwork
Placement Diagram
Aproximately 29" x 29"

Project Specifications

Skill Level: Intermediate
Project Size: Approximately 29" x 29"
Block Size: 3" x 3"
Number of Blocks: 13 Nine-Patch A;
    12 Nine-Patch B and 16 Heart

Materials

- 1/8 yard each blue and brown prints
- 1/4 yard each red and gold prints
- 1/2 yard each tan-on-tan and green prints
- 1 yard vertical stripe for border
- Backing 33" x 33"
- Batting 33" x 33"
- 3 1/2 yards self-made or purchased binding
- All-purpose thread to match fabrics
- Basting spray
- Basic sewing supplies and tools, ruler, rotary cutter and mat

strips into two each 32 1/2" and 11 1/2" segments. Cut two 1" strips into two each 25 1/2" and 18 1/2" segments. Cut the remaining 1" strips into two 4 1/2" segments and fifty 3 1/2" C segments.

Step 7. With right sides together, stitch the 1 1/2" strips together along length as follows: tan-on-tan, gold, tan-on-tan—repeat for two strip sets; tan-on-tan, blue, tan-on-tan—repeat for two strip sets; gold, brown, gold; and blue, gold, blue. Press seams toward darkest fabric for all strip sets.

Step 8. Cut each strip set into 1 1/2" segments; you will cut 13 segments from each strip set.

Step 9. Join one gold-brown-gold segment with two

tan-on-tan-gold-tan-on-tan segments to make a Nine-Patch A block as shown in Figure 1; repeat for 13 blocks.

Step 10. Join one blue-gold-blue segment with two tan-on-tan-blue-tan-on-tan segments to make a Nine-Patch B block as shown in Figure 2; repeat for 12 blocks.

Step 11. Sew a 2" by fabric width tan-on-tan strip to a 2" by fabric width red print strip along length with right sides together; press seams toward red print strip. Cut strip into 2" segments. Cut the 3 1/2" by fabric width red print strip into 2" segments.

Step 12. Sew a red print segment to a red-tan-on-tan segment to make one Heart block as shown in Figure 3; repeat for 16 blocks. Press seams in one direction.

Step 13. Arrange blocks in diagonal rows with green print 3 1/2" C segments and A triangles as shown in Figure 4. Join units in rows.

Step 14. Arrange block rows with green print sashing strips as shown in Figure 5; join rows and sashing strips. Add B triangles to corners to complete pieced

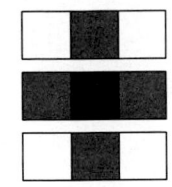

Figure 1
Join segments as shown to make a Nine-Patch A block.

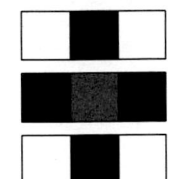

Figure 2
Join segments as shown to make a Nine-Patch B block.

Figure 3
Join segments to make Heart block.

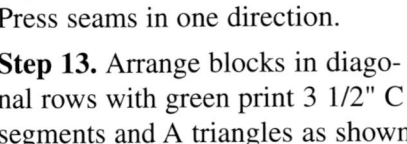

Figure 4
Arrange blocks with A triangles and C pieces as shown.

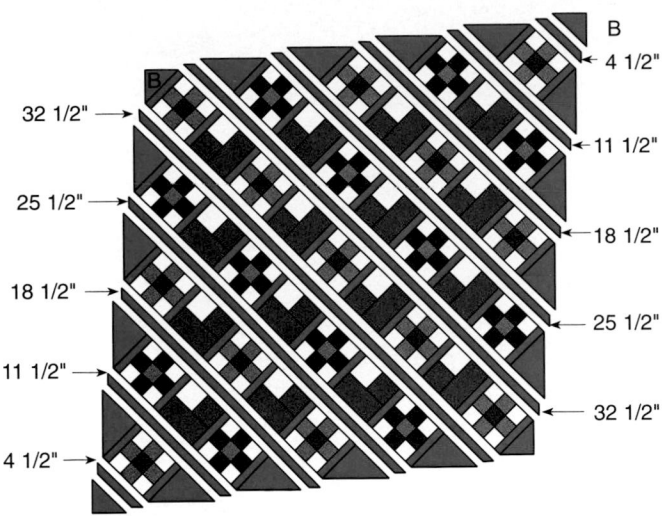

Figure 5
Arrange rows with green print strips and B triangles as shown.

section, again referring to Figure 5; press seams toward green print pieces.

Step 15. Cut four strips border stripe 2 1/2" x 31"; sew a strip to each side of the pieced center, mitering corners. Trim corner seams to 1/4"; press seams toward strips.

Step 16. Prepare quilt for quilting using basting spray on the wrong side of the backing and pieced top to eliminate pins or basting. Quilt and bind edges referring to the General Instructions. ❖

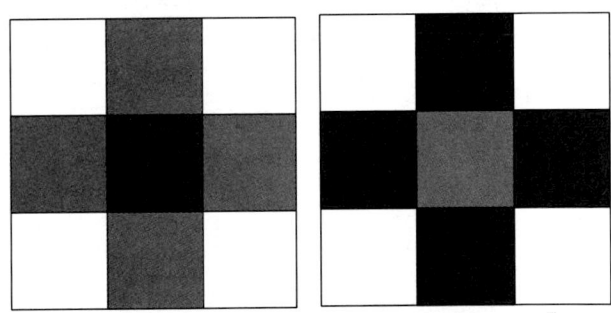

Nine-Patch A Block
3" x 3" Block
Make 13

Nine-Patch B Block
3" x 3" Block
Make 12

Heart
3" x 3" Block
Make 16

Heart in Diamond Chair Back

By Phyllis Dobbs

Make chair-back covers in solid colors and a simple design for an Amish look.

Instructions

Step 1. Cut one square light green solid 6 1/2" x 6 1/2" for A.

Step 2. Prepare template for heart shape using pattern given. Trace shape on the paper side of the 6" x 6" square fusible transfer web. Fuse traced shape on the wrong side of the pink solid; cut out shape on traced line. Remove paper backing.

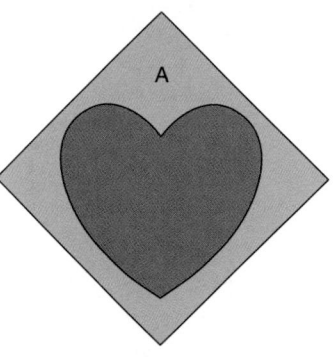

Figure 1
Center heart shape on A.

Step 3. Center the heart shape on the 6 1/2" x 6 1/2" A square as shown in Figure 1; fuse in place. Machine-appliqué around edges of heart shape using pink all-purpose thread.

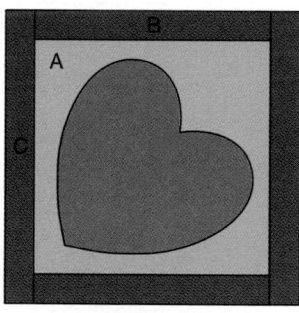

Figure 2
Sew B and C strips to A.

Step 4. Cut two strips each purple solid 1 1/4" x 6 1/2" (B) and 1 1/4" x 8" (C). Sew B to two opposite sides of A and C to the remaining sides referring to Figure 2; press seams toward strips.

Step 5. Cut two squares light green solid 6 1/4" x 6 1/4"; cut each square on one diagonal to make D triangles. Sew D to each side of the A-B-C unit as shown in Figure 3; press seams toward D.

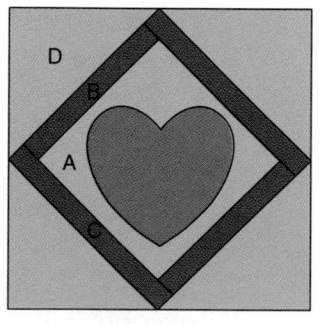

Figure 3
Sew a D triangle to each side of the pieced unit.

Step 6. Cut two strips each pink solid 1 1/4" x 11 1/8" (E) and 1 1/4" x 12 5/8" (F); sew E to two opposite sides of stitched unit and F to the remaining sides

Project Specifications
Skill Level: Beginner
Project Size: 16 1/8" x 16 1/8"

Materials
- 1/4 yard purple solid
- 1/4 yard each light green, dark green and pink solids
- Backing 20" x 20"
- Batting 20" x 20"
- Neutral color and pink all-purpose thread
- Clear nylon monofilament
- 6" x 6" square fusible transfer web
- Basic sewing supplies and tools

referring to Figure 4; press seams toward strips.

Step 7. Cut four strips dark green solid 2 1/2" x 12 5/8" (G) and four squares purple solid 2 1/2" x 2 1/2" (H). Sew G to two opposite sides of the pieced unit; press seams toward G. Sew an H square to each end of the remaining two G strips as shown in Figure 5. Sew a G-H strip to each remaining side of the pieced unit; press seams toward strips.

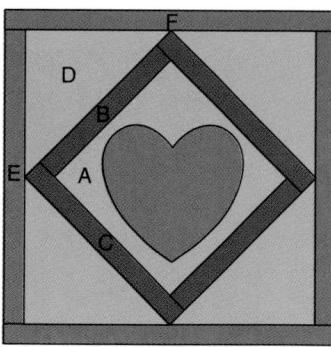

Figure 4
Sew E and F strips to the pieced unit.

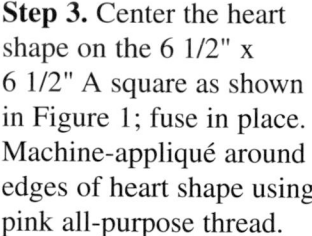

Figure 5
Sew H to each end of G.

Step 8. Cut four strips purple solid 2" x 22" for ties. Fold each strip in half along length with right sides together; stitch together along long raw edges and across one end at a

diagonal as shown in Figure 6. Trim excess on angled ends. Turn right side out through open end; press with seam on edge.

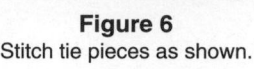

Figure 6
Stitch tie pieces as shown.

1/4"

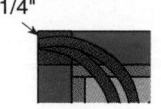

Figure 7
Pin ties at corners as shown.

Step 9. Pin two layered ties to one top side edge 1/4" from top, aligning the open end of the tie to the edge as shown in Figure 7; repeat for second set of ties on other corner.

Step 10. Pin the chair back to the backing, right sides together; lay both pieces on top of batting with chair back next to batting; pin layers together.

Step 11. Stitch around edges, leaving a 4" opening along bottom edge; turn and press. Hand-stitch opening closed.

Step 12. Pin the layers together. Machine-quilt in the

Heart in Diamond Chair Back
Placement Diagram
16 1/8" x 16 1/8"

ditch of seams and around appliquéd heart shape using clear nylon monofilament in the top of the machine and neutral color all-purpose thread in the bobbin. ❖

Heart
Cut 1 pink solid

Happy Easter Coaster Set

By Janice Loewenthal

Pastel fabric scraps and small squares of batting are all you need to make these neat coasters with Easter-design motifs.

Instructions

Step 1. Chose one appliqué motif. Prepare templates for each shape using full-size pattern given.

Step 2. Trace shapes onto paper side of fusible transfer web referring to pattern for number to cut. Cut out shapes leaving a margin beyond traced lines.

Step 3. Fuse shapes to fabric scraps using colors as desired. Cut out shapes on traced lines; remove paper backing.

Step 4. Cut one square light blue print 4 1/2" x 4 1/2". Center motif on square referring to full-size pattern and Placement Diagram for positioning of pieces; fuse in place.

Step 5. Cut a square of fabric stabilizer 4 1/2" x 4 1/2". Using threads to contrast or match fabrics, machine appliqué around each shape. Remove stabilizer when stitching is complete.

Step 6. Cut one square prequilted muslin 4 1/2" x 4 1/2"; pin behind fused motif. Place the appliquéd square on top of the muslin square wrong sides together; pin to hold.

Step 7. Cut two strips each pink print 1" x 4 1/2" and 1" x 6". Sew a 1" x 4 1/2" strip to opposite sides of layered coaster with right sides together. Turn under

Project Specifications
Skill Level: Beginner
Project Size: 4 1/2" x 4 1/2"

Materials
- Fat quarter light blue print for background
- Fat quarter pink print for binding
- Scraps assorted prints for appliqué
- 1/8 yard prequilted muslin
- All-purpose thread to match or contrast fabrics
- 1/8 yard fusible transfer web
- 1/8 yard tear-off fabric stabilizer
- Black and white permanent fabric pens
- Basic sewing supplies and tools

raw edge of strip 1/4" along length; turn to backside. Hand-stitch in place.

Step 8. Sew a 1" x 6" strip pink print to the remaining two sides. Turn under raw edge of each strip 1/4".

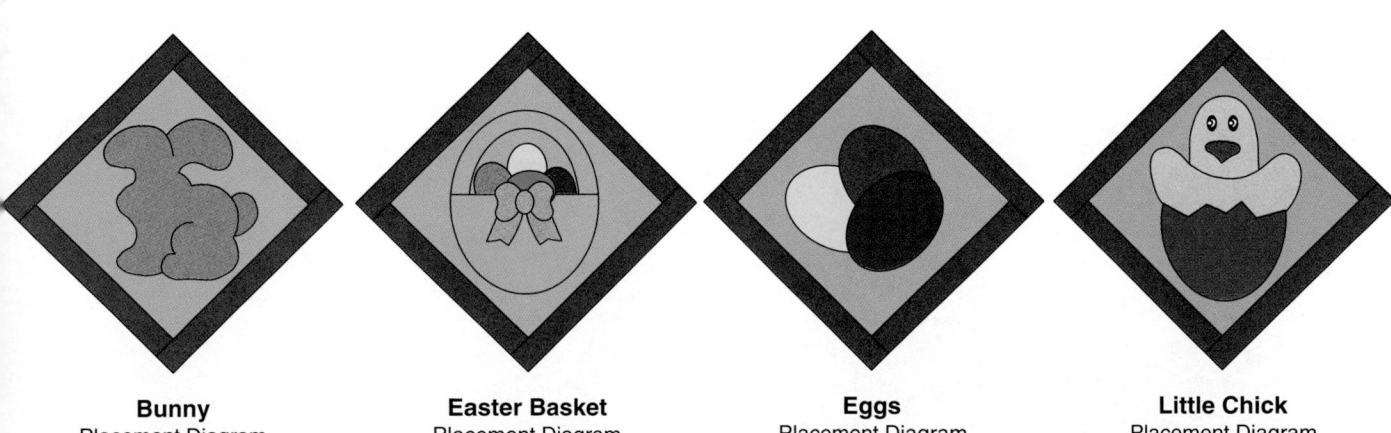

Bunny
Placement Diagram
4 1/2" x 4 1/2"

Easter Basket
Placement Diagram
4 1/2" x 4 1/2"

Eggs
Placement Diagram
4 1/2" x 4 1/2"

Little Chick
Placement Diagram
4 1/2" x 4 1/2"

along length; turn ends under even with square as shown in Figure 1; fold over seam. Hand-stitch in place. Repeat for one coaster in each design. *Note: For Little Chick design, use black and white permanent fabric pens to make eyes referring to pattern for placement.* ❖

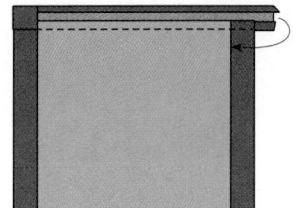

Figure 1
Fold ends under as shown.

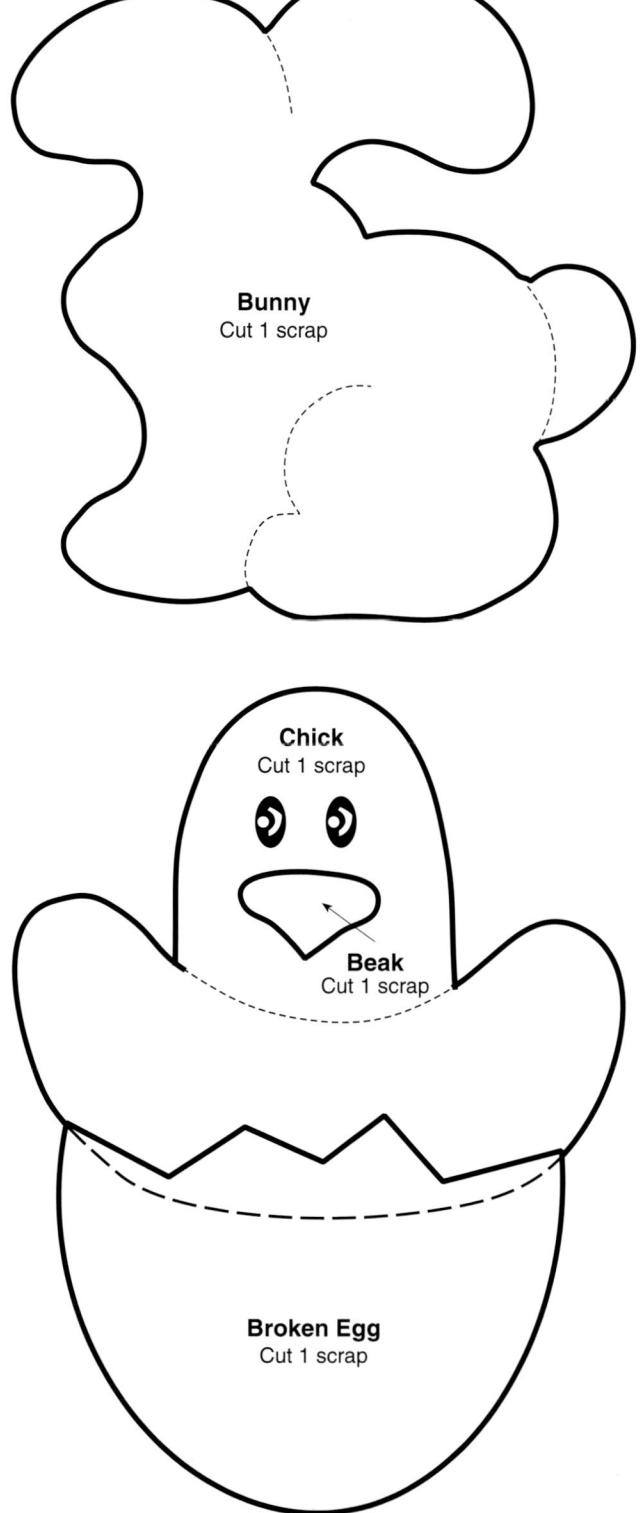

Bunny
Cut 1 scrap

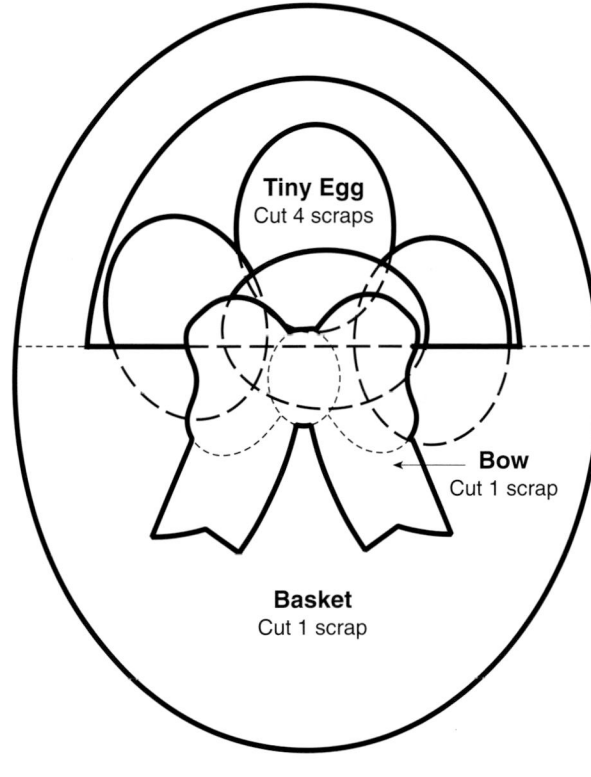

Tiny Egg
Cut 4 scraps

Bow
Cut 1 scrap

Basket
Cut 1 scrap

Chick
Cut 1 scrap

Beak
Cut 1 scrap

Broken Egg
Cut 1 scrap

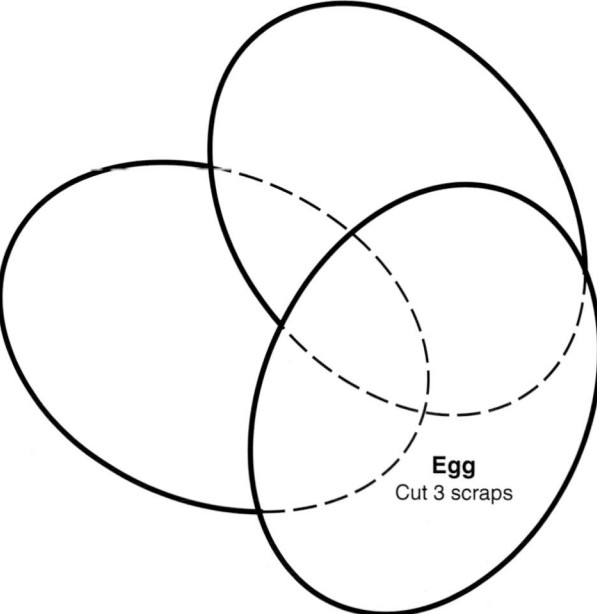

Egg
Cut 3 scraps

Forever Stripes Place Mat

By Phyllis Dobbs

Make some of these patriotic-looking place mats for your Fourth of July celebration this year.

Instructions

Step 1. Cut four strips red solid and two strips muslin 2" by fabric width. Sew the muslin strip between the two red solid strips to make a strip set; repeat for two strips sets.

Step 2. Cut strip sets into four 9 1/2" segments and four 5" segments as shown in Figure 1.

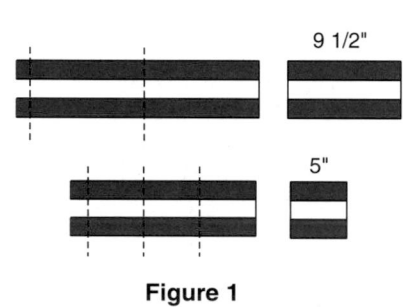

Figure 1
Cut strip sets as shown.

Step 3. Cut one strip navy blue solid 5" by fabric width; cut strip into eight 5" x 5" squares.

Step 4. Cut one strip muslin 5" by fabric width; cut strip into two 9 1/2" segments. Set aside remainder of strip to cut stars.

Step 5. Sew a 5" x 9 1/2" muslin segment between two pieced segments as shown in Figure 2; press. Repeat for second place mat.

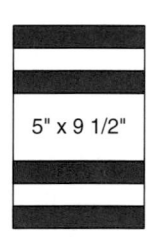

Figure 2
Sew the muslin segment between 2 pieced segments.

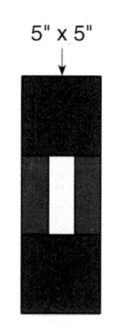

Figure 3
Sew a pieced segment between 2 squares.

Step 6. Sew a 5" pieced segment between two 5" x 5" navy blue solid squares as shown in Figure 3; repeat for two units. Press seams toward squares. Repeat for second place mat.

Step 7. Sew the units pieced in Step 6 to the ends of

Project Specifications
Skill Level: Beginner
Project Size: 14" x 18 1/2" including binding
Number of Place Mats: 2

Materials
- 1/4 yard red solid
- 1/3 yard navy blue solid
- 3/4 yard muslin
- 2 pieces batting 15" x 20"
- Off-white all-purpose thread
- Off-white quilting thread
- Fade-out fabric marker
- Basic sewing supplies and tools

the unit pieced in Step 5 as shown in Figure 4; press. Repeat for second place mat.

Step 8. Prepare template for star shape; cut as directed on pattern piece. *Note: Do not add a seam allowance to star shape.*

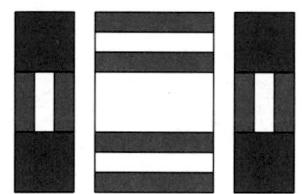

Figure 4
Join pieced sections as shown.

Step 9. Layer two star shapes together. Pin a doubled star set on each navy blue corner square.

Step 10. Cut two backing pieces 15" x 20" from muslin. Sandwich one batting piece between a backing piece and the pieced top; pin or baste layers together to hold flat.

Step 11. Using off-white quilting thread, hand-quilt stars in place 1/4" from edge of star shapes. *Note: Raw edges of stars are left loose. Using star template,*

mark two star shapes in the muslin center of each place mat using fade-out fabric marker. Hand-quilt on marked lines and in the ditch of seams.

Step 12. Trim edges even. Cut four strips navy blue solid 1 1/2" by fabric width. Bind edges referring to General Instructions to finish. ❖

Forever Stripes Place Mat
Placement Diagram
14" x 18 1/2" including binding

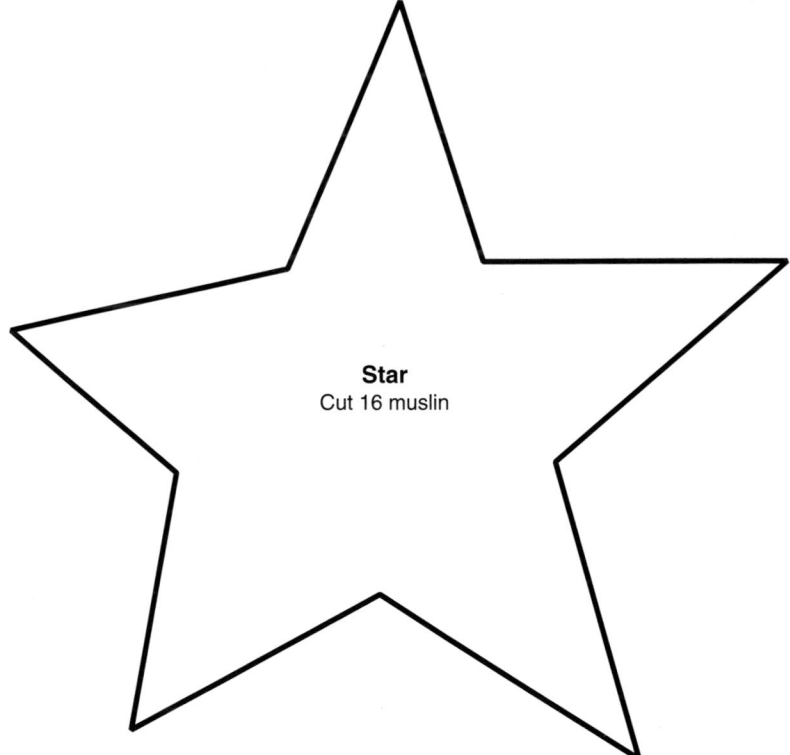

Star
Cut 16 muslin

Maple Leaf Table Runner

By Jill Reber

Fall fabrics combine to make pieced Maple Leaf blocks in this pretty table runner.

Instructions

Step 1. From each of the four dark prints cut four 2 7/8" x 2 7/8" squares, three 2 1/2" x 2 1/2" squares for B, one 4 1/2" x 4 1/2" square for C and one 2" x 8" bias strip. Cut each of the 2 7/8" x 2 7/8" squares in half on one diagonal to make A triangles; you will need eight A triangles of each dark print.

Step 2. From each of the four medium prints cut four 2 1/2" x 4 1/2" rectangles for D.

Step 3. From the tan-on-tan print cut one strip 2 1/2" by fabric width, two strips 4 1/2" by fabric width and one strip 5 1/4" by fabric width. Cut the 2 1/2" by fabric width strip into 2 1/2" squares for B; you will need 12 B squares. Cut one 4 1/2" by fabric width strip into 2 1/2" segments for D; you will need 12 D rectangles. Cut the remaining 4 1/2" by fabric width strips into 4 1/2" square segments for C; you will need six C squares. Cut the 5 1/4" by fabric width strip into 5 1/4" square segments; cut each square on both diagonals to make E triangles. You will need 16 E triangles.

Step 4. To piece one block, sew two matching A triangles to angled sides of E; sew a medium print D to the A side as shown in Figure 1; press. Repeat for four units.

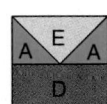

Figure 1
Sew 2 A's to E; add D.

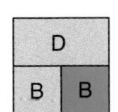

Figure 2
Join 2 B pieces; add D.

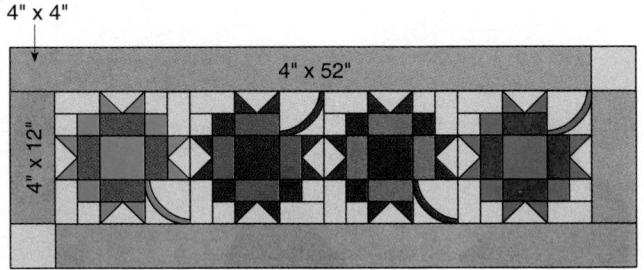

Maple Leaf Table Runner
Placement Diagram
20" x 56"

Project Specifications

Skill Level: Intermediate
Project Size: 20" x 56"
Block Size: 12" x 12"
Number of Blocks: 4

Materials

- 1/2 yard tan-on-tan print
- 1/3 yard each 2 different brown prints for borders
- 4 different fat quarters dark print
- 4 different 5" x 12" rectangles medium print
- Backing 24" x 60"
- Batting 24" x 60"
- 4 1/2 yards self-made or purchased binding
- Neutral color all-purpose thread
- Basic sewing supplies and tools, ruler, rotary cutter and mat

Step 5. Sew a dark print B to a tan-on-tan print B; sew to a tan-on-tan print D as shown in Figure 2; press. Repeat for three units.

Step 6. Join two B-D units with one A-E-D unit to make a row as shown in Figure 3; press.

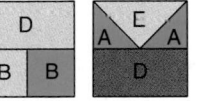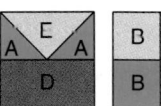

Figure 3
Join 2 B-D units with 1 A-E-D unit.

Step 7. Fold the dark print 2" x 8" bias strip stem piece in thirds as shown in Figure 4; press. Place from corner to corner on a tan-on-tan print C curving slightly in the center again referring to Figure 4, hand- or machine-appliqué in place.

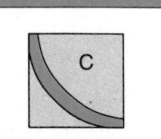

Figure 4
Fold stem strip in thirds;
place on C as shown.

Step 8. Join one B-D unit with one A-E-D unit and the stem unit to make a row as shown in Figure 5; press.

Step 9. Join two A-E-D units with a dark print C to make a row as shown in Figure 6; press.

Step 10. Join rows to complete one block as shown in Figure 7; press. Repeat for four blocks.

Step 11. Join blocks as shown in Figure 8; press seams in one direction.

Step 12. From each brown border print, cut one strip 4 1/2" x 12 1/2" and cut and piece two strips 4 1/2" x 52 1/2".

Step 13. Sew a 4 1/2" x 12 1/2" strip to each end of the pieced unit; press seams toward strips.

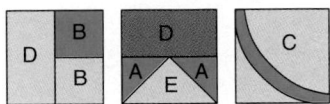

Figure 5
Join 1 B-D unit with 1 A-E-D unit and stem unit.

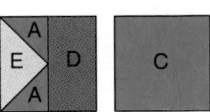

Figure 6
Join 2 A-E-D units with dark print C.

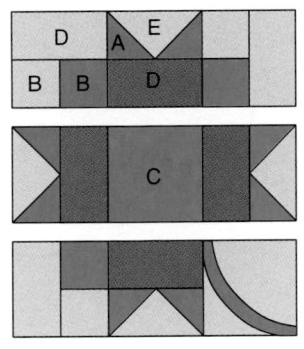

Figure 7
Join rows to complete 1 block.

Figure 8
Join blocks as shown.

Step 14. Sew a tan-on-tan print C square to one end of each 4 1/2" x 52 1/2" border strip; press seams toward strip.

Step 15. Sew a strip to each side of the pieced section referring to the Placement Diagram and photo of project for positioning of strips; press seams toward strips.

Step 16. Prepare quilt for quilting and finish referring to the General Instructions. ❖

Maple Leaf
12" x 12" Block

Autumn Leaves

By Joyce Livingston

There are dozens of autumn leaves hiding in your scrap bag ready to share a message with family and friends.

Project Notes

Use the patterns supplied here or go out in your yard or a nearby park and choose your own patterns right from the trees. This adventure will make your finished leaves even more special.

A number of years ago I began creating these leaves to decorate my Thanksgiving table and the center island in my kitchen. Everyone liked them so well, I went back to my scrap bag and made enough to send at least two to each of our six married children's families and a few to their friends and relatives. This started a new tradition. Now each year I make two new leaves for my own collection and at least two more for each of those on our loved-ones list.

The recipients look forward to receiving the leaves as this signals the arrival of the fall season. I love seeing how the leaves are displayed in their respective homes. Some use them around a floral centerpiece, some on a coffee table or end table. Others lay them around a cornucopia filled with vegetables and gourds, or use them as coasters. They could be hot-glued to a wreath for the front door. There is no end to their usefulness.

Sewing leaves is much more fun than raking them. Sew up a bushel basket full today and begin your own Thanksgiving leaf tradition.

Instructions

Step 1. Prepare template for leaf shape using one of the patterns given or a leaf from your favorite tree. Mark vein lines.

Step 2. Trace shape on the right side of one print square.

Project Specifications

Skill Level: Beginner
Project Size: Size varies

Materials

- An assortment of print scraps each at least 8" x 8" square—2 for each finished leaf
- Scrap pieces of batting 8" x 8" square
- Contrasting all-purpose thread
- Basic sewing supplies and tools and small sharp scissors

Step 3. Place another print square right side down on a flat surface; lay a batting square on top. Place the traced square right side up on the batting; pin the three layers together.

Step 4. Set the sewing machine to a medium-width zigzag stitch. Stitch on the marked lines on the top fabric piece, removing pins as you sew.

Step 5. Stitch vein lines as marked on pattern, backstitching at beginning and end to lock stitches.

Step 6. Using small sharp scissors, trim away excess fabric and batting as close to stitching as possible being careful not to clip into stitching. ***Note:*** *If you slip and cut stitches, a touch of clear nail polish will hold them in place or you may restitch over that area.* ❖

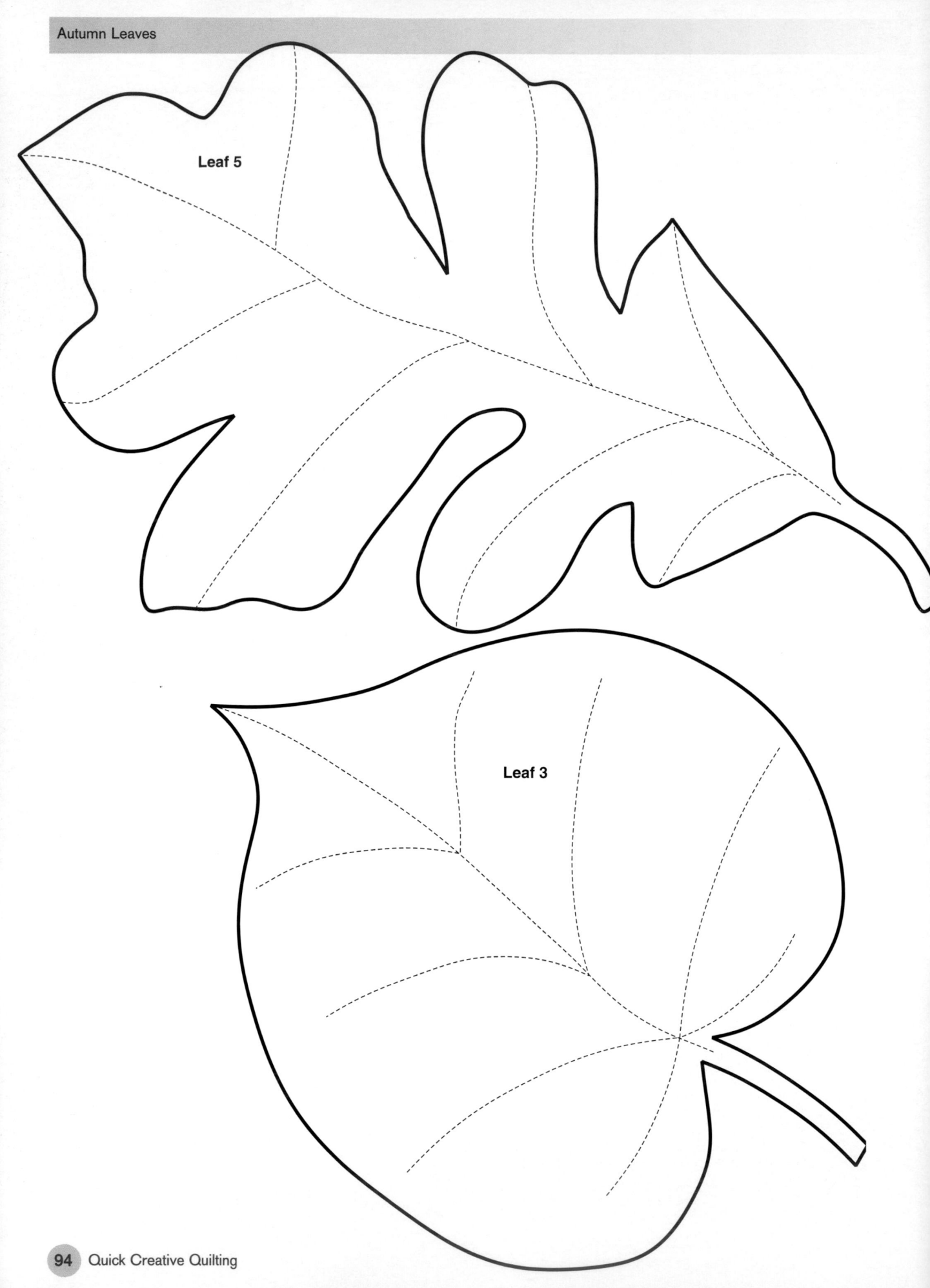

Leaf 5

Leaf 3

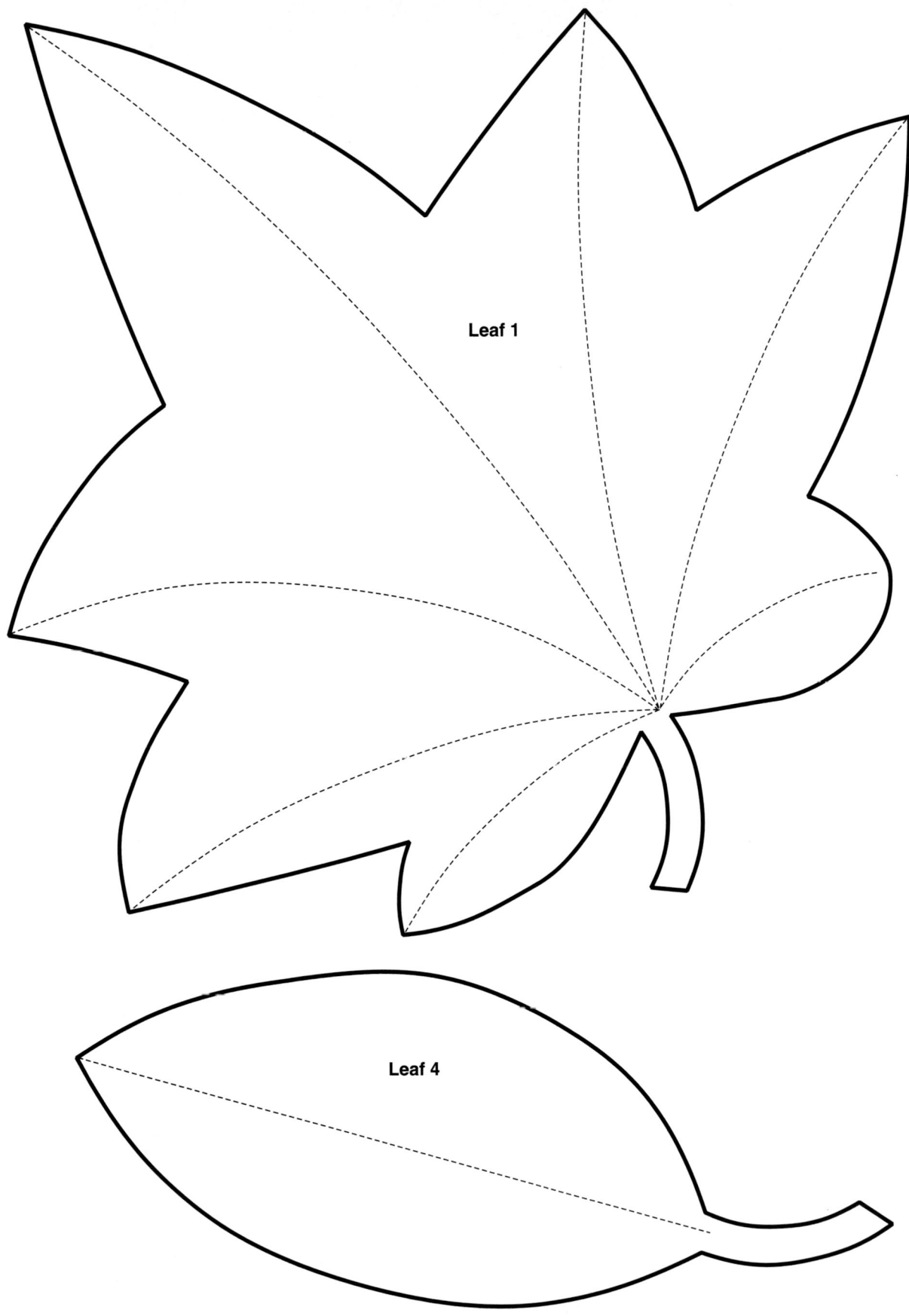

Leaf 1

Leaf 4

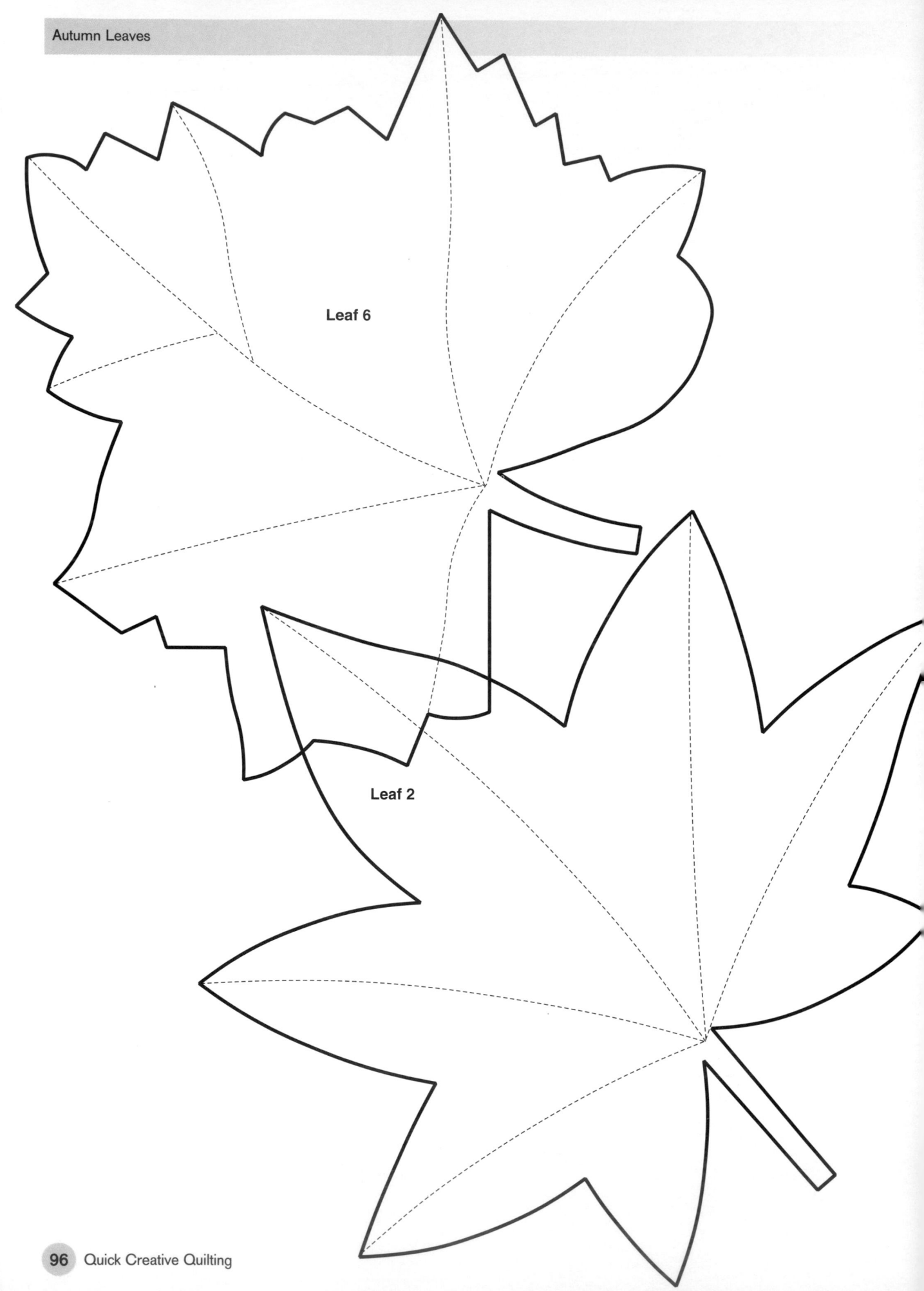

Leaf 6

Leaf 2

Autumn Apples Wall Quilt

By Christine A. Schultz

The apples in this wall quilt are pieced, not appliquéd.
Paper-piecing makes this project easy to stitch.

Instructions

Step 1. Trace or copy paper-piecing patterns for segments A and B using patterns given; make nine copies of each segment, reversing four of each segment by turning pattern over and tracing lines on the wrong side of the paper before copying. ***Note:*** *Patterns are reversed for paper piecing already; reversing the pattern again will complete a reversed block as shown in Figure 1.*

Block   Block reversed

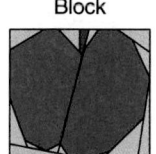 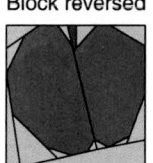

Figure 1
Using patterns as given complete 1 block as shown; reversing patterns as given completes a reversed block as shown.

3" x 21 1/4"

1" x 15 1/4"

3" x 15 1/4"

1" x 13 1/4"

Autumn Apples Wall Quilt
Placement Diagram
21 1/4" x 21 1/4"

Project Specifications

Skill Level: Intermediate
Project Size: 21 1/4" x 21 1/4"
Block Size: 3 3/4" x 3 3/4"
Number of Blocks: 9

Materials

- 1/4 yard apple print
- 1/4 yard beige print
- 1/4 yard brown print
- 1" x 15" strip dark brown print
- 9 assorted 6" x 6" squares red prints
- Backing 25" x 25"
- Thin cotton batting 25" x 25"
- 2 3/4 yards self-made or purchased binding
- All-purpose thread to match fabrics
- Basic sewing supplies and tools and paper

Step 2. To paper-piece segment A, rough-cut fabric patches at least 1/4" larger all around than finished patch referring to pattern for fabric color. Lay patch 1 right side up on the unmarked side of the paper, completely covering the area for patch 1 as shown in Figure 2. Lay patch 2 right side down over patch 1,

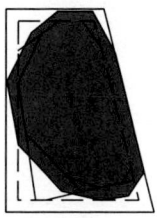 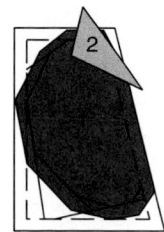

Figure 2
Place patch 1 on paper on space for piece 1.

Figure 3
Place patch 2 right sides together with patch 1.

aligning edges to overlap the seam line between patches 1 and 2 at least 1/4" as shown in Figure 3; pin in place. Flip paper over; stitch on the line through all layers using a small machine stitch as shown in Figure 4. Trim seam allowance to a scant 1/4"; finger-press pieces flat as shown in Figure 5.

Step 3. Cut fabric for patch 3, lay right sides together with bottom edge of patches 1 and 2, overlapping seam line. Stitch and finger-press pieces flat; trim seam allowance. Continue adding pieces, finger-pressing flat

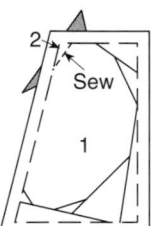

Figure 4
Turn paper over; stitch
on line between
pieces 1 and 2.

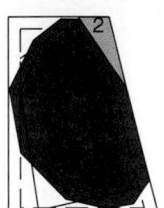

Figure 5
Finger-press
patches 1 and 2 flat.

and trimming seam allowances until all pieces have been stitched. Repeat with segment B. *Note: Do not add patch 9 at this point.*

Step 4. Join segments A and B along center seam. Carefully remove paper seam allowance for this seam only; press. Add patch 9 as shown in Figure 6; press. Carefully trim block on the cutting lines to complete one Apple block; repeat for nine blocks, reversing four blocks.

Patch 9

Figure 6
Stitch patch 9 to the 2 sections after they are joined.

Step 5. Cut six strips apple print 1 1/2" x 4 1/4" for sashing. Join three blocks with two strips to make a row as shown in Figure 7; repeat for three rows referring to the Placement Diagram for positioning of reversed blocks.

Step 6. Cut four strips apple print 1 1/2" x 13 3/4"; join rows with strips beginning and ending with a strip. Press seams toward strips.

Step 7. Cut two strips apple print 1 1/2" x 15 3/4"; sew to the top and bottom of the pieced section. Press seams toward strips.

Step 8. Cut two strips each brown print 3 1/2" x 15 3/4" and 3 1/2" x 21 3/4". Sew the shorter strips to opposite sides and longer strips to the top and bottom; press seams toward strips.

Step 9. Prepare for quilting and finish referring to the General Instructions. ❖

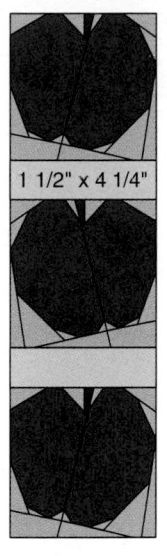

1 1/2" x 4 1/4"

Figure 7
Join 3 blocks with 2 sashing strips to make a row.

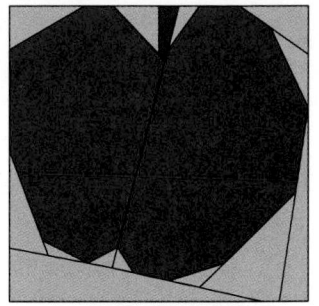

Autumn Apples
3 3/4" x 3 3/4" Block
Make 5

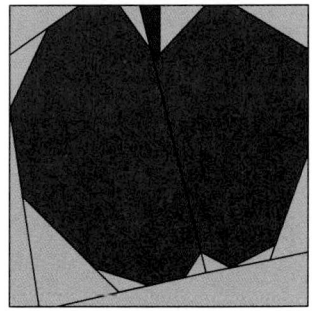

Autumn Apples Reversed
3 3/4" x 3 3/4" Block
Make 4

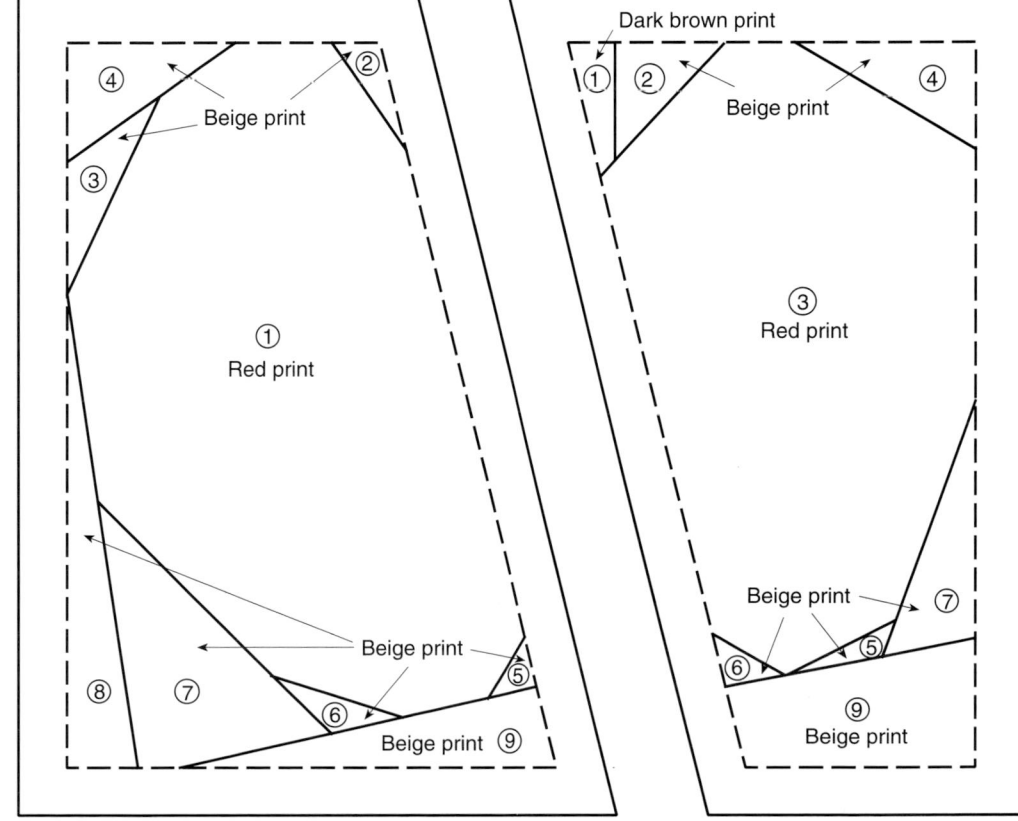

Segment A

Segment B

Harvest Candle Mat

By Holly Daniels

A pumpkin-pie scented candle is the perfect centerpiece for this Harvest Candle Mat.

Instructions

Step 1. Prepare template A using pattern piece given; cut as directed on the piece.

Step 2. Join four different green print A pieces as shown in Figure 1; repeat for four units in the same fabric order. Press seams in one direction.

Step 3. Join two units; repeat. Join these two units as shown in Figure 2 to complete circle; press flat. ***Note:*** *If pieces don't lie flat after stitching, adjust a few seams until it will lie flat.*

Step 4. Trace circle, pumpkin, center and stem onto paper side of the 12" x 16" piece fusible transfer

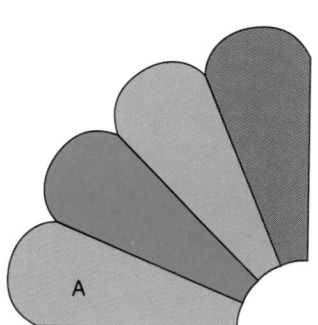

Figure 1
Join 4 different A pieces.

Project Specifications
Skill Level: Beginner
Project Size: Approximately 13 1/2" diameter

Materials
- 7" x 12" pieces of 4 different green prints
- 4" x 4" square green mottled
- Scraps 1 brown and 4 orange prints
- Backing 15" x 15"
- Lightweight batting 15" x 15"
- Green all-purpose thread
- Orange, brown and dark green rayon thread
- 12" x 16" piece fusible transfer web
- 1/4 yard tear-off fabric stabilizer
- Basic sewing supplies and tools

web. Cut out shapes leaving a margin around each shape.

Step 5. Fuse shapes to the wrong side of fabrics as directed on each piece for color and number to cut; remove paper backing.

Step 6. Arrange pumpkin motifs on pieced A section referring to the Placement Diagram and photo of project for positioning suggestions; fuse in place.

Step 7. Cut four pieces tear-off fabric stabilizer 4 1/2" x 4 1/2"; pin one piece behind each fused pumpkin motif. Machine-appliqué shapes in place using matching rayon thread in the top of the

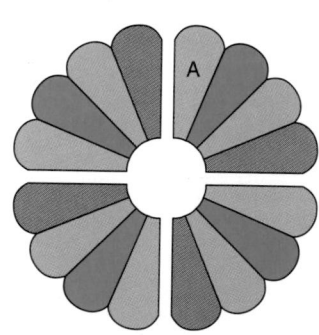

Figure 2
Join pieced units to complete circle.

Harvest Candle Mat
Placement Diagram
Approximately 13 1/2" Diameter

machine and green all-purpose thread in the bobbin.

Step 8. Layer batting and backing right sides up and pieced-and-appliquéd top right side down. Pin along outer edges. Sew all around; trim edges even, clip inner notches. Turn right side out through hole in top center. Smooth and press edges flat.

Step 9. Stitch in the ditch of seams between A pieces to secure layers using green all-purpose thread.

Step 10. Fuse the B circle in place over center hole. Machine-appliqué in place using green rayon thread in the top of the machine and all-purpose thread in the bobbin to finish. ❖

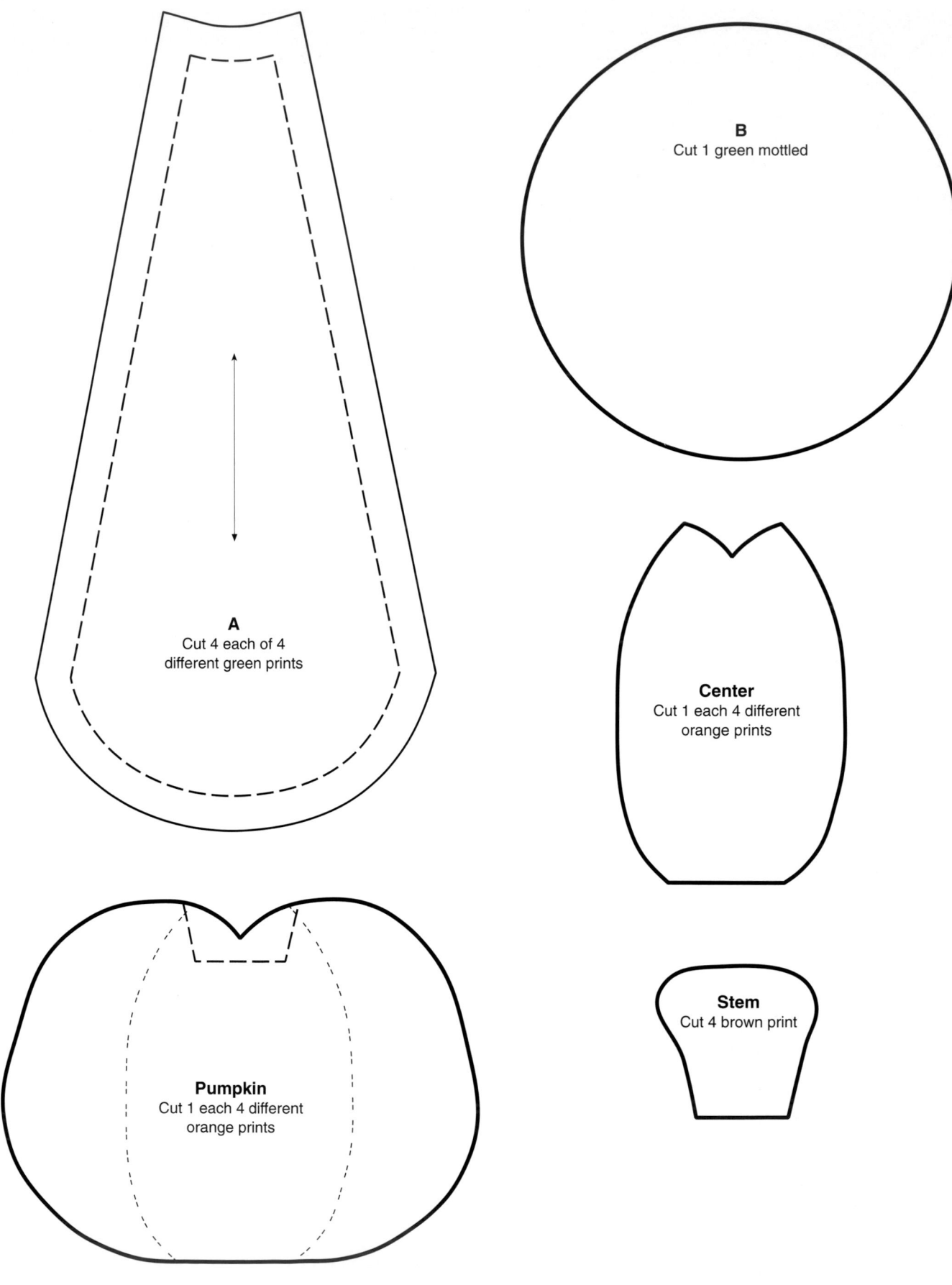

A
Cut 4 each of 4
different green prints

B
Cut 1 green mottled

Center
Cut 1 each 4 different
orange prints

Pumpkin
Cut 1 each 4 different
orange prints

Stem
Cut 4 brown print

Halloween Treat Bag

By Kathy Brown

*Use a simple dish towel to create this little treat bag
for your Halloween trickster this year.*

Instructions

Step 1. Lay the dish towel right side down on a flat surface. Turn the top edge down 1"; pin in place right side down. Turn the bottom edge up 1"; pin in place. Sew a straight seam on each end to make a casing for the shoelace to slip through as shown in Figure 1; remove pins.

Figure 1
Fold over ends 1"; stitch.

Step 2. Fold the dish towel in half with right sides together as shown in Figure 2. Pin the left and right sides closed; turn right side out to reveal basic bag shape.

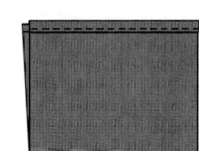

Figure 2
Fold bag in half with
right sides together
as shown

Step 3. Trace the cat, moon and star shapes onto the paper side of the fusible transfer web. Cut out shapes leaving a margin beyond traced lines.

Project Specifications
Skill Level: Beginner
Project Size: 14" x 12"

Materials
- 15" x 26" black-and-white check dish towel
- Scraps black solid, gold check and orange print
- All-purpose thread to match fabrics
- 9" x 12" piece fusible transfer web
- Small amount of white and pink acrylic paints
- Small flat paintbrush
- Black permanent fabric pen
- 36"-long black round shoelace
- 8" x 8" piece freezer paper
- Basic sewing supplies and tools

Step 4. Fuse shapes to the wrong side of fabrics as directed on pattern pieces for color; cut out shapes on traced lines. Remove paper backing.

Step 5. Arrange shapes on bag front referring to the Placement Diagram and photo of project for positioning suggestions. Unpin sides of bag; fuse shapes in place.

Step 6. Iron the 8" x 8" piece of freezer paper to the backside of the bag with shiny side down. Turn bag right side up.

Step 7. Using thread to match fabrics, machine-appliqué pieces in place referring to the General Instructions. Remove freezer paper when stitching is complete.

Step 8. Fold the bag in half again with right sides together. Pin left and right sides closed. Stitch down

Halloween Treat Bag
Placement Diagram
14" x 12"

sides, starting stitching below the casing and ending at the bottom of the bag as shown in Figure 3; backstitch at the beginning and end to secure stitching.

Step 9. Turn bag right side out; run the 36"-long black round

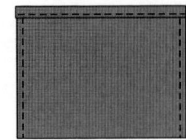

Figure 3
Stitch along sides, starting below casing.

shoelace through the casing and tie ends together.

Step 10. Using a small amount of white acrylic paint, make dots for cat's eyes and freckles, make mouth line and highlight cheeks. With a small amount of pink acrylic paint, make cat's nose. Draw on the whiskers and dot in eyes with the black permanent fabric pen. ❖

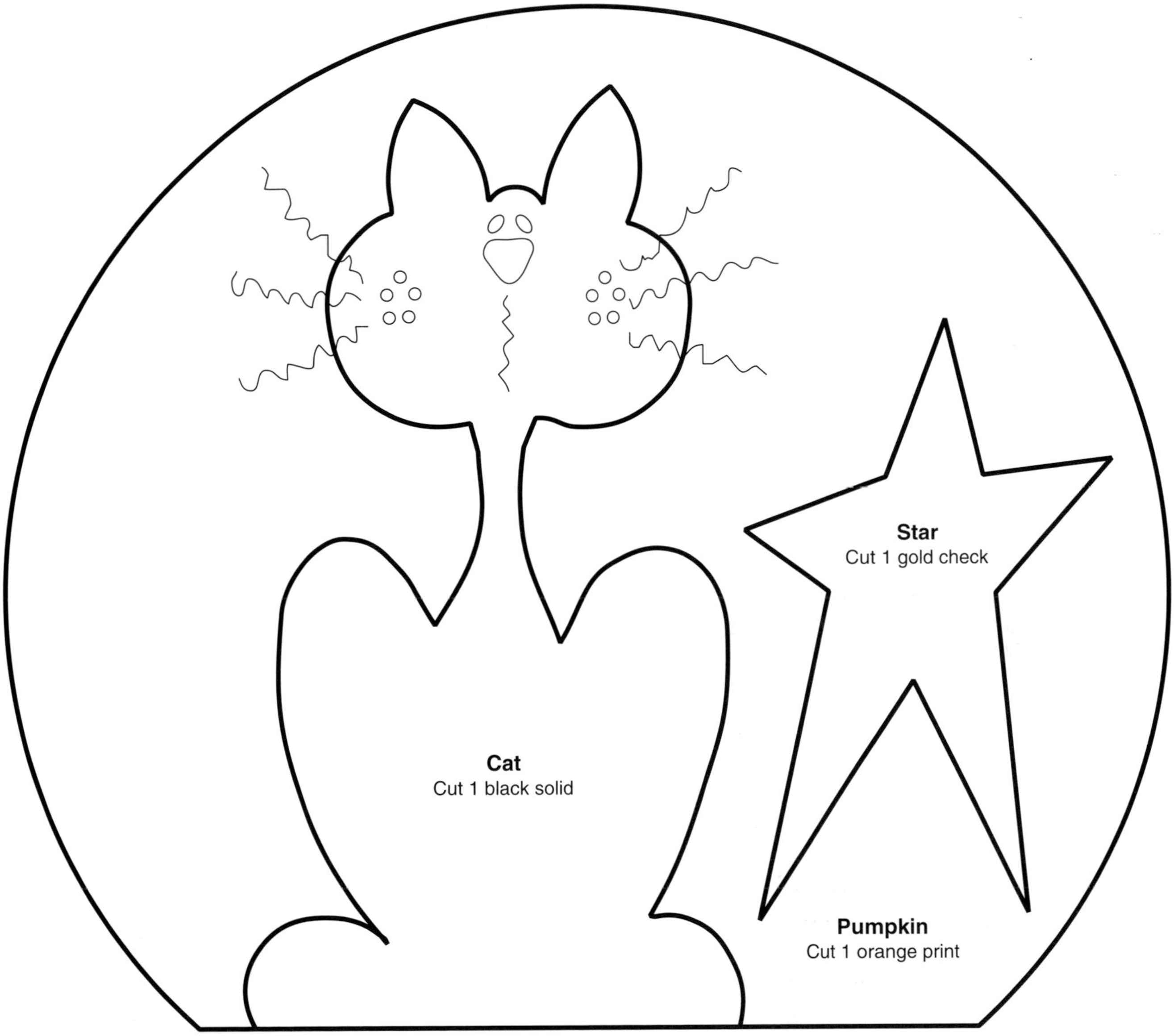

Star
Cut 1 gold check

Cat
Cut 1 black solid

Pumpkin
Cut 1 orange print

Jack-o'-Lantern Bib

By Kathy Brown

Mr. Jack-o'-Lantern never looked so sweet as he smiles for the baby wearing this Halloween bib.

Instructions

Step 1. Prepare template for bib using pattern piece given. Cut as directed on the pattern piece.

Step 2. Fuse the 6" x 6" square fusible transfer web to the wrong side of the 6" x 6" square black solid. Trace shapes for face on the paper side of the fused square. Cut out shapes on traced lines; remove paper backing.

Step 3. Arrange face shapes on the right side of one fabric bib piece referring to Figure 1 for placement of pieces. Fuse shapes in place.

Step 4. Pin the batting to the wrong side of the fused bib piece. Machine-appliqué face shapes in place with matching thread.

Project Specifications
Skill Level: Beginner
Project Size: 11 1/2" x 13 1/4"

Materials
- 1/2 yard orange print
- 6" x 6" square black solid
- Batting 13" x 16"
- All-purpose thread to match fabrics
- 6" x 6" square fusible transfer web
- 1" x 1" square stick-on hook-and-loop tape
- Basic sewing supplies and tools

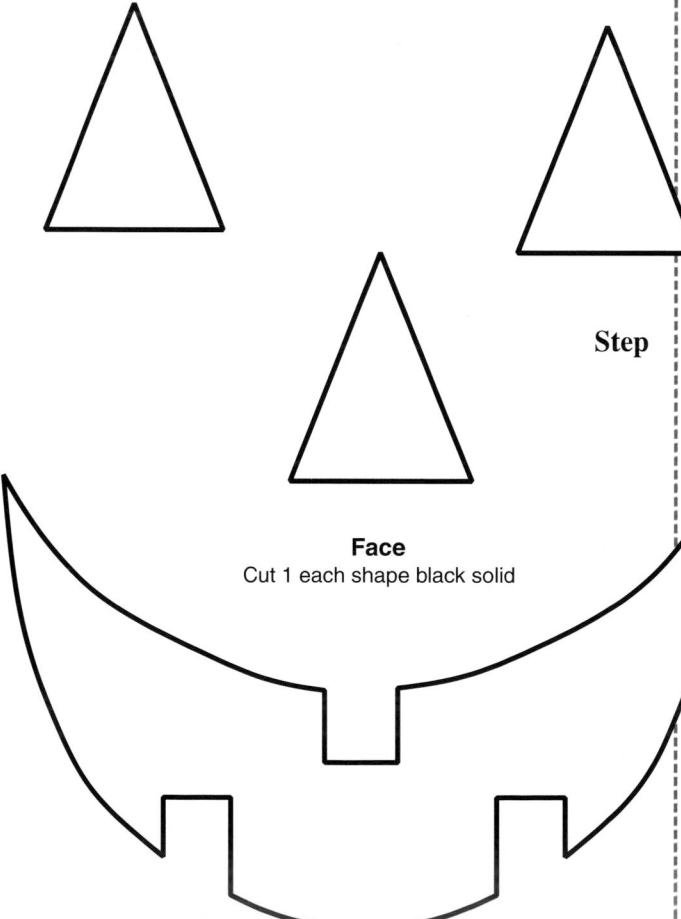

Step

Face
Cut 1 each shape black solid

5. Place remaining fabric bib piece right sides together with the appliquéd layers. Stitch around the entire bib, leaving a 2" opening as marked on pattern. When stitching is complete, turn right side out through opening; press flat. Hand-stitch opening closed.

Step 6. Topstitch 1/4" from edge with thread to match bib.

Step 7. Place hook-and-loop tape pieces at top edges of bib on the wrong side of one end and the right side of the other end referring to Figure 2 and pattern for placement. ❖

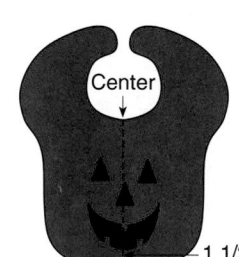

Figure 1
Arrange shapes on fabric bib piece as shown.

Figure 2
Place hook-and-loop tape as shown.

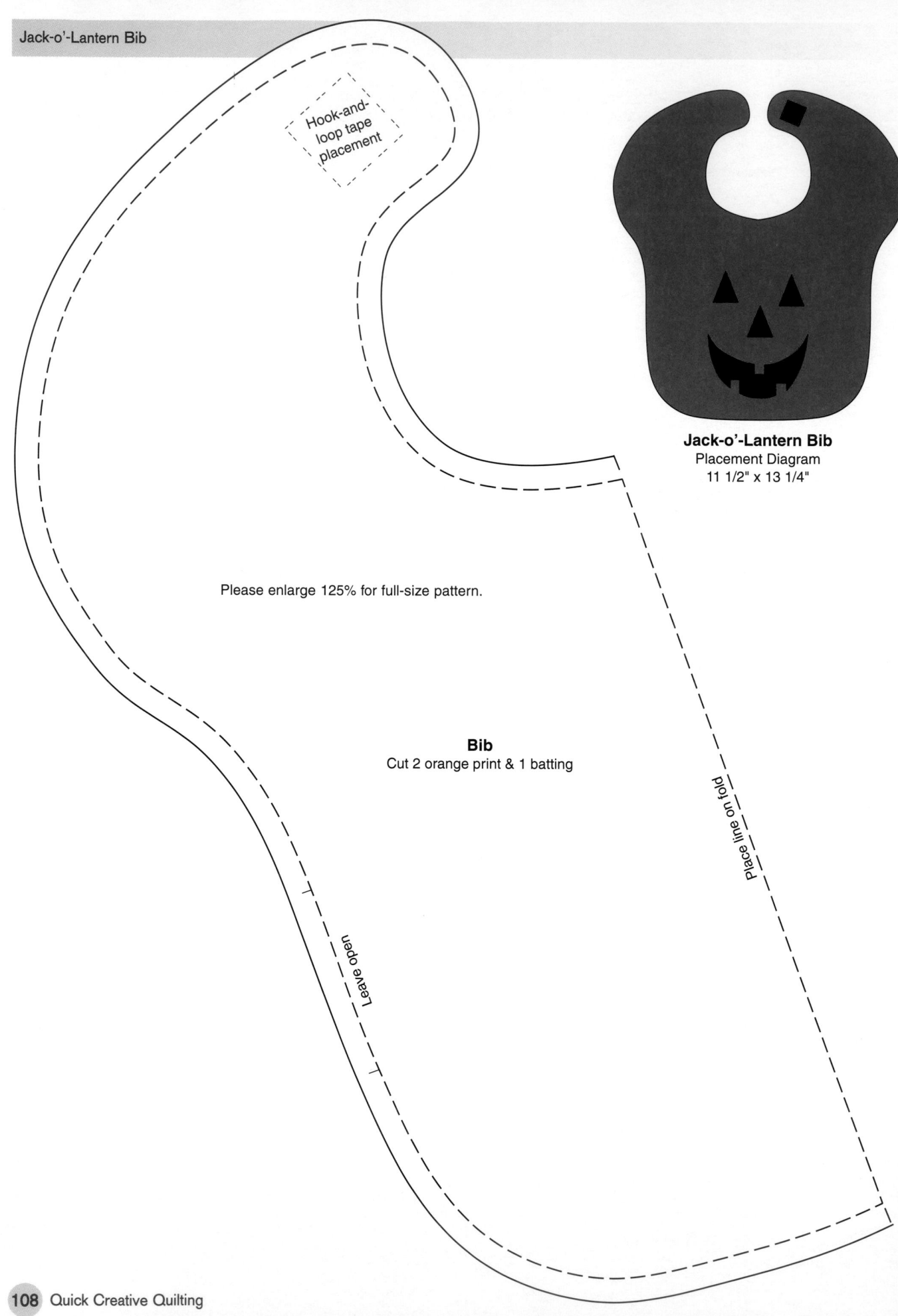

Hook-and-loop tape placement

Jack-o'-Lantern Bib
Placement Diagram
11 1/2" x 13 1/4"

Please enlarge 125% for full-size pattern.

Bib
Cut 2 orange print & 1 batting

Place line on fold

Leave open

Ho-Ho Santa Pillow

By Kathy Brown

This Santa pillow is the perfect accent to help bring holiday cheer to a small corner of any room.

Instructions

Step 1. Lay the dish towel on a flat surface right side up. Mark the center of the length. Fold the bottom edge up to the center; fold the top edge to 1" beyond the center, overlapping bottom edge as shown in Figure 1. Pin at sides to hold; turn right side out.

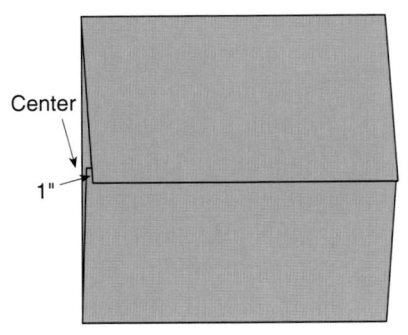

Figure 1
Fold dish towel as shown.

Step 2. Prepare templates for appliqué pieces using pattern pieces given. Trace shapes onto paper side of fusible transfer web. Cut out shapes leaving a margin beyond traced lines.

Step 3. Fuse paper shapes to the wrong side of fabrics as directed on pattern pieces for number and color to cut. Cut out shapes on traced lines; remove paper backing.

Step 4. Center and layer fabric pieces on front of folded and pinned dish towel referring to the Placement Diagram, pattern and photo of project for

Ho-Ho Santa Pillow
Placement Diagram
12" x 12"

Project Specifications
Skill Level: Beginner
Project Size: 12" x 12"

Materials
- 15" x 26" green-and-white check dish towel
- Scraps red and yellow prints
- 3" x 5" rectangle tan solid
- 8" x 8" square white chenille
- 12" x 12" pillow form
- All-purpose thread to match fabrics
- 1/2 yard fusible transfer web
- 7" x 9" piece freezer paper
- Small amount of pink and white acrylic paint
- Small flat paintbrush
- Black permanent fabric pen
- Make-up blusher and cotton swab
- 4 (1 1/8") buttons to cover
- 1 (7/8") button to cover
- 1 (1 1/2") button to cover
- 1 green ceramic star button
- Basic sewing supplies and tools

positioning of pieces; fuse shapes in place.

Step 5. Unpin sides of pillow. Iron the 7" x 9" piece freezer paper to the backside of the fused area.

Step 6. Machine-appliqué shapes in place using all-purpose thread to match fabrics. When appliqué is complete, remove freezer paper from backside.

Step 7. Using make-up blusher and a cotton swab, make cheeks on face area.

Step 8. Fold dish towel again as in Step 1; pin sides closed. Stitch sides, enclosing any stitching on the towel in seam; remove pins. Turn right side out through overlapped opening.

Step 9. Cover two 1 1/8" buttons with red print and two with yellow print. Sew a button on each corner so buttons just barely meet the pillow edge as shown in Figure 2.

Step 10. Cover 1 1/2" button with yellow print; sew to hat brim

Figure 2
Sew a button to each corner as shown.

referring to the Placement Diagram. Cover the 7/8" button with red print; sew to Santa appliqué for nose referring to mark on pattern for placement.

Step 11. Using a small amount of pink acrylic paint, paint mouth shape in place referring to pattern for placement. Highlight mouth and nose button with white acrylic paint. Mark eyes and eyebrows with black permanent fabric pen, referring to pattern for placement; highlight with white acrylic paint.

Step 12. Sew the green ceramic star button to hat brim, referring to the pattern for placement.

Step 13. Insert pillow form through opening in pillow back to finish. ❖

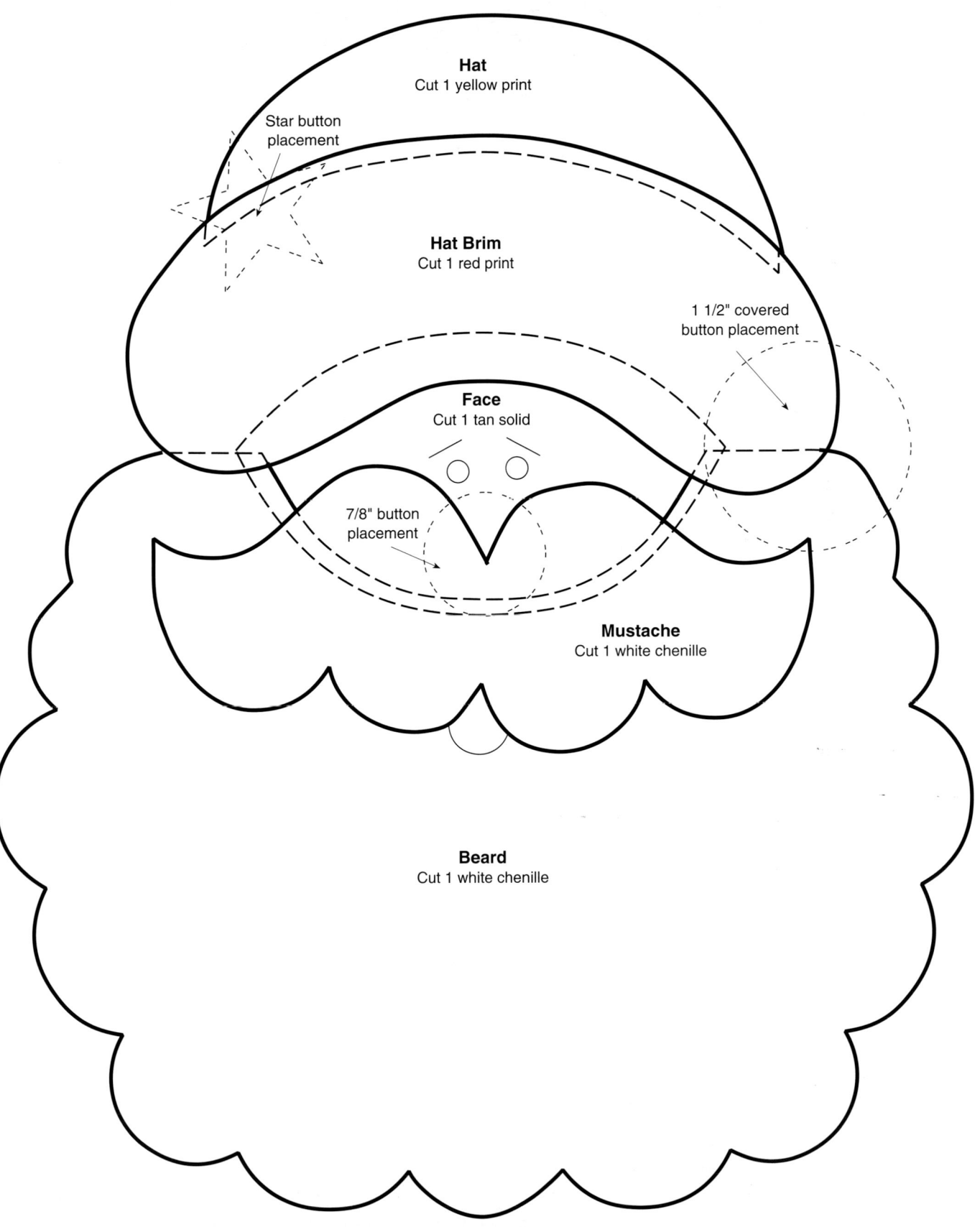

Hat
Cut 1 yellow print

Star button
placement

Hat Brim
Cut 1 red print

1 1/2" covered
button placement

Face
Cut 1 tan solid

7/8" button
placement

Mustache
Cut 1 white chenille

Beard
Cut 1 white chenille

Eight Tiny Reindeer

By Judith Sandstrom

These pieced reindeer look ready to do their job on Christmas Eve.
In the meantime, let them adorn your table or wall.

Instructions

Step 1. From the cream-on-cream print, cut eight each of the following size pieces: 3 1/2" x 4 1/2" (A); 2 1/2" x 3 1/2" (B); 2 1/2" x 2 1/2" (C); and 1 1/2" x 2 1/2" (D).

Step 2. Cut four 1 1/2" by fabric width strips from the cream-on-cream print. Subcut into three 27 1/2", two 15 1/2" and six 6 1/2" segments for sashing and border strips.

Step 3. Cut three strips brown print 1 1/2" by fabric width. Subcut into sixteen each 3 1/2" (E) and 2 1/2" (D) segments.

Step 4. Cut one 1 1/2" by fabric width strip tan print. Subcut strip into eight 2 1/2" (D) segments.

Step 5. To piece one block, sew a tan print D to a cream-on-cream print D; add a brown print D to the bottom to complete Unit 1 as shown in Figure 1. Press seams toward darker fabrics.

Step 6. Sew a brown print D to C as shown in Figure 2; sew E to the top and side of the D-C unit as shown in Figure 3 to complete Unit 2. Press seams toward darker fabrics.

Step 7. Join Units 1 and 2 with pieces A and B as shown in Figure 4 to complete one block; repeat for eight blocks. Press seams toward darker fabrics.

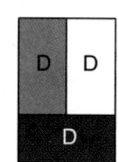

Figure 1
Piece Unit 1 as shown.

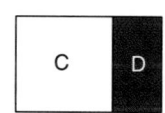

Figure 2
Sew D to C as shown.

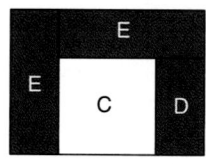

Figure 3
Piece Unit 2 as shown.

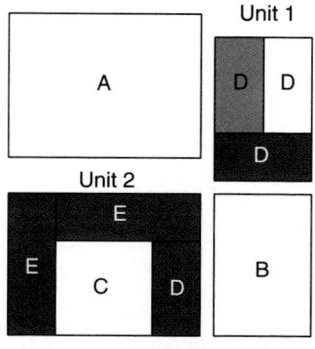

Figure 4
Join A and B with Units 1 and 2 to complete 1 block.

Step 8. Join four blocks with three 1 1/2" x 6 1/2" cream-on-cream print strips to make a row as shown in Figure 5; repeat for two rows. Press seams toward strips.

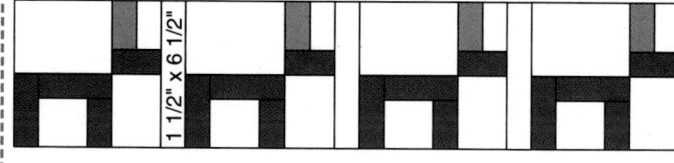

Figure 5
Join 4 blocks with 3 sashing strips to make a row.

Step 9. Join the two rows with three 1 1/2" x 27 1/2" cream-on-cream print strips as shown in Figure 6; press seams toward strips.

Step 10. Sew a 1 1/2" x 15 1/2" cream-on-cream print strip to each short end of pieced center; press seams toward strips.

Step 11. Cut two strips each 2" x 29 1/2" and 2" x 18 1/2" red-and-green check. Sew the longer strips to opposite long sides and shorter strips to opposite short sides. Press seams toward strips.

Step 12. Prepare quilt for quilting using basting spray on the wrong side of the backing and pieced top to eliminate pins or basting. Quilt and bind edges referring to the General Instructions.

Step 13. Cut eight 9" lengths from the 1/8"-wide red satin ribbon. Tie each length into a bow; tack a bow on each block referring to the block drawing for positioning of bow.

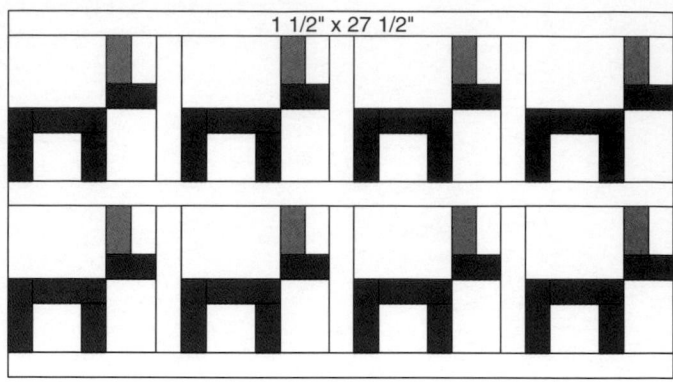

Figure 6
Join rows with 3 sashing strips as shown.

Step 14. Stitch a 1/2" tan button on each block for eyes referring to the block drawing for positioning. ❖

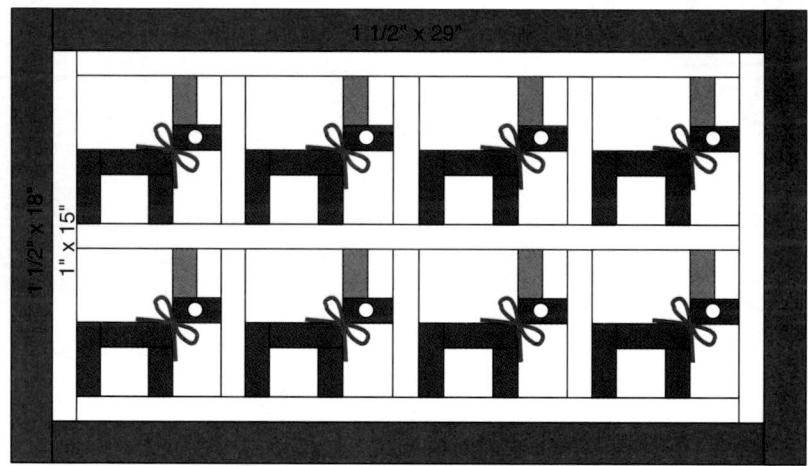

Eight Tiny Reindeer
Placement Diagram
18" x 32"

Reindeer
6" x 6" Block

Holly & Angel Tree Skirt

By Judith Sandstrom

Fusing shapes in place works well for a quick project that will not require frequent washing like this angelic tree skirt.

Instructions

Step 1. To make circle for background, fold the 44" x 44" piece of blue print in half along length and width to form a square as shown in Figure 1. Measure and mark a dot 2" and 21" away from the center point at

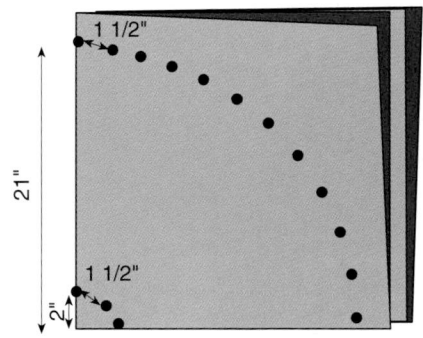

Figure 1
Fold fabric for background as shown.
Mark dots as shown.

1 1/2" intervals, again referring to Figure 1. Connect the dots to make solid lines; cut along both lines to make center circle and outside circular edge. Unfold and cut along one fold line for back slit.

Step 2. Place the batting on a large flat surface; press

Holly & Angel Tree Skirt
Placement Diagram
43" Diameter

Project Specifications

Skill Level: Beginner
Project Size: 43" diameter

Materials

- Scraps green, gold, rust and brown prints or solids
- 7" x 8" rectangle of 9 different small plaids or checks
- 1/4 yard cream-on-cream print
- 1 1/4 yards 44"-wide blue print
- Backing 44" x 44"
- Thin cotton batting 44" x 44"
- All-purpose thread to match fabrics
- 2 yards fusible transfer web
- 2 yards 1/8"-wide red satin ribbon
- Very-fine-point brown permanent fabric pen
- Basting spray
- Basic sewing supplies and tools

backing piece. Apply the basting spray to the wrong side of the backing piece following manufacturer's instructions. Center the backing right side up on top of batting; smooth any wrinkles. Center the background circle right side down on the backing; pin layers together every 2" around inside circle, on each side of the slit and around outer edges.

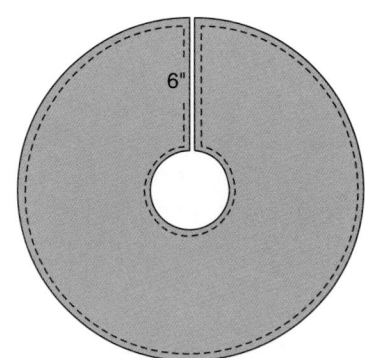

Figure 2
Stitch all around, leaving a 6" opening
on 1 side of slit as shown.

Step 3. Stitch all around, leaving a 6" opening on one side of the slit as shown in Figure 2. Trim excess batting and backing even with background edge; cut center circle and slit, leaving a 1/4" seam allowance. Clip to seam at center circle. Turn right side out through opening; press edges flat.

Step 4. Press seam inside opening; hand-stitch opening closed.

Step 5. Prepare templates using pattern pieces given. Trace shapes onto paper side of fusible transfer web as directed on each piece for number to cut. Cut out shapes leaving a margin all around traced lines.

Step 6. Fuse shapes to wrong side of fabric scraps as directed on pattern pieces. Cut out shapes on traced lines; remove paper backing.

Step 7. Transfer facial features and lines on wings to fabric pieces using the very-fine-point brown permanent fabric pen and referring to pattern pieces for placement.

Step 8. Referring to Figure 3, position angel motifs 1 1/2" from edge of blue print background and 6 1/2" apart at dress edges, layering pieces in numerical order as marked on pattern and alternating hair colors; pin in place. Place and pin a halo above each angel's head.

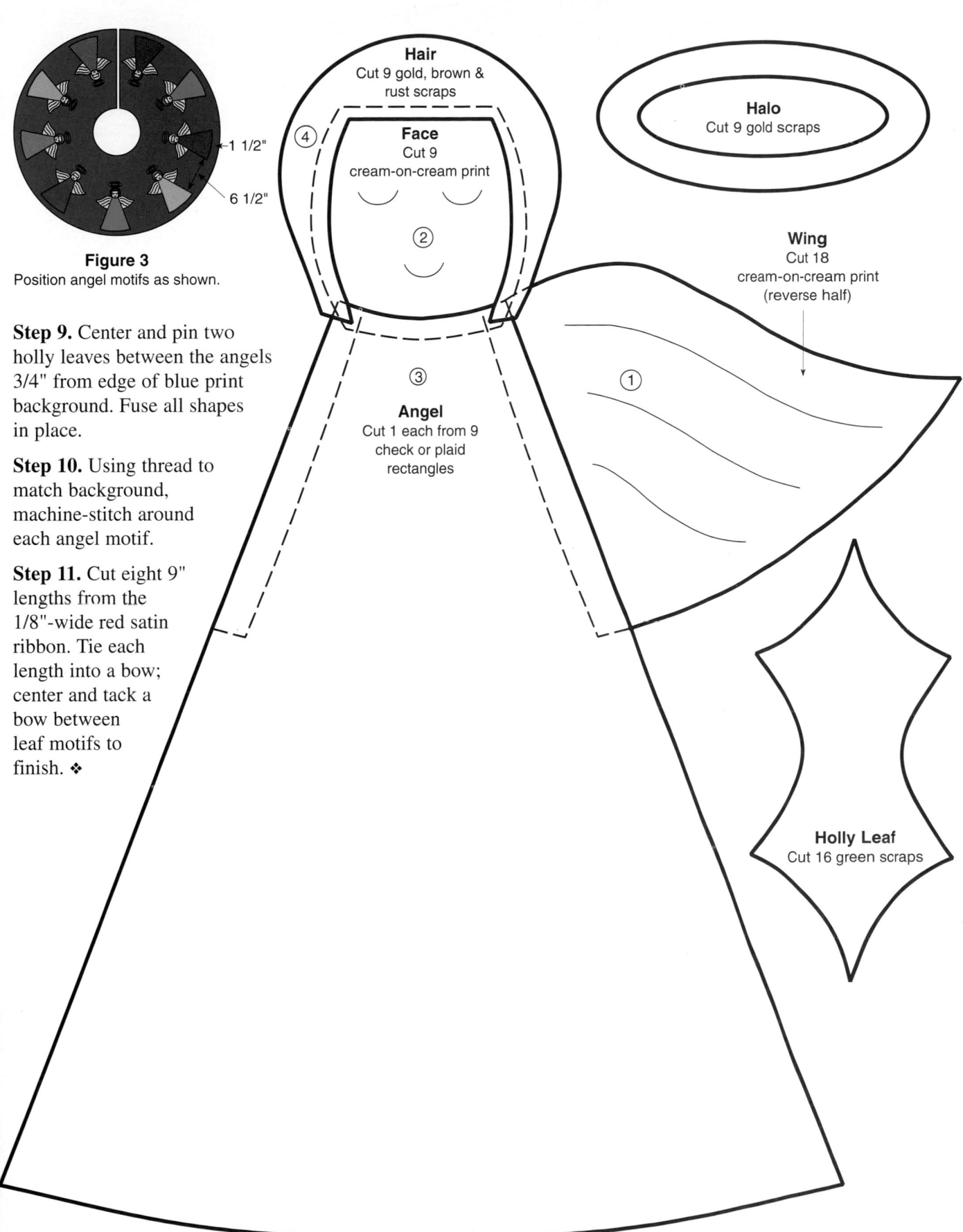

Figure 3
Position angel motifs as shown.

1 1/2"

6 1/2"

Hair
Cut 9 gold, brown & rust scraps

④

Face
Cut 9
cream-on-cream print

②

③

Angel
Cut 1 each from 9
check or plaid
rectangles

①

Halo
Cut 9 gold scraps

Wing
Cut 18
cream-on-cream print
(reverse half)

Holly Leaf
Cut 16 green scraps

Step 9. Center and pin two holly leaves between the angels 3/4" from edge of blue print background. Fuse all shapes in place.

Step 10. Using thread to match background, machine-stitch around each angel motif.

Step 11. Cut eight 9" lengths from the 1/8"-wide red satin ribbon. Tie each length into a bow; center and tack a bow between leaf motifs to finish. ❖

Weekend Quilts

If you have prepared your fabric and read through the instructions, you can make one of these beautiful quilts, even the full-size bed quilts, in 20 hours or less by using quick-cutting, -piecing and -applique methods. What a great way to spend a weekend!

Flowers for Mother Teresa

By Lucy A. Fazely

Mother Teresa's name evokes a spirit of sacrifice and kindness.
Make this wall quilt as a tribute to her.

Instructions

Step 1. Prepare templates for pieces A and B using pattern pieces given.

Step 2. Cut the following strips: one strip each floral print 4 1/2" by fabric width—subcut into three 4 1/2" x 4 1/2" square segments for C; one strip each of medium green and dark green print 4 1/2" by fabric width —subcut dark green print strip into eight and medium green print strip into four 4 1/2" x 4 1/2" square segments for C; two strips white-on-white print 4 1/2" by fabric width—subcut into sixteen 4 1/2" x 4 1/2" square segments for C; and two strips white-on-white print 2 1/2" by fabric width—subcut into four 4 1/2" segments for G and twenty 2 1/2" segments for F.

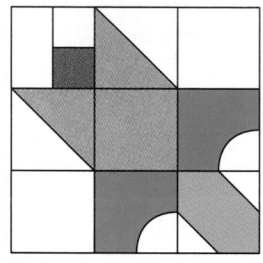

Flowers for Mother Teresa
12" x 12" Block

Step 3. To piece one block, sew a white-on-white print F to a coordinating print F; sew G to the F unit as shown in Figure 1.

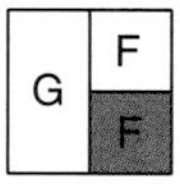

Figure 1
Sew F to F; add G.

Step 4. Draw a diagonal line on the wrong side of two white-on-white print C squares. With right sides together, layer white-on-white print C with a floral print C; stitch on the diagonal line. Trim 1/4" away from seam as shown in Figure 2; press pieces open to complete one C unit referring to Figure 3. Repeat for two units.

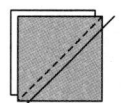
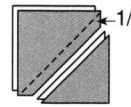
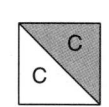
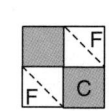

Figure 2
Trim 1/4" away from seam.

Figure 3
Press open to complete 1 C unit.

Figure 4
Stitch on diagonal lines as shown.

Step 5. Draw a diagonal line through two white-on-white print F squares. Lay both squares on a medium green print C square and stitch on the lines as shown in Figure 4. Trim 1/4" from seam; press to complete one C-F unit as shown in Figure 5.

Project Specifications

Skill Level: Intermediate
Project Size: 31" x 31"
Block Size: 12" x 12"
Number of Blocks: 4

Materials

- 1/6 yard 4 floral prints for flowers
- 4 squares 2 1/2" x 2 1/2" coordinating prints for F
- 1/6 yard dark green print
- 1/6 yard medium green print
- 1/6 yard light green print
- 1/6 yard medium green print 2
- 1/6 yard dark green print 2
- 1/2 yard white-on-white print
- Backing 35" x 35"
- Batting 35" x 35"
- 4 yards self-made or purchased green binding
- Neutral color all-purpose thread
- Basic sewing supplies

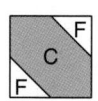
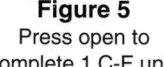
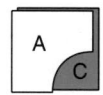

Figure 5
Press open to complete 1 C-F unit.

Figure 6
Lay A on a dark green print C; trim

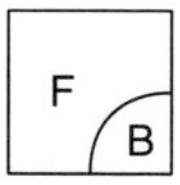

Figure 7
Lay B on a white-on-white print F; trim.

Step 6. Lay template A on a dark green print C square as shown in Figure 6; cut into A shape. Repeat for two A pieces. Lay template B on a white-on-white print F square as shown in Figure 7; cut to B shape. Repeat for two B pieces.

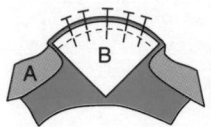

Figure 8
Sew B to A.

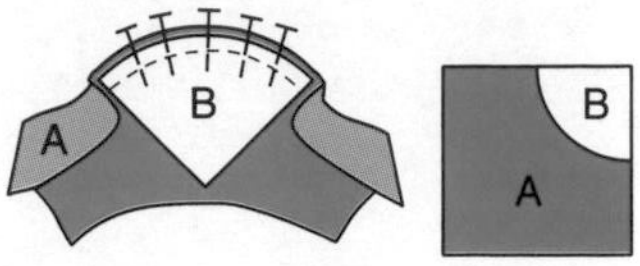

Step 7. Sew B to A as shown in Figure 8; repeat for two units.

Step 8. Lay out pieced units with one floral print and two white-on-white print C squares in rows as shown in Figure 9. Join units in rows; join rows to complete one block. Repeat for four blocks.

Step 9. Join the four pieced blocks as shown in Figure 10 to complete pieced center; press.

Step 10. Cut two strips each light green print 1 1/2" x 24 1/2" and 1 1/2" x 26 1/2". Sew the shorter strips to opposite sides and the longer strips to the top and bottom of the pieced center; press seams toward strips.

Step 11. Cut two strips each 1 1/2" x 26 1/2" and 1 1/2" x 28 1/2" medium green print 2. Sew the shorter strips to opposite sides and the longer strips to the top and bottom of the pieced center; press seams toward strips.

Step 12. Cut two strips each 2" x 28 1/2" and 2" x 31 1/2" dark green print 2. Sew the shorter strips to opposite sides and the longer strips to the top and bottom of the pieced center; press seams toward strips.

Step 13. Prepare quilt top for quilting and finish referring to the General Instructions. ❖

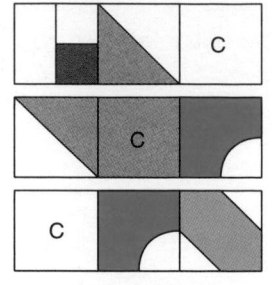

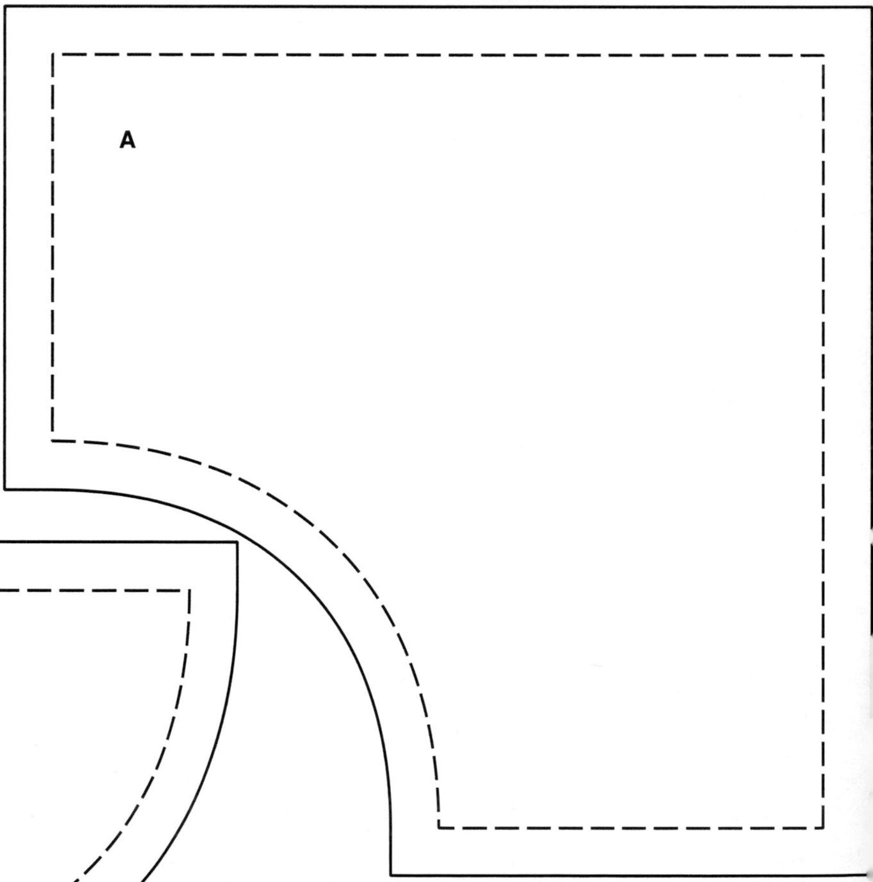

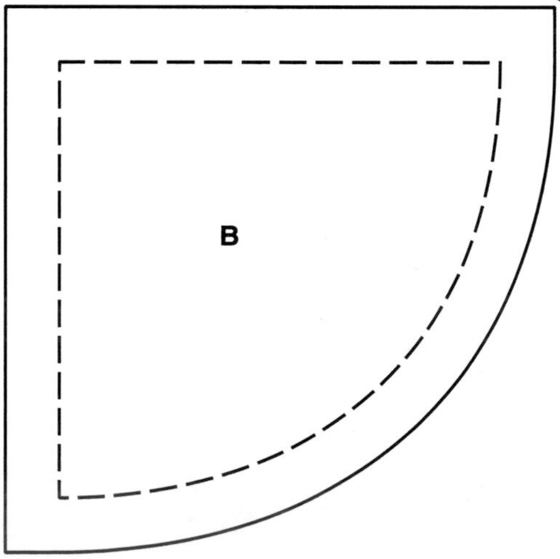

Figure 9
Lay out pieced units in rows; join to complete 1 block.

Figure 10
Join 4 pieced blocks to complete pieced center.

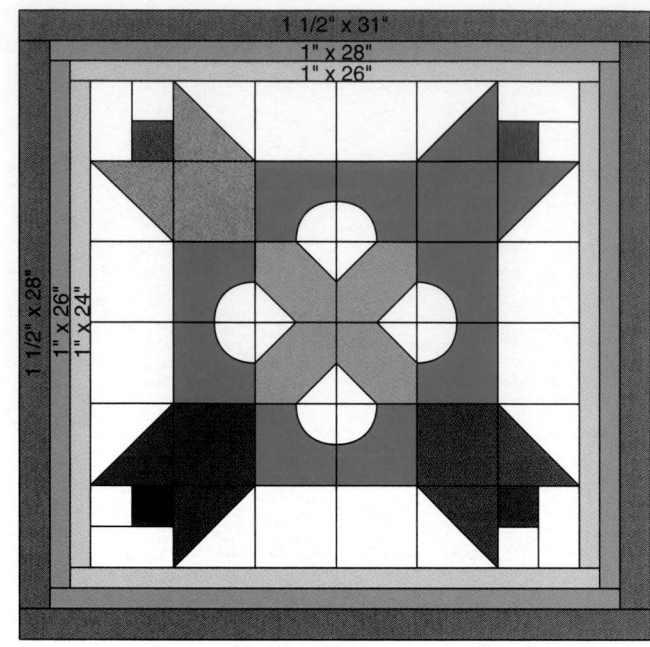

Flowers for Mother Teresa
Placement Diagram
31" x 31"

A

B

Love of Patchwork Friendship Quilt

By Judith Sandstrom

Friendship quilts are wonderful reminders of special people and can be made for someone of any age. The quilt shown has children's signatures and will be a reminder of friends for many years in the future.

Instructions

Step 1. Cut three strips white-on-white print 3 1/2" by fabric width; subcut into 3 1/2" square segments. Set aside 32 squares for signatures. Cut seven squares white-on-white print 3 7/8" x 3 7/8"; cut each square in half on one diagonal to make 14 A triangles for edges. Cut one square white-on-white print 4 1/4" x 4 1/4"; cut in half on both diagonals to make four small B triangles for corners.

Stripe
3" x 3" Block
Make 40

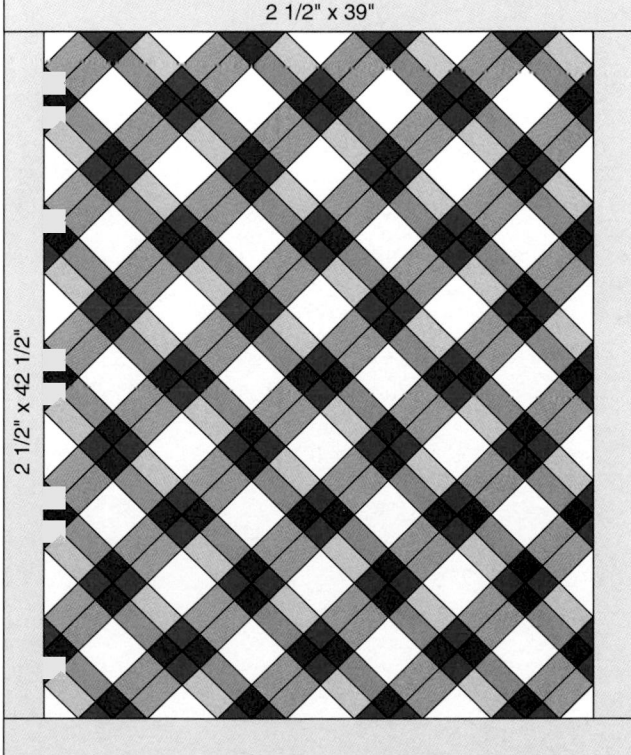

Love of Patchwork Friendship Quilt
Placement Diagram
39" x 47 1/2"

Project Specifications

Skill Level: Beginner
Project Size: 39" x 47 1/2"
Block Size: 3" x 3" and 3" x 3" x 4 1/4"
Number of Blocks: 31 Four-Patch, 40
  Stripe and 18 Half Four-Patch

Materials

- 1/4 yard each dark green, dark blue, light green, yellow, and light blue prints
- 3/8 yard floral print for border
- 1/2 yard white-on-white print
- 5/8 yard rose print
- Backing 43" x 52"
- Batting 43" x 52"
- Neutral color all-purpose thread
- 3 or 4 colored extra-fine-point fabric marking pens
- Quilt basting spray
- Basic sewing supplies, rotary cutter, self-healing mat and acrylic ruler

Four-Patch
3" x 3" Block
Make 31

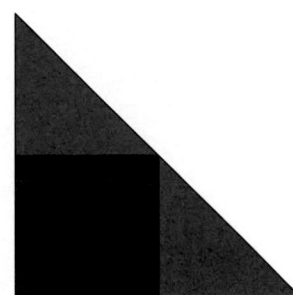

Half Four-Patch
3" x 4 1/4" Block
Make 18

Step 2. Cut three strips each dark green and dark blue prints and four strips each light green, yellow, light blue and rose prints 2" by fabric width.

Step 3. Stitch strips with right sides together along length as follows: dark green/dark blue; light green/yellow and light blue/rose. Repeat for three strip sets dark green/dark blue and four strip sets of the remaining combinations.

Step 4. Cut dark green/dark blue strip sets in 2" segments; repeat for 62 segments.

Figure 1
Join 2 segments to make a Four-Patch block.

Step 5. Join two dark green/dark blue segments to make a Four-Patch block as shown in Figure 1; press. Repeat for 31 blocks.

Step 6. Cut the light green/yel-low and the light blue/rose strip sets into 3 1/2" segments; repeat for 40 segments of each combination referring to Figure 2.

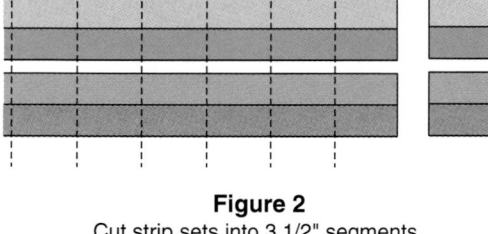

Figure 2
Cut strip sets into 3 1/2" segments.

Step 7. Cut one strip dark blue print 2" by fabric width. Subcut into 18 squares 2" x 2". Cut nine 2 3/8" x 2 3/8" squares dark green print; cut each square in half on one diagonal. Join two dark green print triangles with one dark blue print square as shown in Figure 3; repeat to make 18 Half Four-Patch blocks.

Figure 3
Join 2 dark green print triangles with 1 dark blue print square to make a Half Four-Patch block as shown.

Step 8. Using colored extra-fine-point fabric marking pens, collect signatures on the 32 white-on-white print squares, placing signatures on point as shown in Figure 4. *Note: If you find it difficult to write on the fabric squares, press freezer paper to the wrong side of the square for a stabilizer; remove*

Julie Norman

Figure 4
Signature should be written on point.

paper after signature has been added. Press all squares to permanently set the ink.

Step 9. Join seven white-on-white print signature squares with eight light green/yellow segments and one A triangle in a diagonal row, reversing the yellow and green sequence as shown in Figure 5.

Figure 5
Join units as shown to make a diagonal row.

Step 10. Join seven light blue/rose segments with six dark green/dark blue Four-Patch blocks and two Half Four-Patch blocks in a diagonal row, reversing color sequence as shown in Figure 6.

Figure 6
Join units as shown to make a diagonal row.

Step 11. Stitch remaining rows referring to Figure 7 for color sequence and number of units in a row.

Step 12. Lay out rows in the proper sequence, again referring to Figure 7; sew A tri-angles to ends of rows. Join rows; sew a B trian-gle to each corner to complete pieced center.

Figure 7
Stitch all rows; add A triangles and Half Four-Patch blocks to ends and B triangles to corners as shown.

Step 13. Cut two strips each floral print 3" x 39 1/2" and 3" x 43". Sew the longer strips to opposite long sides and shorter strips to the top and bottom; press seams toward strips.

Step 14. Prepare 5 1/2 yards self-made binding from rose print, prepare quilt for quilting and finish referring to the General Instructions. ❖

Sugar Bowl Baskets

By Jill Reber

*Pastel-colored fabrics combine to make this pretty wall quilt with basket blocks.
The pieced borders and appliquéd floral corner squares complement the blocks.*

Instructions

Step 1. Cut one strip each across the width of the fabric from the beige-on-beige print: 4 1/2"—subcut into eight 2 1/2" segments for A rectangles and four 4 1/2" segments for corner squares; 4 7/8"—subcut into four 4 7/8" square segments for B; and 2 7/8"—subcut into eight 2 7/8" square segments for C. Cut the 4 7/8" and the 2 7/8" square segments in half on one diagonal to make B and C triangles.

Step 2. Cut one strip each across the width of the fabric from the blue print: 4 7/8"—subcut into four 4 7/8" square segments for B; trim remaining strip to 2 1/2"—subcut into four 2 1/2" square segments for D; and 2 7/8"—subcut into twelve 2 7/8" square segments for C. Cut the 4 7/8" and the 2 7/8" square segments in half on one diagonal to make B and C triangles.

Step 3. Sew a beige-on-beige print C to a blue print C; repeat for 16 units. Sew a blue print C to one end of A as shown in Figure 1; repeat for four units. Sew a blue print C to one end of A, again referring to Figure 1; repeat for four units. Sew a beige-on-beige print B to a blue print B; repeat for four units.

Step 4. To piece one block, join two C units as shown in Figure 2; sew the pieced unit to a B unit as shown in Figure 3.

Step 5. Join two C units and add D as shown in Figure 4. Sew this unit to the

Sugar Bowl
8" x 8" Block

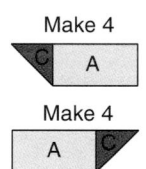

Make 4

Make 4

Figure 1
Sew a blue print
C to 1 end of A.

Figure 2
Join 2 C units.

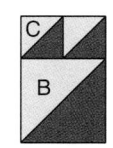

Figure 3
Sew a C unit
to a B unit.

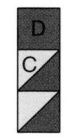

Figure 4
Join 2 C units;
add D.

Project Specifications

Skill Level: Intermediate
Project Size: 36" x 36"
Block Size: 8" x 8"
Number of Blocks: 4

Materials

- 3" x 4" scrap green print
- 1/4 yard pink print 1
- 1/3 yard blue print
- 1/2 yard pink print 2
- 5/8 yard floral print
- 1 yard beige-on-beige print
- Backing 40" x 40"
- Batting 40" x 40"
- All-purpose thread to match fabrics
- 1/8 yard fusible transfer web
- 1/8 yard tear-off fabric stabilizer
- Basic sewing supplies, rotary cutter, self-healing mat and acrylic ruler

previously pieced unit referring to Figure 5. Sew an A-C unit to adjacent B sides of the pieced unit; add a beige-on-beige print B to the corner to complete one block as shown in Figure 6; repeat for four blocks.

Step 6. Join two blocks to make a row as shown in Figure 7; repeat for two rows.

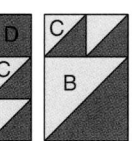

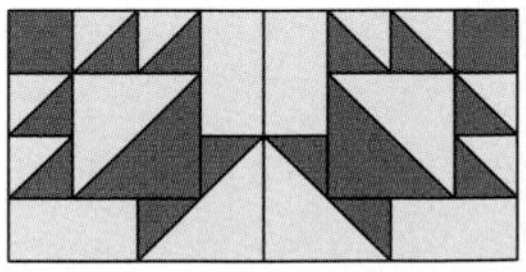

Figure 5
Sew the C-D unit
to the B-C unit.

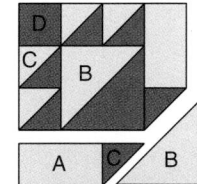

Figure 6
Sew A-C units to the pieced
unit; add B to the corner to
complete 1 block.

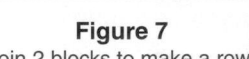

Figure 7
Join 2 blocks to make a row.

Join the rows referring to the Placement Diagram for positioning of rows; press.

Step 7. Cut two strips each 2 1/2" x 16 1/2" and 2 1/2" x 20 1/2" beige-on-beige print. Sew the shorter strips to the top and bottom and longer strips to sides; press seams toward strips.

Step 8. Prepare template for E using pattern given. Cut two strips 2 1/2" by fabric width each pink prints 1 and 2. Cut 20 E pieces from each fabric referring to Figure 8.

Figure 8
Cut E pieces from 2 1/2" strips as shown.

Step 9. Cut three strips beige-on-beige print 2 7/8" by fabric width. Subcut into 2 7/8" square segments for C; you will need 40 segments. Cut each square segment in half on one diagonal to make 80 C triangles.

Step 10. Sew a C triangle to opposite long sides of E as shown in Figure 9; repeat for 40 units.

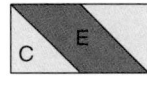 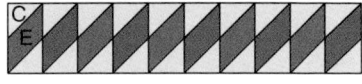

Figure 9
Sew C to opposite sides of E.

Figure 10
Join 10 C-E units to make a strip.

Step 11. Join 10 C-E units to make a strip, alternating pink prints as shown in Figure 10; repeat for four strips.

Step 12. Sew a pieced strip to two opposite sides of the pieced center; press seams toward strips.

Step 13. Prepare templates for appliqué shapes using patterns given. Trace shapes onto paper side of fusible transfer web as directed on patterns for number to cut. Cut out shapes leaving a margin beyond traced lines.

Step 14. Fuse paper shapes to the wrong side of fabrics as directed on patterns for color. Cut out shapes on traced lines; remove paper backing.

Step 15. Fuse one flower motif to each 4 1/2" x 4 1/2" beige-on-beige print square using pattern as a guide for placement.

Step 16. Sew an appliquéd square to each end of each remaining pieced strip referring to the Placement Diagram for positioning of squares. Sew these strips to the remaining sides of the pieced center; press seams toward strips.

Step 17. Cut a piece of tear-off fabric stabilizer to fit behind appliquéd squares. Using all-purpose thread to match fabric, machine-appliqué shapes in place. Tear off stabilizer when appliqué is complete.

Step 18. Cut two strips each floral print 4 1/2" x 28 1/2" and 4 1/2" x 36 1/2". Sew shorter strips to top and bottom and longer strips to opposite sides; press seams toward strips.

Step 19. Prepare quilt for quilting and quilt referring to the General Instructions.

Step 20. Cut four strips 2" by fabric width pink print 2. Prepare as double-fold, straight-grain binding; bind quilt edges referring to the General Instructions. ❖

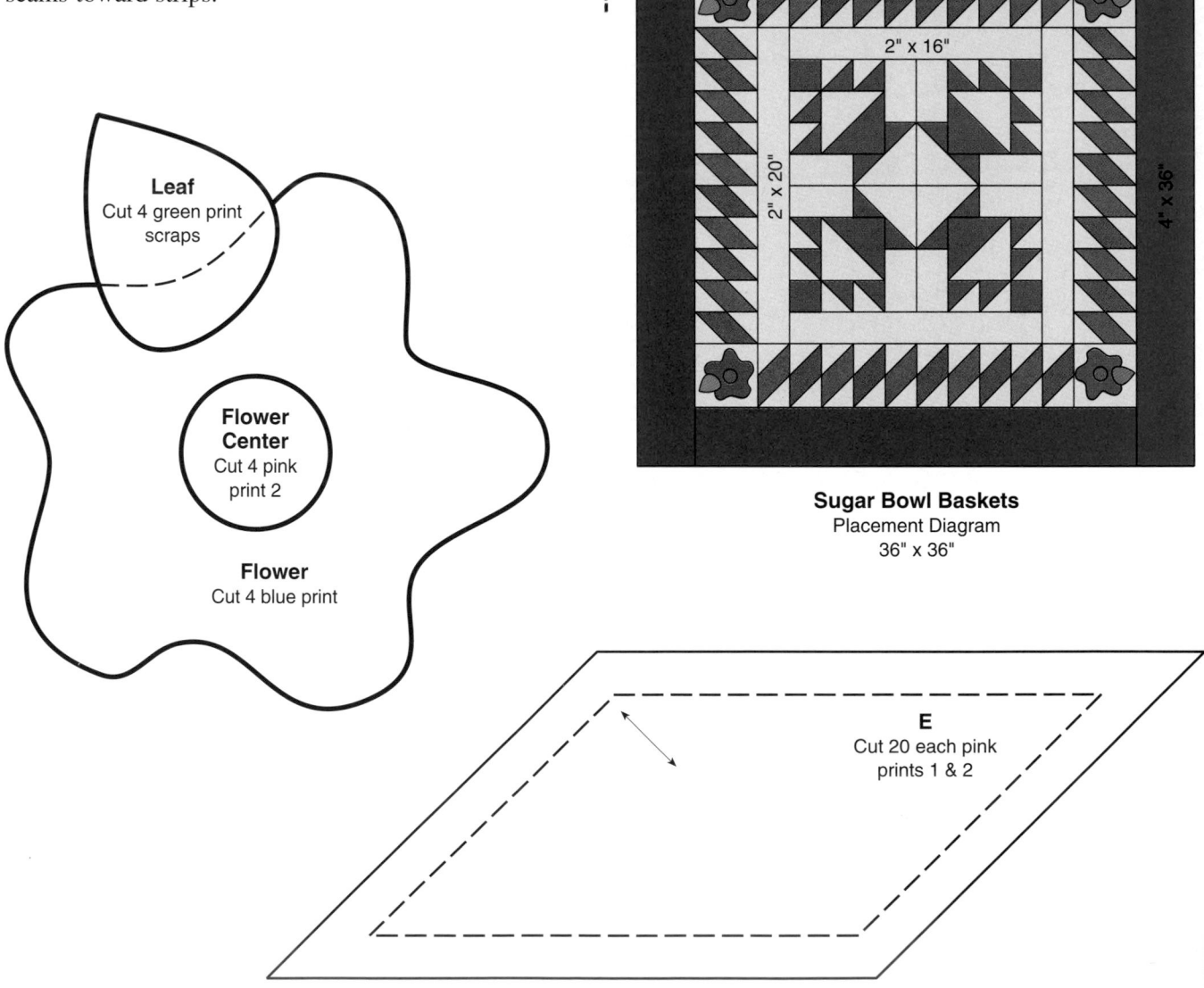

Sugar Bowl Baskets
Placement Diagram
36" x 36"

Leaf
Cut 4 green print scraps

Flower Center
Cut 4 pink print 2

Flower
Cut 4 blue print

E
Cut 20 each pink prints 1 & 2

Field of Sunflowers

By Ruth M. Swasey

Sunflower prints have been popular for the past few years. This quilt uses a preprinted sunflower-print panel with coordinated fabrics and can be quickly stitched for that gift you need in a hurry.

Project Notes

The quilt shown used only 20 preprinted sunflower blocks. The half blocks were made by cutting a whole block in half on the diagonal. In so doing, the half blocks become less then half of the whole blocks because the seam allowance has not been added. Instructions to complete the quilt as it was made by the designer are complicated because of the sizes of the fill-in triangles. In order to make the half blocks fit together as shown in the Placement Diagram, the whole blocks have to be cut with an added seam allowance as the Instructions state.

Project Specifications

Skill Level: Intermediate
Project Size: 71 1/2" x 86 3/8"

Materials

- 20 preprinted sunflower blocks 12" x 12"
- 2 1/8 yards small sunflower print
- 2 1/2 yards sunflower border stripe
- Backing 76" x 91"
- Batting 76" x 91"
- 9 1/4 yards self-made or purchased binding
- Neutral color all-purpose thread
- Basic sewing supplies, rotary cutter, self-healing mat and acrylic ruler

Instructions

Step 1. Trim 13 preprinted sunflower blocks to 11" x 11".

Step 2. Trim remaining sunflower blocks to 11 3/8" x 11 3/8". Cut each block in half on one diagonal to

Field of Sunflowers
Placement Diagram
71 1/2" x 86 3/8"

make triangles for half blocks; you will need 14 half blocks for A.

Step 3. Cut seven squares small sunflower print 16 1/8" x 16 1/8". Cut each square in half on both diagonals as shown in Figure 1 to make B triangles.

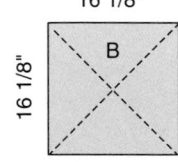

Figure 1
Cut square in half on both diagonals.

Step 4. Cut four squares small sunflower print 8 1/4" x 8 1/4". Cut each square in half on one diagonal to make C triangles.

Step 5. Sew a B triangle to opposite sides of a sunflower block as shown in Figure 2; repeat for 11 units.

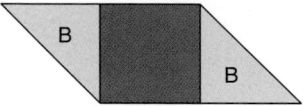

Figure 2
Sew B triangles to opposite
sides of a sunflower block.

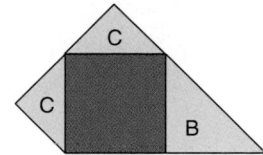

Figure 3
Sew C and B to sunflower block.

Step 6. Sew C triangles to adjacent sides of a sunflower block; add a B triangle as shown in Figure 3; repeat for two units.

Step 7. Join three units pieced in Step 5 with the two units pieced in Step 6 to make the center row as shown in Figure 4; press seams in one direction.

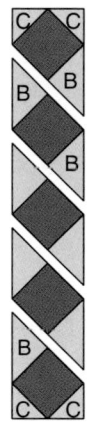

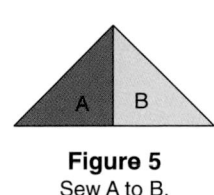

Figure 5
Sew A to B.

Figure 4
Join units to make
the center row.

Step 8. Sew an A piece to a B piece as shown in Figure 5; repeat for four units.

Step 9. Join four units pieced in Step 5 with two units pieced in Step 8 to make a side row as shown in

Figure 6
Join units to make
a side row; repeat
for other side.

Make 1 Make 1

Figure 7
Join units to make
pieced border strips;
repeat for other side.

Figure 6; repeat for a second row, again referring to Figure 6. Press seams in one direction.

Step 10. Join the three rows referring to the Placement Diagram for positioning of rows; press seams in one direction.

Step 11. Join five A pieces with four B pieces and add C to ends as shown in Figure 7 to make side border strip; repeat for second strip again referring to Figure 7.

Step 12. Sew side border strips to opposite long sides of pieced center; press seams toward strips.

Step 13. Cut two strips each sunflower border stripe 6 1/2" x 74" and 6 1/2" x 89" from length of fabric. Sew shorter strips to top and bottom and longer strips to sides, mitering corners; trim seams and press toward strips.

Step 14. Prepare quilt for quilting and finish referring to the General Instructions. ❖

A Walk in Spring

By Ruth M. Swasey

Bright prints combine to make this easy-to-strip-piece quilt. Free up an afternoon and evening to stitch the top and finish in your favorite method to make a colorful quilt with a spring look.

Instructions

Step 1. Cut six strips each yellow, green, orange and floral prints 6 1/2" by fabric width.

Step 2. Sew one strip of each fabric together along length to make a strip set; repeat for six strip sets keeping fabrics in same color order in each set. Press seams in one direction.

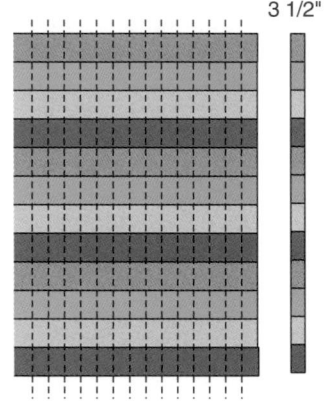

Figure 1
Cut strip set into 3 1/2" segments.

Step 3. Join three strip sets along length; press. Repeat to make two strip sets. Cut each strip set into 3 1/2" segments as shown in Figure 1; you will need 20 strip segments.

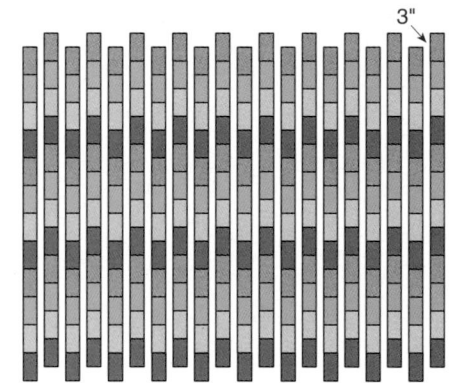

Figure 2
Join strips, moving every other segment up 3".

Step 4. Sew the strip segments together along length, moving every other segment up 3" to make a zigzag pattern as shown in Figure 2. Press seams in one direction.

Step 5. Trim ends even as shown in Figure 3. Trim 1 1/2" off top and bottom rows as shown in Figure 4.

Step 6. Cut and piece four

Figure 3
Trim ends even.

Project Specifications

Skill Level: Intermediate
Project Size: 72" x 78"

Materials

- 1 1/4 yards orange print
- 1 3/4 yards floral print
- 2 1/8 yards each yellow and green prints
- Backing 76" x 82"
- Batting 76" x 82"
- 8 3/4 yards self-made or purchased binding
- All-purpose thread to match fabrics
- Basic sewing supplies, rotary cutter, self-healing mat and acrylic ruler

strips 3 1/2" x 66 1/2" floral print. Sew strips to opposite long sides and then to top and bottom; press seams toward strips.

Step 7. Prepare templates for pieces A and B using pattern pieces given; cut as directed on each piece.

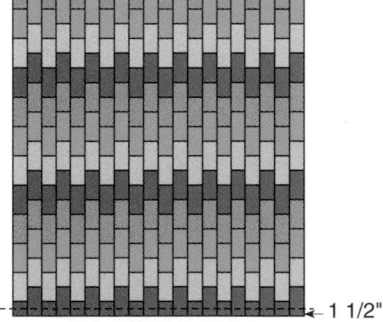

Figure 4
Trim 1 1/2" off top and bottom rows as shown.

Step 8. Join 10 yellow print A pieces with 11 green print A pieces to make a strip as shown in Figure 5; sew a yellow print B to each end, again referring to Figure 5. Repeat for second strip. Sew a pieced strip to the top and bottom referring to the Placement

3" x 66"

3" x 66"

A Walk in Spring
Placement Diagram
72" x 78"

Figure 5
Join 10 yellow print and 11 green print A pieces; add
yellow print B pieces to ends as shown.

Diagram for positioning. Press seams toward strips.

Step 9. Join 13 yellow print A pieces with 12 green
print A pieces to make a strip. Sew a green print B to
each end; repeat for second strip. Sew a pieced strip to
opposite long sides referring to the Placement Diagram
for positioning of strips; press seams toward strips.

Step 10. Prepare quilt for quilting and finish referring
to the General Instructions. ❖

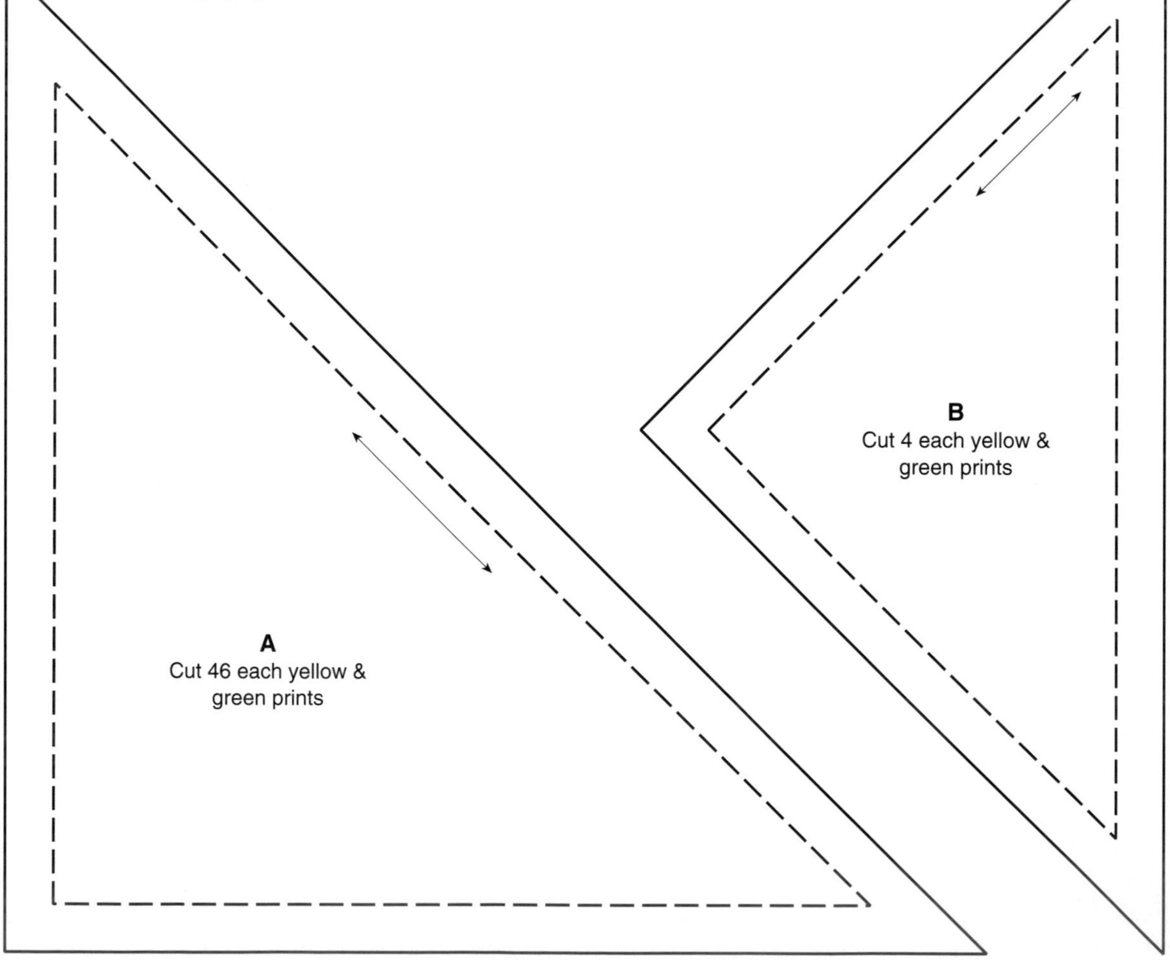

B
Cut 4 each yellow &
green prints

A
Cut 46 each yellow &
green prints

Garden of Flowers

By Holly Daniels

Pastel colors are used to create this simple bed-size quilt using the Nine-Patch block with the Greek Cross block.

Nine-Patch Blocks

Step 1. Cut 10 strips lavender print 4 1/2" x 44". Cut eight strips floral print 4 1/2" x 44".

Step 2. Sew a lavender print strip to a floral print strip to a lavender print strip to make an A strip set; repeat for four A strip sets. Sew a floral print strip to a lavender print strip to a floral print strip to make a B strip set; repeat for two B strip sets.

Step 3. Cut A and B strip sets into 4 1/2" segments as shown in Figure 1; you will need 36 A segments and 18 B segments.

Nine-Patch
12" x 12" Block
Make 18

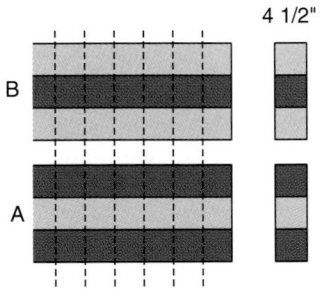
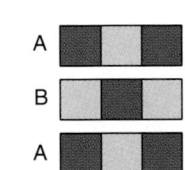

Figure 1
Cut strip sets into 4 1/2" segments.

Figure 2
Join 2 A segments with 1 B segment to make a Nine-Patch block.

Step 4. Sew a B segment between two A segments to complete one Nine-Patch block as shown in Figure 2; repeat for 18 blocks.

Greek Cross Blocks

Step 1. Cut two strips lavender print 4 1/2" x 44". Cut eight strips each peach print and white solid 2 1/2" x 44".

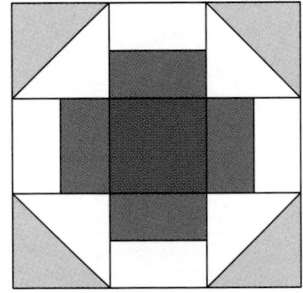

Greek Cross
12" x 12" Block
Make 17

Project Specifications

Skill Level: Beginner
Project Size: 72" x 96"
Block Size: 12" x 12"
Number of Blocks: 18 Nine-Patch; 17 Greek Cross

Materials

- 1 1/4 yards peach print
- 1 1/2 yards white solid
- 1 3/4 yards floral print
- 2 3/4 yards lavender print
- Backing 76" x 100"
- Batting 76" x 100"
- 9 3/4 yards self-made or purchased binding
- All-purpose thread to match fabrics
- Clear nylon monofilament
- Basic sewing supplies, disappearing marker, rotary cutter, self-healing mat and acrylic ruler

Step 2. Sew a peach print strip to a white solid strip to make a C strip set; press seam toward the peach print strip; repeat for eight C strip sets.

Step 3. Sew a C strip set to each side of a lavender print strip to make a D strip set as shown in Figure 3; press seams toward C strip set. Repeat for two D strip sets.

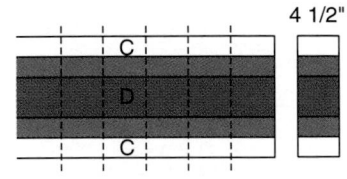

Figure 3
Sew a C strip set to opposite sides of a D strip; cut into 4 1/2" segments to make D-C units.

Step 4. Cut D strip sets into 4 1/2" segments, again referring

to Figure 3 to make D-C units. You will need 17 D-C units.

Step 5. Cut remaining C strip sets into 4 1/2" units as shown in Figure 4; you will need 34 C units.

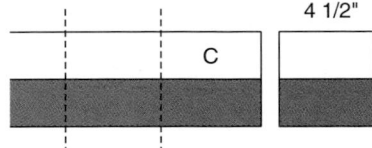

Figure 4
Cut remaining C strip sets into 4 1/2" segments to make C units.

Step 6. Cut five strips each floral print and white solid 4 7/8" x 44". Cut each strip into 4 7/8" square segments for E. You will need 34 squares of each color.

Step 7. Lay a floral print square right sides together with a white solid square. Draw a line through one diagonal of the white solid square using the disappearing marker as shown in Figure 5. Stitch 1/4" away on each side of the line as shown in Figure 6; cut apart on drawn line to make E units as shown in Figure 7. Repeat for all floral print and white solid squares; you will need 68 E units.

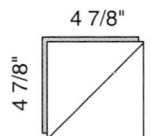
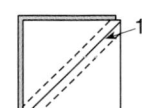

Figure 5
Draw a line through the diagonal on the white solid side of the layered squares.

Figure 6
Stitch 1/4" on each side of the line.

Step 8. Open each E unit; press seam toward floral print triangle.

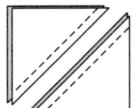
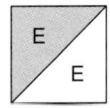
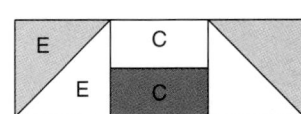

Figure 7
Cut apart on drawn line to make E units.

Figure 8
Sew an E unit to opposite sides of a C unit.

Step 9. Sew an E unit to opposite sides of a C unit as shown in Figure 8; repeat for all C and E units.

Step 10. Sew a D-C unit between two E-C units to complete one Greek Cross block as shown in Figure 9; repeat for 17 blocks.

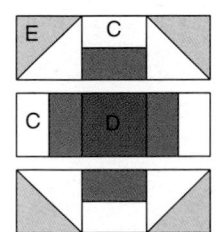

Figure 9
Sew a D-C unit between 2 E-C units to complete 1 Greek Cross block.

Garden of Flowers
Placement Diagram
72" x 96"

Assembly

Step 1. Join three Nine-Patch blocks with two Greek Cross blocks to make an A row; repeat for four A rows. Press seams in one direction.

Step 2. Join three Greek Cross blocks with two Nine-Patch blocks to make a B row; repeat for three B rows. Press seams in the opposite direction of A rows.

Step 3. Join A and B rows, beginning and ending with A rows; press seams in one direction.

Step 4. Cut and piece two strips each peach print 2 1/2" x 88 1/2" and 2 1/2" x 60 1/2". Sew the shorter strips to the top and bottom and longer strips to the longer sides; press seams toward strips.

Step 5. Cut and piece two strips each lavender print 4 1/2" x 96 1/2" and 4 1/2" x 64 1/2". Sew the shorter strips to the top and bottom and longer strips to the longer sides; press seams toward strips.

Step 6. Prepare quilt for quilting and finish referring to the General Instructions. ***Note:*** *The quilt shown was machine-quilted using clear nylon monofilament in the top of the machine and all-purpose thread in the bobbin.* ❖

Lazy Log Cabin Bed Quilt

By Ann Boyce

Scrap strips combine to make this quick and easy Log Cabin bed-size quilt.

Instructions

Step 1. Cut all fabrics into 2" by fabric width strips; you will need 88 strips each light and dark prints.

Step 2. Choose four strips dark prints. Sew strips together along length to make a strip set as shown in Figure 1; press seams in one direction. Repeat for 22 strip sets each light and dark prints.

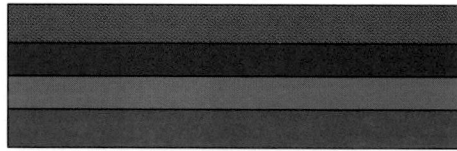

Figure 1
Join 4 dark print strips to make a strip set.

Step 3. Prepare template for A triangle using pattern given. Place the A template on a strip set as shown in Figure 2. Cut 128 each light and dark A triangles.

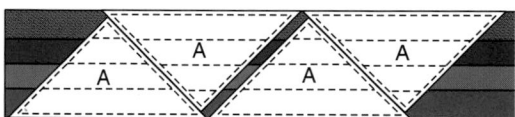

Figure 2
Cut A triangles from strip sets as shown.

Step 4. Sew two dark print A triangles together as shown in Figure 3. Repeat with all dark and light print triangles, sewing dark to dark and light to light.

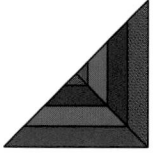

Figure 3
Join 2 dark print triangles.

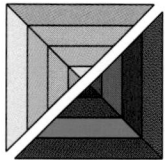

Figure 4
Join triangle units as shown to complete 1 block.

Step 5. Join a dark print triangle pair to a light print triangle pair to complete one block as shown in Figure 4; repeat for 64 blocks.

Step 6. Arrange blocks in eight rows of eight blocks each, making a Barn-Raising design referring to the

Project Specifications

Skill Level: Beginner
Project Size: 87" x 87"
Block Size: 10 7/8" x 10 7/8"
Number of Blocks: 64

Materials

- 5 yards total light prints
- 5 yards total dark prints
- Backing 91" x 91"
- Batting 91" x 91"
- All-purpose thread to match fabrics
- Basic sewing supplies, rotary cutter, self-healing mat and acrylic ruler

Placement Diagram for positioning of blocks. Join blocks in rows; join rows to complete quilt top. Press seams in one direction.

Step 7. Prepare quilt top for quilting and finish referring to the General Instructions. ❖

Using Scraps

If you have 2" scrap strips of varying lengths, cut strips into 4", 8", 12" and 14" lengths. Join the strips as shown in Figure 5. Cut individual triangles from these stitched sections referring to Figure 6.

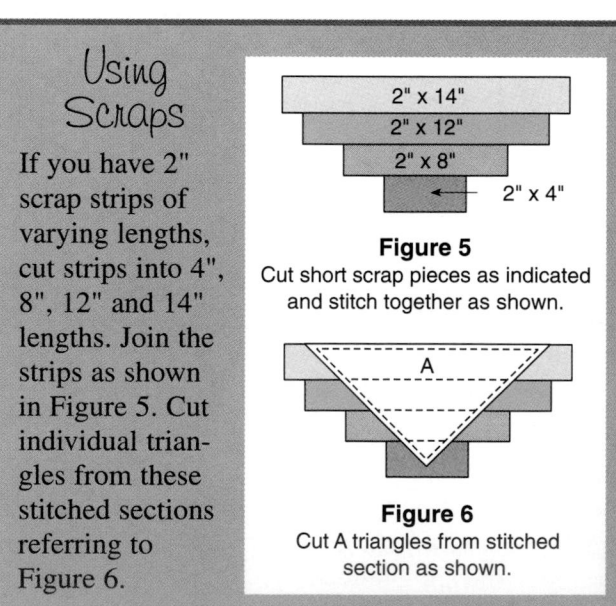

Figure 5
Cut short scrap pieces as indicated and stitch together as shown.

Figure 6
Cut A triangles from stitched section as shown.

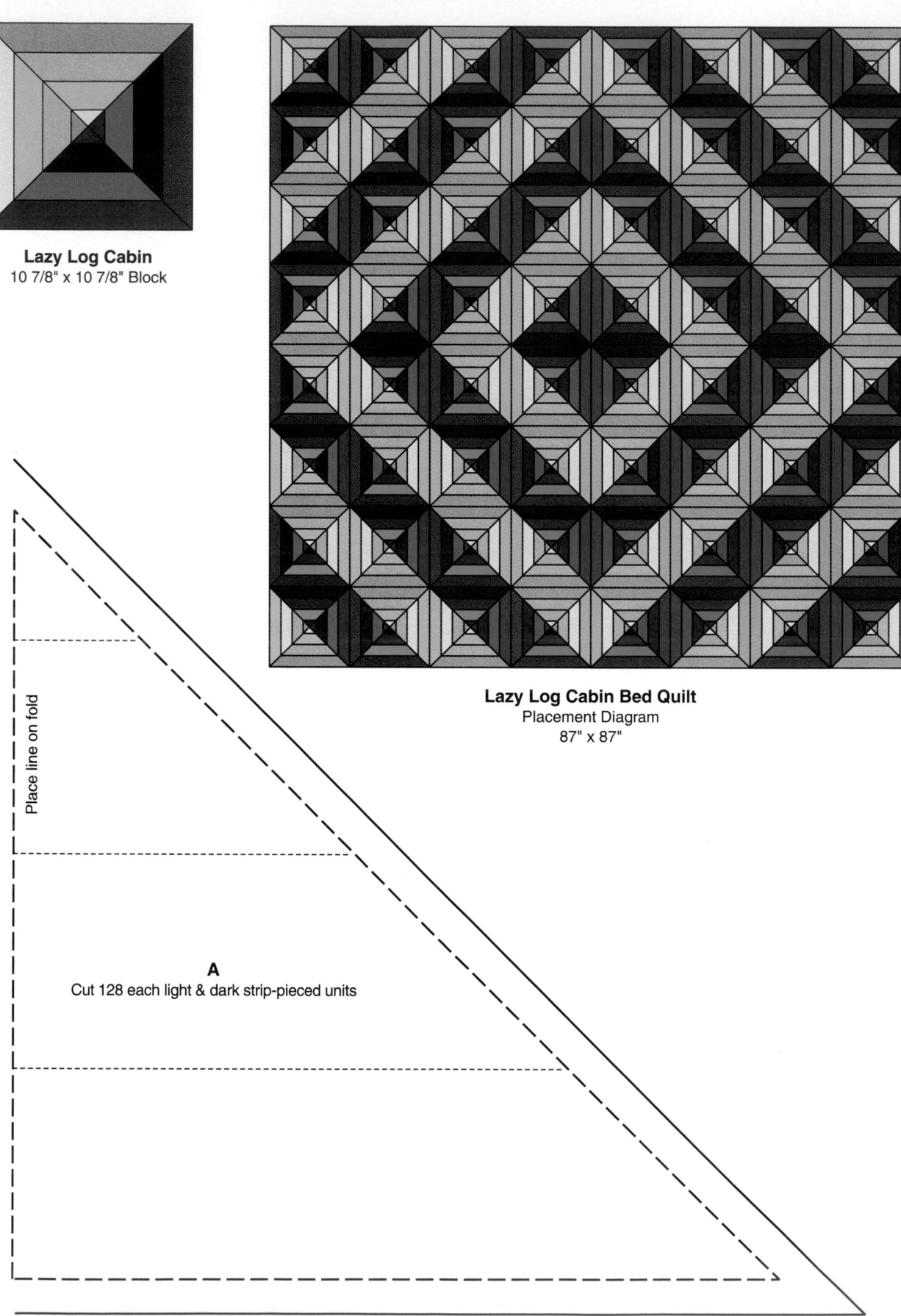

Lazy Log Cabin
10 7/8" x 10 7/8" Block

Lazy Log Cabin Bed Quilt
Placement Diagram
87" x 87"

Place line on fold

A
Cut 128 each light & dark strip-pieced units

Petite Pineapple

By Lucy A. Fazely

Without foundation-piecing, the Pineapple pattern is hard to make accurately. Try this technique and see what a beautiful wall quilt you can make.

Instructions

Step 1. Press fabric stabilizer; cut into nine 7" x 7" squares.

Step 2. Center one square over block design drawing given. Using a ruler and pencil, trace all lines on stabilizer square; mark numbers in each area as marked on pattern. Draw the seam allowance around the outside; repeat for all squares.

Pineapple
6" x 6" Block

Step 3. Mark the colors needed for each area on the unmarked side of the stabilizer on each square.

Step 4. Cut nine squares light background print 2" x 2" for center piece 1.

Step 5. For pieces 2–10, subcut the following strips and then cut as directed. Cut six strips tan print 1 1/4" by fabric width. Subcut into 18 pieces each size as follows: 2 1/2" for piece 3; 2 1/2" for piece 5; 3" for piece 7; and 3 1/2" for piece 9.

Step 6. Cut six strips dark print 1 1/4" by fabric width. Subcut into 18 pieces each size as follows: 2 1/2" for piece 2; 2 1/2" for piece 5; 3" for piece 7; and 3 1/2" for piece 9.

Step 7. Cut 12 strips light background print 1 1/4" by fabric width. Subcut into 36 pieces each size as follows: 2 1/2" for piece 4; 3" for piece 6; 3 1/2" for piece 8; and 4" for piece 10.

Step 8. Cut nine squares each dark print and tan print 3" x 3". Cut each square in half on one diagonal to make triangles for piece 11.

Step 9. Lay background piece 1 square centered under the section marked 1, wrong side next to stabilizer (on the side marked with color, not numbers). Lay a dark print piece 2 right sides together on piece 1. Pin along line between 1 and 2; fold piece 2 over at pin to be sure it generously covers area 2 marked on stabilizer.

Project Specifications

Skill Level: Intermediate
Project Size: 25 1/2" x 25 1/2"
Block Size: 6" x 6"
Number of Blocks: 9

Materials

- 1/3 yard tan print
- 2/3 yard light background print
- 3/4 yard dark print
- Backing 30" x 30"
- Batting 30" x 30"
- All-purpose thread to match fabrics
- 18" x 36" piece fabric stabilizer
- Basic sewing supplies and tools, rotary cutter and ruler

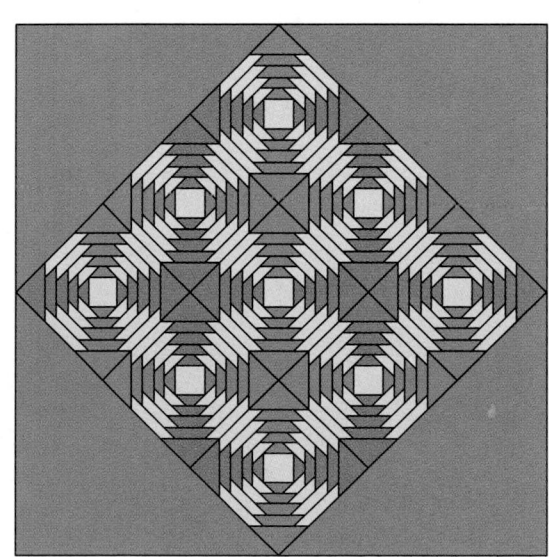

Petite Pineapple
Placement Diagram
25 1/2" x 25 1/2"

Step 10. Remove pin; re-pin away from the line. Stitch on line extending the line 1/8" before and after the line—no backstitching is necessary.

Step 11. Turn over piece; trim seam allowance to 1/4" if necessary. Press piece 2 over; repeat with second piece 2 on opposite side of center. Add piece 3 in the same manner using the dark fabric. ***Note:*** *When adding pieces 5, 7, 9 and 11, be careful to sew dark print pieces to the dark corners of the block and tan print pieces to the tan corners of the block.*

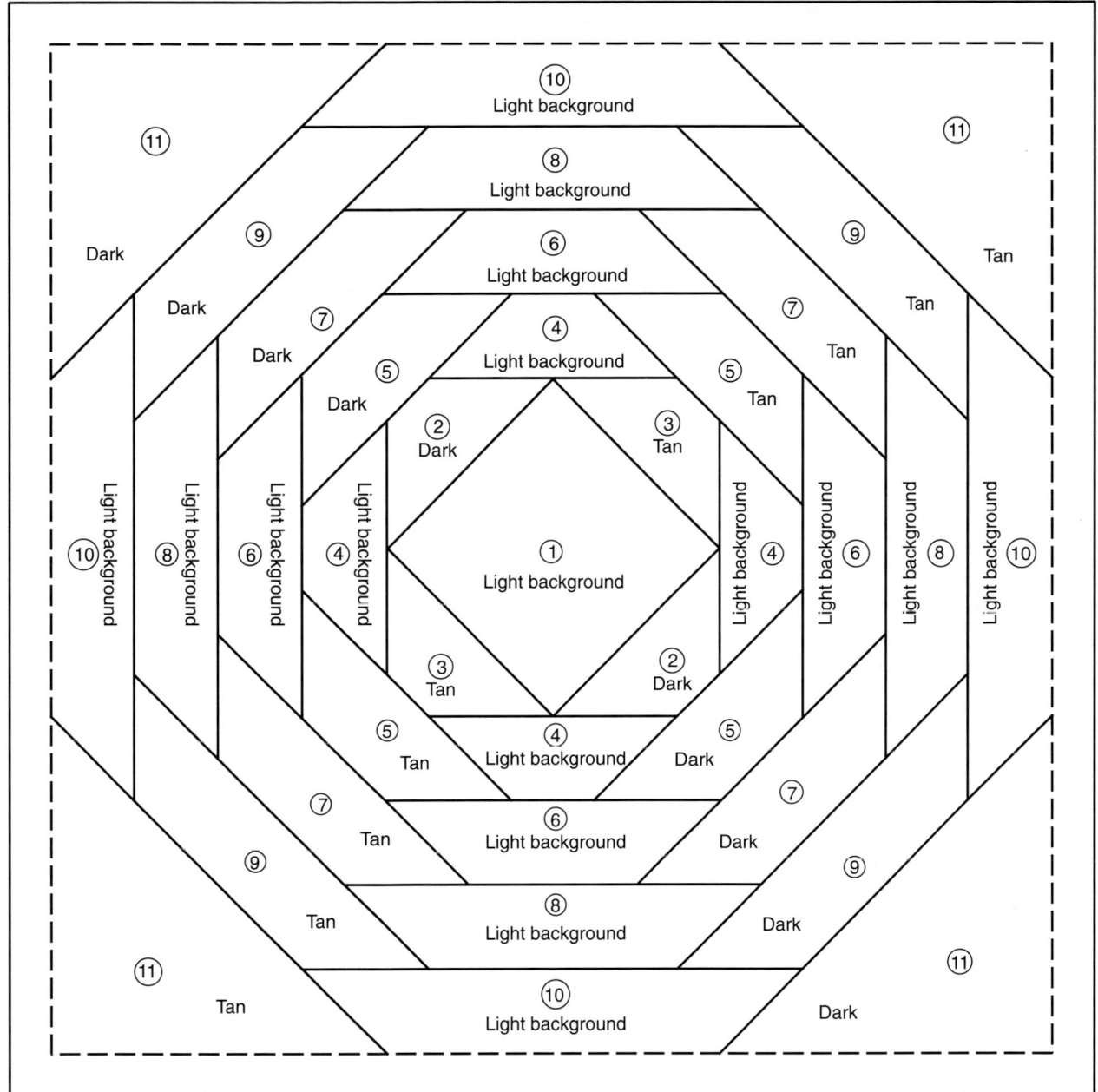

Foundation Pattern

Step 12. Continue adding pieces in numerical order completing all pieces using the same number before moving on to the next number until blocks are complete. *Note: Do not remove stabilizer at this time.*

Step 13. Trim blocks to 1/4" seam allowance line.

Step 14. Lay out blocks in three rows of three blocks each referring to the Placement Diagram for positioning of blocks. Join in rows; join rows to complete pieced center.

Step 15. Cut two squares dark print 13 5/8" x 13 5/8". Cut

each square in half on one diagonal to make triangles. Sew a triangle to each side of the pieced center; press seams toward triangles. Remove stabilizer from stitched section.

Step 16. Prepare for quilting and quilt as desired referring to the General Instructions.

Step 17. When quilting is complete, trim batting only even with top edge. Trim backing 5/8" larger than quilt top all around. Turn backing edge over even with edge of quilt top; turn edge under 1/4" slipstitch in place all around to finish edges. ❖

Bear Paw Jewels

By Lucy A. Fazely

Jewel-tone fabrics are used to make the Bear Paw blocks in this quilt. These colors are set off against a black background giving the project an Amish look.

Instructions

Step 1. Cut 20 strips black solid 2 1/2" by fabric width. Subcut eight of the strips into 2 1/2" segments for B squares; you will need 120 B squares; set aside. Subcut four strips into 6 1/2" segments for C; you will need 24 C segments. Subcut two strips into 14 1/2" segments for D sashing strips; you will need four D strips. Cut and piece the remaining strips to make three 2 1/2" x 46 1/2" strips and two 2 1/2" x 34 1/2" strips.

Step 2. Choose six jewel-tone prints for large squares in each block. Cut four 4 1/2" x 4 1/2" squares from each of these fabrics for A.

Step 3. Cut one 2 1/2" by fabric width strip from each of the remaining six jewel-tone prints; subcut into 2 1/2" square segments for B. You will need 17 B squares from each jewel-tone print.

Step 4. Place one jewel-tone print B square right sides together with a black solid B square. Draw a diagonal line on the print square; sew along line. Trim 1/4" beyond seam; press pieces open with seam toward the black solid B as shown in Figure 1. Repeat for 16 B units in each color.

Bear Paw
14" x 14" block

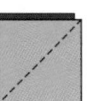  

Figure 1
Stitch, trim to 1/4" beyond seam and press open as shown.

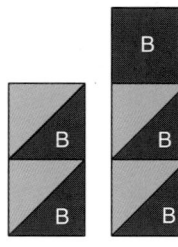

Figure 2
Join B units; sew a black solid B to a pieced B unit.

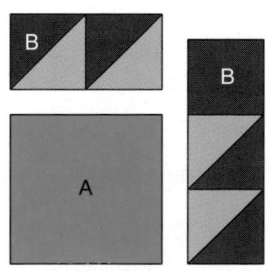

Figure 3
Join pieced units with A to complete 1 A-B unit as shown.

Step 5. Join two same-fabric B units; sew a black solid B to one unit as shown in Figure 2.

Step 6. Join the pieced units with A to complete one A-B unit as shown in Figure 3; repeat for four units of the same fabrics.

Step 7. Sew two A-B units to C as shown in Figure 4; repeat. Sew the remaining B square between two C rectangles. Join the pieced units as shown in Figure 5 to complete one block. Repeat for six blocks.

Step 8. Join three blocks with two D sashing strips to make a row as shown in Figure 6; repeat for two rows. Press seams toward strips.

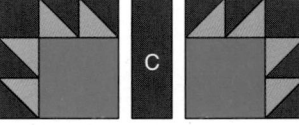

Figure 4
Sew 2 A-B units to C as shown.

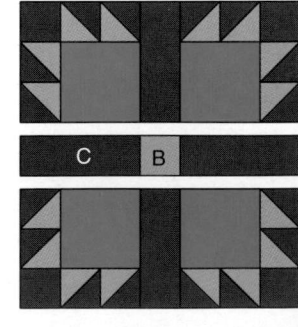

Figure 5
Join the pieced units as shown.

Step 9. Join the rows with three 2 1/2" x 46 1/2" black solid strips; press seams toward strips. Sew a 2 1/2" x 34 1/2" strip black solid to the top and bottom; press seams toward strips.

Step 10. Cut two strips of each jewel-tone print 2 1/2" by fabric width. Join one strip of each color along length with right sides together to make a panel; press seams in one direction. Repeat for a second panel in the same color order as the first one.

Step 11. Cut six 6 1/2" segments from each panel as shown in Figure 7. Join two segments to make a border strip as shown in Figure 8; repeat for four border strips.

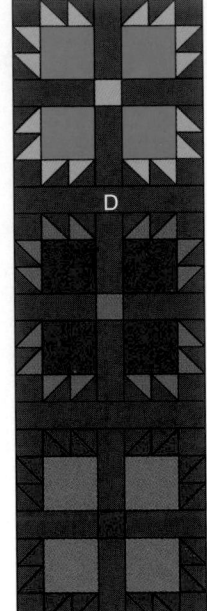

Figure 6
Join 3 blocks with 2 D strips.

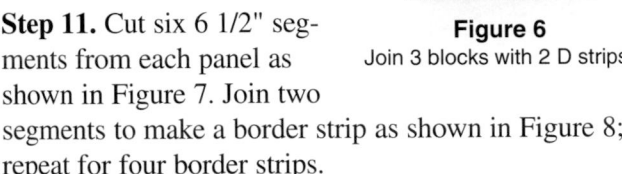

6 1/2"

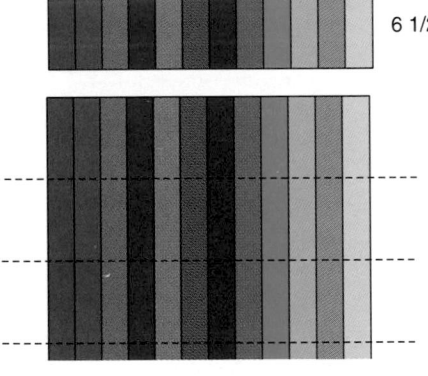

Figure 7
Cut panel into 6 1/2" segments as shown.

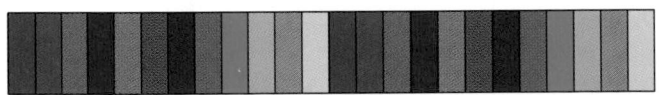

Figure 8
Join 2 segments as shown.

Step 12. Lay a border strip along each side of the pieced center with the colors flowing in a clockwise direction as shown in Figure 9. Remove the last strips from the top right and bottom left side border strips. Add these pieces to the side strip adjacent to it,

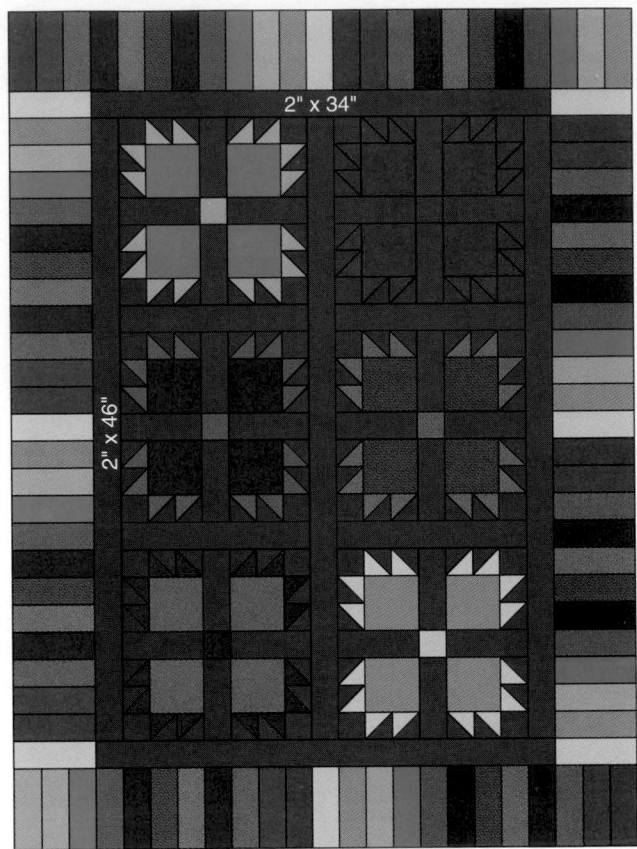

Bear Paw Jewels
Placement Diagram
46" x 62"

again referring to Figure 9.

Step 13. Sew longer strips to longer sides and shorter strips to the top and bottom of the pieced center; press seams toward strips. *Note: If the strips do not fit exactly, adjust seam allowance between strips as needed.*

Move this piece to top edge of right border strip.

Move this piece to bottom edge of left border strip.

Figure 9
Sew strips to pieced center as shown.

Step 14. Prepare 6 1/2 yards self-made black binding, prepare quilt top for quilting and finish referring to the General Instructions. ❖

Ohio Bear Paw

By Christine Carlson

Although complicated looking, this wall quilt is surprisingly easy to assemble and makes for a perfect weekend project. Subdued earth tones and a variety of traditional prints all contribute to the country look so popular today.

Instructions

Step 1. Cut the 18" x 22" piece dark tan solid to make two 11" x 18" rectangles. Layer these with right sides up. Cut five 1 1/2"-wide A bias strips as shown in Figure 1; you will need 10 bias strips. From remaining fabric, cut four 1 1/2" x 1 1/2" B squares.

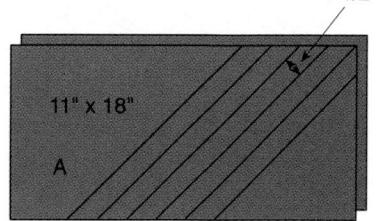

Figure 1
Cut 5 A bias strips 1 1/2" wide from layered pieces.

Step 2. Lay the 11" x 18" piece dark green print wrong side up on a flat surface. Lay the 11" x 18" piece gold print wrong side up on top. Cut three each 1 1/2"-wide C (dark green print) and E (gold print) bias strips from the layered fabrics.

Ohio Bear Paw
Placement Diagram
20 1/2" x 20 1/2"

Project Specifications

Skill Level: Intermediate
Project Size: 20 1/2" x 20 1/2"
Block Size: 3" x 3" and 4" x 4"
Number of Blocks: 4 Bear Paw, 4 Corner and 4 Four X

Materials

- 18" x 22" piece dark tan solid
- 11" x 18" dark green print
- 11" x 18" piece gold print
- 11" x 18" piece light beige print
- 12" x 12" square light tan solid
- 12" x 12" square red stripe
- 16" x 16" square green/gold print
- Backing 24" x 24"
- Thin batting 24" x 24"
- 2 3/4 yards narrow dark green print self-made or purchased binding
- All-purpose thread to match fabrics
- Basic sewing supplies, rotary cutter, self-healing mat and acrylic ruler

Step 3. Cut six 2 1/2" x 2 1/2" D squares from the remaining dark green print and four 2 1/2" x 2 1/2" F squares from the remaining gold print.

Step 4. Cut two 1 1/2"-wide G bias strips from the 11" x 18" piece light beige print. Cut two 2 1/2" x 2 1/2" H squares and two 5 1/4" x 5 1/4" M squares from the remaining light beige print.

Step 5. Cut eight 2 1/2" x 2 1/2" I squares from the 12" x 12" square light tan solid. Cut two 5 1/4" x 5 1/4" J squares from remaining light tan solid.

Step 6. Cut four 5 1/4" x 5 1/4" K squares from the 12" x 12" square red stripe.

Step 7. Sew an A bias strip to a C bias strip; repeat for four A/C sets. Cut 24 A/C bias squares 1 1/2" x 1 1/2" as shown in Figure 2.

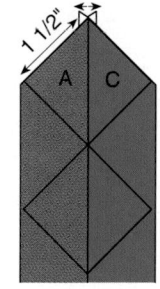

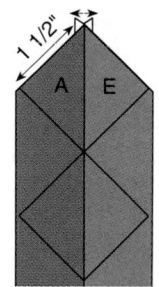

Figure 2
Cut 24 A/C 1 1/2" x 1 1/2" bias squares from stitched sets as shown.

Figure 3
Cut 16 A/E 1 1/2" x 1 1/2" bias squares from stitched sets as shown.

Step 8. Sew an A bias strip to an E bias strip; repeat for three A/E sets. Cut 16 A/E bias squares 1 1/2" x 1 1/2" as shown in Figure 3.

Step 9. Sew an A bias strip to a G bias strip; repeat for three A/G sets. Cut eight A/G bias squares 1 1/2" x 1 1/2" as shown in Figure 4.

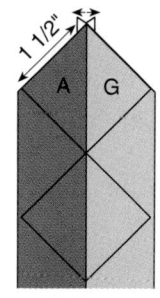

Figure 4
Cut 8 A/G 1 1/2" x 1 1/2" bias squares from stitched sets as shown.

Step 10. Join two A/C bias squares as shown in Figure 5; repeat for 12 sets.

Step 11. Sew an A/C set to the left side of D as shown in Figure 6; repeat for four sets.

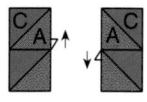

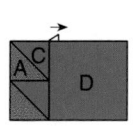

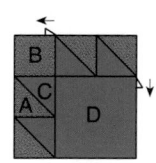

Figure 5
Join 2 A/C bias squares.

Figure 6
Sew an A/C set to the left side of D.

Figure 7
Sew a B-A/C unit to an A/C-D unit to complete 1 Bear Paw block.

Step 12. Sew B to one end of an A/C set; sew to the A/C-D unit to complete one Bear Paw block as shown in Figure 7. Repeat for four blocks.

Step 13. Join two A/E bias squares; sew to I as shown in Figure 8; repeat for four units.

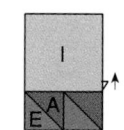

Figure 8
Sew an A/E bias square to I.

Step 14. Sew an A/E-I unit to a dark green print Bear Paw block as shown in Figure 9; repeat for four units.

Step 15. Join two A/E bias squares. Sew an I square to one side and an F square to the opposite side of the A/E set as shown in Figure 10; repeat for four units.

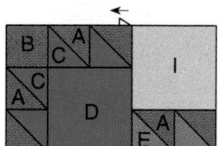

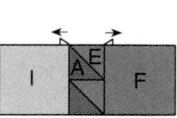

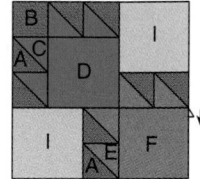

Figure 9
Sew an A/E-I unit to a Bear Paw block.

Figure 10
Sew I and F to opposite sides of an A/E set.

Figure 11
Sew the A/E-I-F unit to the pieced unit.

Step 16. Sew the A/E-I-F unit to the bottom of the unit pieced in Step 14 as shown in Figure 11; repeat for four units.

Step 17. Cut J, K and M squares in half on both diagonals to make eight each J, K and M triangles. Sew a J triangle to a K triangle as shown in Figure 12; repeat for eight units. Join two units to complete one Four X block as shown in Figure 13; repeat for four blocks. *Note: Set aside remaining K triangles and M triangles for use in Corner blocks.*

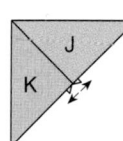

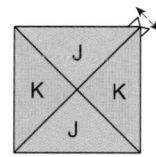

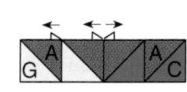

Figure 12
Sew J to K.

Figure 13
Join two J-K units to complete 1 Four X block.

Figure 14
Join two A/G bias squares with 1 A/C set.

Step 18. Join two A/G bias squares with one A/C bias square set as shown in Figure 14; repeat for two units.

Step 19. Sew an A/G-A/C unit to one J edge of a Four X block as shown in Figure 15; repeat for two blocks.

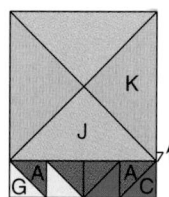

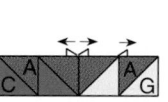

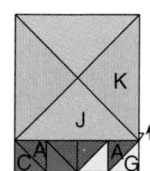

Figure 15
Sew an A/G-A/C unit to a Four X block.

Figure 16
Join 1 A/C set with 2 A/G bias squares.

Figure 17
Sew an A/C-A/G unit to a Four X block.

Step 20. Join one A/C bias square set with two A/G bias squares as shown in Figure 16; repeat for two units. Sew an A/C-A/G unit to one J edge of a Four X block as shown in Figure 17; repeat for two blocks.

Step 21. Sew H to D; repeat. Join two H-D units to make a Four-Patch unit as shown in Figure 18.

Step 22. Lay blocks and pieced units out in rows as shown in Figure 19. Join in rows; join rows to complete pieced center.

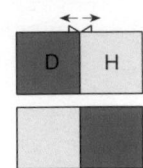

Figure 18
Join H-D units to make a Four-Patch unit.

Figure 19
Lay out blocks and units in rows.

Step 23. Sew M to K as shown in Figure 20; repeat for eight units. Join two units to complete a block as shown in Figure 21. Trim block to 3 1/2" x 3 1/2"

Figure 20
Sew M to K as shown.

square as shown in Figure 22; repeat to complete four Corner blocks.

Step 24. Cut four strips green/gold print 3 1/2" x 14 1/2". Sew a strip to two opposite sides of the pieced center. Sew a Corner block to each end of the remaining two strips as shown in Figure 23. Sew a strip to each remaining side, referring to the Placement Diagram for positioning; press seams toward strips.

Step 25. Prepare for quilting and finish referring to the General Instructions. ❖

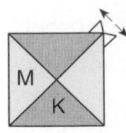
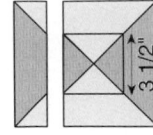

Figure 21
Join 2 M-K units as shown.

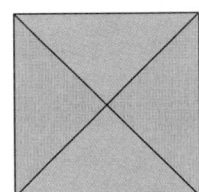

Figure 22
Trim Corner blocks to 3 1/2" x 3 1/2" as shown.

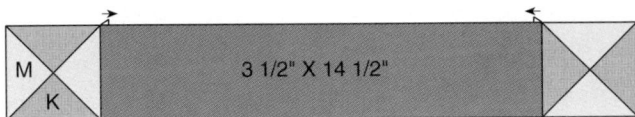

Figure 23
Sew Corner blocks to strip as shown.

Bear Paw
3" x 3" Block

Corner
3" x 3" Block

Four X
4" x 4" Block

Country Garden Quilt

By Vicki Blizzard

Flowers are growing everywhere on this pretty yo-yo flower quilt. Collect a variety of bright buttons to decorate your quilt while being used to tie the layers together.

Instructions

Step 1. Cut a piece of white-on-white print 52 1/2" x 76 1/2" for center background.

Step 2. Cut three red print and two each yellow and blue print circles 11" in diameter for yo-yo flowers.

Step 3. Turn under edges of each circle 1/8". Hand-sew a running stitch around folded edge and gather into a tight circle as shown in Figure 1; knot thread securely. Flatten into a circle.

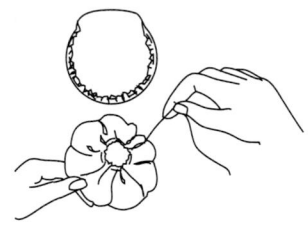

Figure 1
Make yo-yo flower as shown.

Step 4. Using yo-yo flower as a pattern, trace seven circles onto paper side of fusible transfer web. Cut out along traced lines.

Country Garden
Placement Diagram
88" x 94"

Project Specifications
Skill Level: Beginner
Project Size: 88" x 94"

Materials
Note: Fabrics must be 44" wide.

- 3/4 yard each green solid and blue print
- 1 1/2 yards yellow print
- 1 1/2 yards 108"-wide white-on-white print
- 2 1/4 yards red print
- 2 3/4 yards 108"-wide muslin for backing
- Batting 92" x 98"
- 10 1/4 yards dark red 2"-wide pre-made binding
- Red and white all-purpose thread
- Clear nylon monofilament
- 1 yard lightweight fusible transfer web
- 8 yards green jumbo rickrack
- 2 ladybug buttons
- 3 bumblebee buttons
- 1/4 pound each assorted red, yellow and blue buttons
- 18 assorted green buttons
- 1 ball size 10 crochet cotton
- Sharp needle for tying
- Basic sewing supplies, rotary cutter, self-healing mat and acrylic ruler

Fuse to the wrong side of each yo-yo flower referring to manufacturer's instructions; remove paper backing.

Step 5. Prepare template for leaf shape. Trace shape onto paper side of fusible transfer web referring to pattern for number to cut. Iron fusible transfer web to the wrong side of the green solid referring to manufacturer's instructions. Cut out shapes; remove paper backing

Step 6. Cut green jumbo rickrack into the following

lengths: one each 23", 30", 36" and 43" and three 50".

Step 7. Baste rickrack lengths in place on white-on-white print background referring to Figure 2. Using clear nylon monofilament in the top of the machine and white all-purpose thread in the bobbin, machine-stitch rickrack pieces in place.

Step 8. Pin a yo-yo flower in place at the top of each rickrack stem and leaves along stems referring to the

Placement Diagram and photo of quilt for positioning of colors; fuse in place and stitch as for rickrack in Step 7. *Note: Set aside two leaves to be placed after borders are added.*

Step 9. Cut seven strips each yellow and red prints 2 1/2" by fabric width. Sew a red print strip to a yellow print strip along length; press seams toward red print strip. Repeat for all strips. Cut strip sets into 2 1/2" segments as shown in Figure 3; you will need 106 segments.

Step 10. Join two segments as shown in Figure 4; continue stitching segments in this order until the strip has 38 segments; press seams in one direction. Repeat for a second strip. Sew a pieced strip to opposite long sides of the appliquéd center.

Step 11. Stitch another strip with 30 segments; press seams in one direction. Sew this strip to the bottom of the appliquéd center.

Step 12. Pin remaining two leaves in place overlapping checkerboard border on each side referring to the Placement Diagram for positioning. Fuse in place and stitch as instructed in Step 8.

Step 13. Cut nine strips red print and three strips each yellow and blue prints and green solid 4 1/2" by fabric width. Sew a red print strip to each colored strip; press seams toward red print.

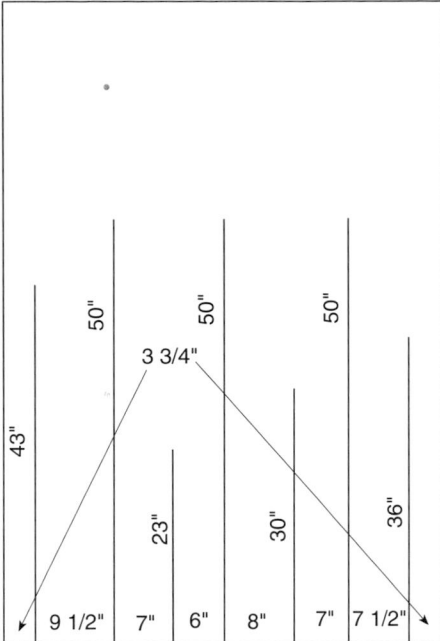

Figure 2
Baste pieces of rickrack to background as shown.

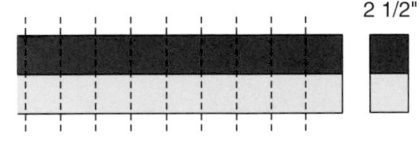

Figure 3
Cut strip sets into 2 1/2" segments.

Figure 4
Join 2 segments.

Step 14. Cut strip sets into 14 1/2" segments. You will need nine segments each red/green, red/blue and red/yellow.

Step 15. Join four red/blue and three each red/green and red/yellow segments on the 14 1/2" sides to make a strip as shown in Figure 5. Join four red/green, three red/blue and red/yellow segments on the 14 1/2" sides to make a strip as shown in Figure 6. Join three red/yellow and two each red/green and red/blue segments on the 14 1/2" sides to make a bottom border strip referring to Figure 7. Sew the longer strips to opposite long sides; set aside bottom strip.

Step 16. Cut four strips each red and yellow prints 2 1/2" by fabric width. Cut each strip in half to make shorter strips. Sew strips together along length as follows: red/yellow/red/yellow/red/yellow/red for A strip set and yellow/red/yellow/red/yellow/red/yellow for B strip set. Press seams in one direction on each strip set.

Step 17. Cut each strip set apart into 2 1/2" segments. Join four A segments with three B segments to make a checkerboard section as shown in Figure 8. Repeat for second checkerboard section.

Step 18. Sew a checkerboard section to each end of the remaining pieced border strip referring to the Placement Diagram for placement of checkerboard sections; press.

Step 19. Sew the border strip with checkerboard corners to the bottom of the appliquéd center; press seams toward strip.

Step 20. Prepare quilt top for finishing referring to the General Instructions.

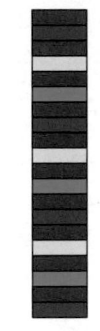

Figure 5
Join segments on the 14 1/2" sides to make a side border strip.

Figure 6
Join segments on the 14 1/2" sides to make a second side border strip.

Figure 7
Join segments on the 14 1/2" sides to make a bottom border strip.

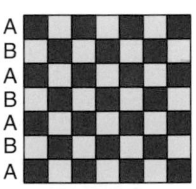

Figure 8
Join 4 A segments with 3 B segments to make a checkerboard section.

Step 21. Lay quilt layers on a clean floor. Scatter green buttons on the bottom background area; leave buttons where they land. Thread needle with a long single length of crochet cotton. Go down through one hole in the button and through all layers of the quilt; come up through all layers into second hole in button. Cut thread leaving 4" ends for tying. Tie a square knot to secure each button.

Step 22. Scatter remaining buttons on quilt background, having more blue buttons on the top areas of the background. Sew in place as for green buttons. Sew a red button in the center of each red yo-yo flower and yellow buttons in the remaining yo-yo flowers.

Step 23. Sew a bumblebee button to one blue and two red yo-yo flowers as desired. Sew a ladybug button to two leaves.

Step 24. Tie between squares on borders and along seams of border strips to hold layers together.

Step 25. When tying is complete, prepare quilt for binding and bind edges using purchased premade binding referring to the General Instructions.

Optional Pillow Cover

Project Specifications
Skill Level: Beginner
Project Size: 36" x 68"

Materials
- 1/2 yard each blue and yellow prints and green solid
- 1 1/4 yards red print
- 1 1/4 yards 108"-wide muslin for backing
- White all-purpose thread
- Basic sewing supplies and tools, rotary cutter, self-healing mat and acrylic ruler

Instructions
Step 1. Cut nine strips red print, three strips each blue and yellow prints and two strips green solid 4 1/2" x 36 1/2".

Step 2. With right sides together, sew a red strip to each colored strip along length of strips; press seams toward red print.

Step 3. Join strip sets with remaining red print strip to complete pillow cover top referring to the Placement Diagram for color arrangement; press seams in one direction.

Step 4. Place pillow top right sides together with the muslin backing; trim edges of backing even with pillow top.

Step 5. Stitch around all sides leaving a 12" opening on one side. Turn right side out through opening; press seams flat at edges. Hand-stitch opening closed. ❖

Country Garden Pillow Cover
Placement Diagram
36" x 68"

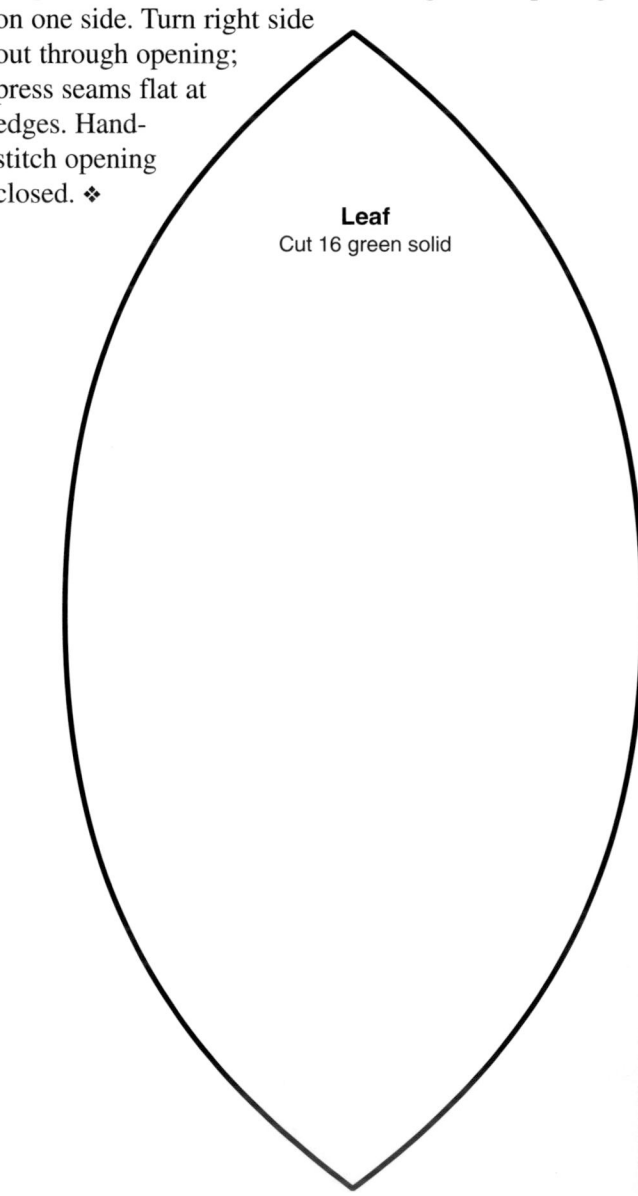

Leaf
Cut 16 green solid

Tantalizing Tulips Bed Quilt

By Judith Sandstrom

*Machine-appliqué these pretty tulip blocks to make
a bright quilt for a spring bedroom decor.*

Instructions

Step 1. Cut 20 squares beige-on-beige print 12 1/2" x 12 1/2". Fold each square on one diagonal and crease.

Step 2. Cut 10 strips light green print 9 3/8" by fabric width. Subcut strips into 9 3/8" segments to make squares; you will need 40 squares. Cut each square in half on one diagonal to make triangles for corners of squares.

Tantalizing Tulips
17" x 17" Block

Step 3. Sew a triangle to each side of a beige-on-beige print square; press seams toward triangles.

Tantalizing Tulips Bed Quilt
Placement Diagram
76" x 93"

Project Specifications

Skill Level: Intermediate
Project Size: 76" x 93"
Block Size: 17" x 17"
Number of Blocks: 20

Materials

- 3/8 yard each dark green, peach, lavender and gold prints
- 2 1/8 yards black print (must be at least 43" wide)
- 2 1/2 yards beige-on-beige print
- 2 2/3 yards light green print
- Backing 72" x 89"
- Thin cotton batting 90" x 108"
- All-purpose thread to match fabrics
- 1 1/2 yards fusible transfer web
- 1 roll of 1/2"-wide fusible transfer web
- Quilt basting spray
- Basic sewing supplies, rotary cutter, self-healing mat and acrylic ruler

Step 4. Prepare template for tulip shape using pattern piece given.

Step 5. Cut four 13" x 17" rectangles fusible transfer web. Fuse one piece to the wrong side of each of the dark green, peach, lavender and gold prints. Trace tulip shapes on the paper side of the fused fabrics referring to pattern for color and number to cut. Cut out shapes on traced lines; remove paper backing.

Step 6. Remove paper backing from the dark green print. Using the rotary cutter, cut twenty 1/4" x 8" stems and forty 1/4" x 7" stems.

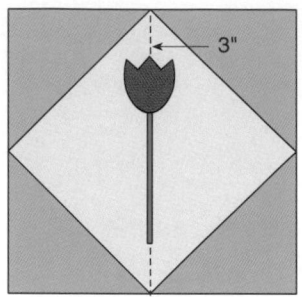

Figure 1
Arrange tulip on the center
diagonal of the square.

Step 7. Referring to Figure 1, arrange one lavender print tulip shape with one 1/4" x 8" stem on the center diagonal of each beige-on-beige print square. Position a peach and gold print tulip on each side with 1/4" x 7" stems, overlapping center stem over side stems referring to Figure 2; fuse shapes in place.

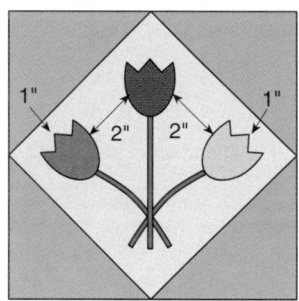

Figure 2
Place tulips on each side; center
stem overlaps side stems.

Step 8. Arrange blocks in five rows of four blocks each. Join blocks in rows. Press seams in one direction. Join rows to complete pieced center.

Step 9. Cut four 4 1/4" x 90" strips batting; spread remaining piece of batting out flat.

Step 10. Referring to manufacturer's instructions, apply basting spray to the wrong side of the prepared backing piece; smooth out over the batting. Turn the batting over, spray quilt front and position it over the batting to align all three layers. Hand-baste close to the edge around outside edges; trim away excess batting and backing.

Step 11. Using matching all-purpose thread, machine satin-stitch all tulips and stems in place. ***Note:** You will be stitching through all layers adding machine quilting at the same time as appliquéing.*

Step 12. Cut eight 9" x 45" strips black print. Join two strips on the 9" sides with right sides together to make one long strip; repeat. Press seams open.

Step 13. Iron the 1/2"-wide fusible transfer web to the *right* side of one long edge of each border strip referring to Figure 3. Place the raw edge without the fusible web right side down on one long side of the basted quilt front referring to Figure 4.

Figure 3
Fuse 1/2"-wide fusible
strip to edge as shown.

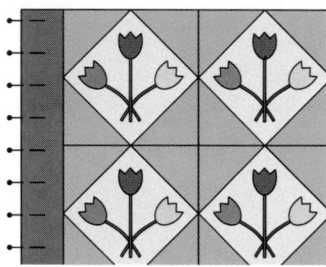

Figure 4
Pin strip without fusible
edge to edge of quilt.

Step 14. Place a 4 1/4" x 90" batting strip on top of the border strip; pin and stitch the three layers together referring to Figure 5. Trim excess border strip and batting even with top and bottom edges of quilt; finger-press seam toward border strip.

Figure 5
Place a 4 1/4" x 90" batting strip
on top of pinned strip as shown;
stitch through all layers.

Step 15. Turn the border strip over the batting to the backside. Fold under the 1/2" fused edge so it extends slightly over and covers the stitching line; fuse in place as shown in Figure 6. From the front side of the quilt, stitch in the ditch of border seam to secure and catch strip on backside as shown in Figure 7. Repeat on opposite long side.

Step 16. When pinning the top and bottom border strips, extend the strips 1/2" beyond quilt edge; trim batting even with quilt edge referring to Figure 8. Iron

Figure 6
Fold under fused edge on backside;
fuse in place to cover seam.

Figure 7
Stitch in the ditch of border seam
on front to secure and catch
border strip on the backside.

1/2"

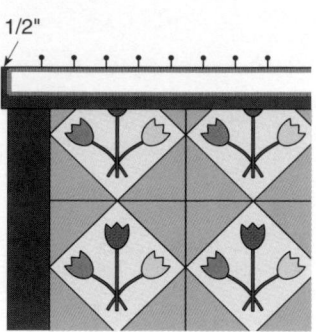

Figure 8
Trim batting even with end.

a 1/2"-wide fusible strip to the right side of the 9"
border strip edge. Stitch as directed for side borders.
Fold under border ends; fuse together to finish. ❖

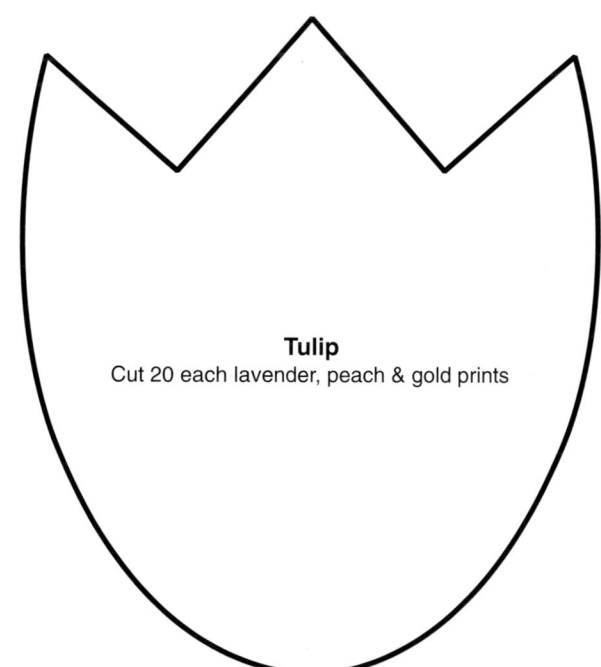

Tulip
Cut 20 each lavender, peach & gold prints

Square Within a Square

By Ruth Swasey

The Log Cabin Courthouse Step design is simply a square within a square design.
It is simple to piece using quick-piecing methods with fabric strips.

Instructions

Step 1. Cut light-colored prints into 2" by fabric width strips. Each block requires two strips each in the following sizes with each round of strips from the same fabric. You will need two 3 1/2" strips for pieces 1 and 2, four 6 1/2" strips for pieces 3, 4, 5 and 6 (pieces 3 and 4 the same fabric as pieces 1 and 2) and two 9 1/2" strips for

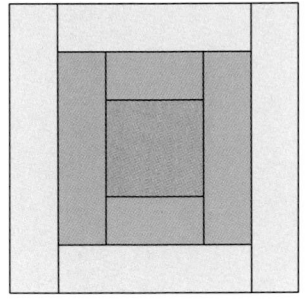

Square Within a Square
9" x 9" Block

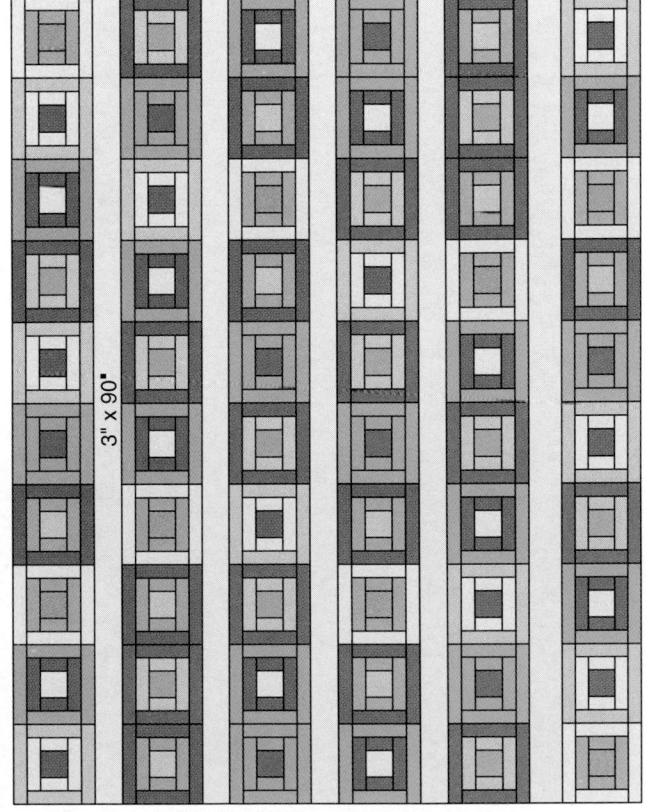

Square Within a Square
Placement Diagram
69" x 90"

Project Specifications

Skill Level: Beginner
Project Size: 69" x 90"
Block Size: 9" x 9"
Number of Blocks: 60

Materials

- 2/3 yard floral print
- 1 1/2 yards white print
- 4 1/2 yards total light-colored prints for strips
- Backing 73" x 94"
- Batting 73" x 94"
- 9 1/4 yards self-made or purchased binding
- Neutral color all-purpose thread
- Neutral color quilting thread
- Basic sewing supplies and tools, rotary cutter , mat and ruler

pieces 7 and 8 from the same fabric as pieces 5 and 6 for each block.

Step 2. Cut five strips 3 1/2" by fabric width floral print. Cut strips into 3 1/2" segments for A; you will need 60 A squares.

Step 3. Sew pieces 1 and 2 to opposite sides of the A square; press seams toward strips. Sew remaining pieces to this unit referring to Figure 1 for order of piecing; press seams toward strips. Repeat for 60 blocks.

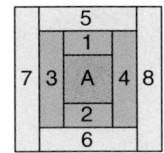

Figure 1
Sew pieces to the A square in the order shown.

Step 4. Join 10 blocks to make a row as shown in Figure 2; repeat for six rows.

Step 5. Cut and piece five strips white print 3 1/2" x 90 1/2". Join block rows with strips to complete pieced top; press seams toward strips.

Step 6. Prepare quilt top for quilting and finish referring to the General Instructions. ❖

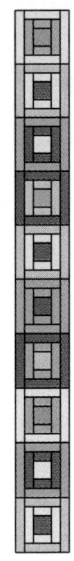

Figure 2
Join 10 blocks
to make a row.

Quiltmaking Basics

Materials & Supplies

Fabrics

Fabric Choices. Quilts and quilted projects combine fabrics of many types, depending on the project. It is best to combine same-fiber-content fabrics when making quilted items.

Buying Fabrics. One hundred percent cotton fabrics are recommended for making quilts. Choose colors similar to those used in the quilts shown or colors of your own preference. Most quilt designs depend more on contrast of values than on the colors used to create the design.

Preparing the Fabric for Use. Fabrics may be prewashed or not depending on your preference. Whether you do or don't, be sure your fabrics are colorfast and won't run onto each other when washed after use.

Fabric Grain. Fabrics are woven with threads going in a crosswise and lengthwise direction. The threads cross at right angles—the more threads per inch, the stronger the fabric.

The crosswise threads will stretch a little. The lengthwise threads will not stretch at all. Cutting the fabric at a 45-degree angle to the crosswise and lengthwise threads produces a bias edge which stretches a great deal when pulled (Figure 1).

If templates are given with patterns in this book, pay careful attention to

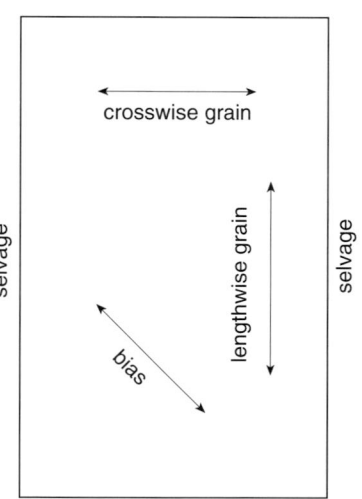

Figure 1
Drawing shows lengthwise, crosswise and bias threads.

the grain lines marked with arrows. These arrows indicate that the piece should be placed on the lengthwise grain with the arrow running on one thread. Although it is not necessary to examine the fabric and find a thread to match to, it is important to try to place the arrow with the lengthwise grain of the fabric (Figure 2).

Thread

For most piecing, good-quality cotton or cotton-covered polyester is the thread of choice. Inexpensive polyester threads are not recommended because they can cut the fibers of cotton fabrics.

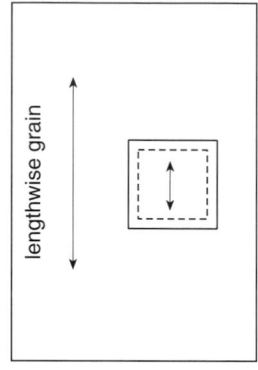

Figure 2
Place the template with marked arrow on the lengthwise grain of the fabric.

Choose a color thread that will match or blend with the fabrics in your quilt. For projects pieced with dark and light color fabrics choose a neutral thread color, such as a medium gray, as a compromise between colors. Test by pulling a sample seam.

Batting

Batting is the material used to give a quilt loft or thickness. It also adds warmth.

Batting size is listed in inches for each pattern to reflect the size needed to complete the quilt according to the instructions. Purchase the size large enough to cut the size you need for the quilt of your choice.

Some qualities to look for in batting are drapeability, resistance to fiber migration, loft and softness.

If you are unsure which kind of batting to use, purchase the smallest size batting available in the type you'd like to try. Test each sample on a small project. Choose the batting that you like working with most and that will result in the type of quilt you need.

Tools & Equipment

There are few truly essential tools and little equipment required for quiltmaking. The basics include needles (hand-sewing and quilting betweens), pins (long, thin sharp pins are best), sharp scissors or shears, a thimble, template materials (plastic or cardboard), marking tools (chalk marker, water-erasable pen and a No. 2

pencil are a few) and a quilting frame or hoop. For piecing and/or quilting by machine, add a sewing machine to the list.

Other sewing basics such as a seam ripper, pincushion, measuring tape and an iron are also necessary. For choosing colors or quilting designs for your quilt, or for designing your own quilt, it is helpful to have graph paper, tracing paper, colored pencils or markers and a ruler on hand.

For making strip-pieced quilts, a rotary cutter, mat and specialty rulers are often used. We recommend an ergonomic rotary cutter, a large self-healing mat and several rulers. If you can choose only one size, a 6" x 24" marked in 1/8" or 1/4" increments is recommended.

Construction Methods

Templates

Traditional Templates. While most quilt instructions in this book use rotary-cut strips and quick-sewing methods, a few patterns require templates. Templates are like the pattern pieces used to sew a garment. They are used to cut the fabric pieces which make up the quilt top. There are two types—templates that include a 1/4" seam allowance and those that don't.

Choose the template material and the pattern. Transfer the pattern shapes to the template material with a sharp No. 2 lead pencil. Write the pattern name, piece letter or number, grain line and number to cut for one block or whole quilt on each piece as shown in Figure 3.

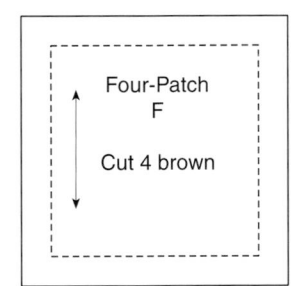

Figure 3
Mark each template with the pattern name and piece identification.

Some patterns require a reversed piece (Figure 4). These patterns are labeled with an R after the piece letter; for example, A and AR. To reverse a template, first cut it with the labeled side up and then with the labeled side down. Compare these to the right and left fronts of a blouse. When making a garment, you accomplish reversed pieces

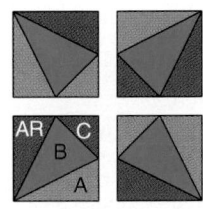

Figure 4
This pattern uses reversed pieces.

when cutting the pattern on two layers of fabric placed with right sides together. This can be done when cutting templates as well.

If cutting one layer of fabric at a time, first trace the template onto the backside of the fabric with the marked side down; turn the template over with the marked side up to make reverse pieces.

Appliqué patterns given in this book do not include a seam allowance. Most designs are given in one drawing rather than individual pieces. This saves space while giving you the complete design to trace on the background block to help with placement of the pieces later. Make templates for each shape using the drawing for exact size. Remember to label each piece as for piecing templates.

For hand appliqué, add a seam allowance when cutting pieces from fabric. You may trace the template with label side up on the right side of the fabric if you are careful to mark lightly. The traced line is then the guide for turning the edges under when stitching.

If you prefer to mark on the wrong side of the fabric, turn the template over if you want the pattern to face the same way it does on the page.

For machine appliqué, a seam allowance is not necessary. Trace template onto the right side of the fabric with label facing up. Cut around shape on the traced line.

Piecing

Hand-Piecing Basics. When hand-piecing it is easier to begin with templates which do not include the 1/4" seam allowance. Place the template on the wrong side of the fabric, lining up the marked grain line with lengthwise or crosswise fabric grain. If the piece does not have to be reversed, place with labeled side up. Trace around shape; move, leaving 1/2" between the shapes, and mark again.

When you have marked the appropriate number of pieces, cut out pieces, leaving 1/4" beyond marked line all around each piece.

To piece, refer to assembly drawings to piece units and blocks, if provided. To join two units, place the patches with right sides together. Stick a pin in at the beginning of the seam through both fabric patches, matching the beginning points

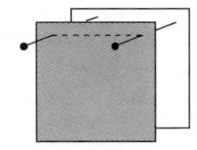

Figure 5
Stick a pin through fabrics to match the beginning of the seam.

(Figure 5); for hand-piecing, the seam begins on the traced line, not at the edge of the fabric (see Figure 6).

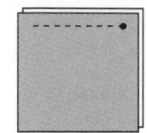

Figure 6
Begin hand-piecing at seam, not at the edge of the fabric. Continue stitching along seam line.

Thread a sharp needle; knot one strand of the thread at the end. Remove the pin and insert the needle in the hole; make a short stitch and then a backstitch right over the first stitch.

Continue making short stitches with several stitches on the needle at one time. As you stitch, check the back piece often to assure accurate stitching on the seam line. Take a stitch at the end of the seam; backstitch and knot at the same time as shown in Figure 7.

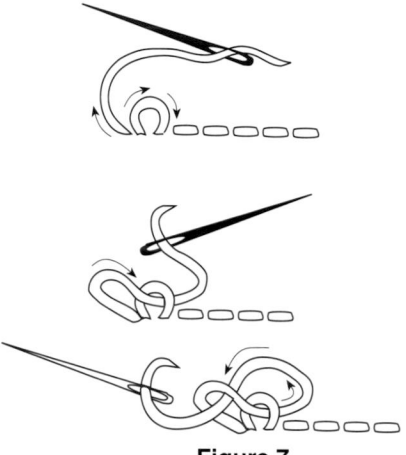

Figure 7
Make a loop in a backstitch to make a knot.

Seams on hand-pieced fabric patches may be finger-pressed toward the darker fabric.

To sew units together, pin fabric patches together, matching seams. Sew as above except where seams meet; at these intersections, backstitch, go through seam to next piece and backstitch again to secure seam joint.

Not all pieced blocks can be stitched with straight seams or in rows. Some patterns require set-in pieces.

To begin a set-in seam on a star pattern, pin one side of the square to the proper side of the star point with right sides together, matching corners. Start stitching at the seam line on the outside point; stitch on the marked seam line to the end of the seam line at the center referring to Figure 8.

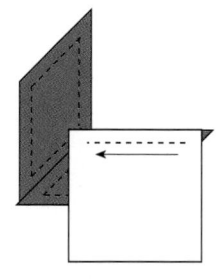

Figure 8
To set a square into a diamond point, match seams and stitch from outside edge to center.

Bring around the adjacent side and pin to the next star point, matching seams. Continue the stitching line from the adjacent seam through corners and to the outside edge of the square as shown in Figure 9.

Machine-Piecing.
If making templates, include the 1/4" seam allowance on the template for machine-piecing. Place template on the wrong side of the fabric as for hand-piecing except butt pieces against one another when tracing.

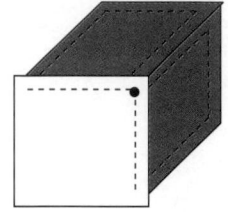

Figure 9
Continue stitching the adjacent side of the square to the next diamond shape in 1 seam from center to outside as shown.

Set machine on 2.5 or 12–15 stitches per inch. Join pieces as for hand-piecing for set-in seams; but for other straight seams, begin and end sewing at the end of the fabric patch sewn as shown in Figure 10. No backstitching is necessary when machine-stitching.

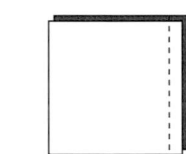

Figure 10
Begin machine-piecing at the end of the piece, not at the end of the seam.

Join units as for hand-piecing referring to the piecing diagrams where needed. Chain piecing (Figure 11—sewing several like units before sewing other units) saves time by eliminating beginning and ending stitches.

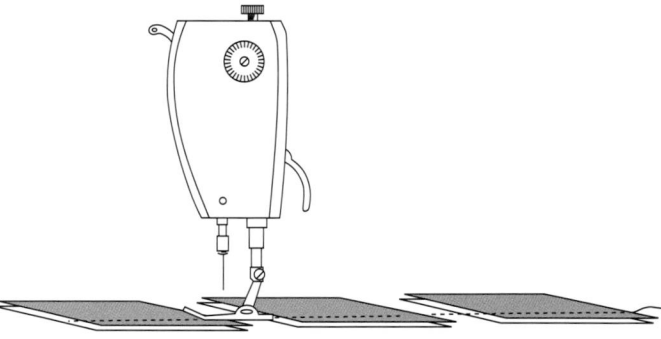

Figure 11
Units may be chain-pieced to save time.

When joining machine-pieced units, match seams against each other with seam allowances pressed in opposite directions to reduce bulk and make perfect matching of seams possible (Figure 12).

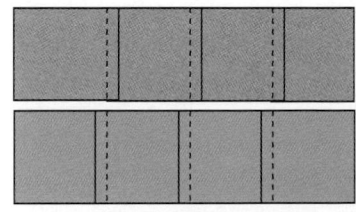

Figure 12
Sew machine-pieced units with seams pressed in opposite directions.

Cutting

Quick-Cutting. Quick-cutting and piecing strips are recommended for making many of the projects in this book. Templates are completely eliminated; instead, a rotary cutter, plastic ruler and mat are used to cut fabric pieces.

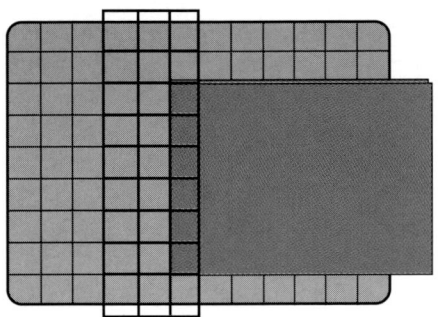

Figure 13
Fold fabric and straighten as shown.

When rotary-cutting strips, straighten raw edges of fabric by folding fabric in fourths across the width as shown in Figure 13. Press down flat; place ruler on fabric square with edge of fabric and make one cut from the folded edge to the outside edge. If strips are not straightened, a wavy strip will result as shown in Figure 14.

Figure 14
Wavy strips result if fabric is not straightened before cutting.

Always cut away from your body, holding the ruler firmly with the non-cutting hand. Keep fingers away from the edge of the ruler as it is easy for the rotary cutter to slip and jump over the edge of the ruler if cutting is not properly done.

For many strip-pieced blocks two strips are stitched together as shown in Figure 15. The strips are stitched, pressed and cut into segments as shown in Figure 16.

Figure 15
Join 2 strips as shown.

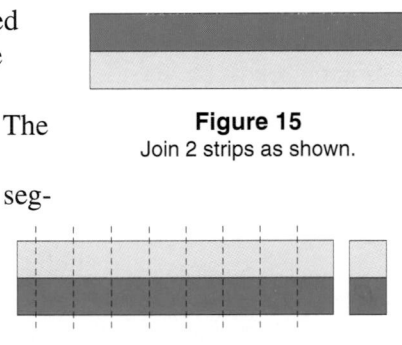

Figure 16
Cut segments from the stitched strip set.

The cut segments are arranged as shown in Figure 17 and stitched to complete, in this example, one Four-Patch block.

Although the block shown is very simple, the same methods may be used for more complicated patterns.

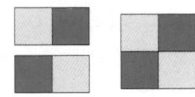

Figure 17
Arrange cut segments to make a Four-Patch block.

The direction to press seams on strip sets is important for accurate piecing later. The normal rule for pressing is to press seams toward the darker fabric to keep the colors from showing through on lighter colors later. For joining segments from strip sets, this rule doesn't always apply.

It is best if seams on adjacent rows are pressed in opposite directions. When aligning segments to stitch rows together, if pressed properly, seam joints will have a seam going in both directions as shown in Figure 18.

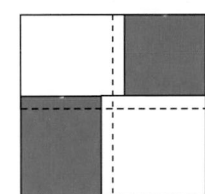

Figure 18
Seams go in both directions at seam joints.

If a square is required for the pattern, it can be subcut from a strip as shown in Figure 19.

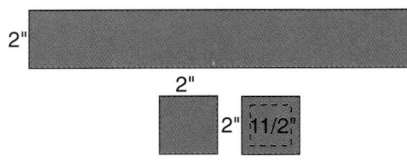

Figure 19
If cutting squares, cut proper-width strip into same-width segments. Here, a 2" strip is cut into 2" segments to create 2" squares. These squares finish at 1 1/2" when sewn.

If you need right triangles with the straight grain on the short sides, you can use the same method, but you need to figure out how wide to cut the strip. Measure the finished size of one short side of the triangle. Add 7/8" to this size for seam allowance. Cut fabric strips this width; cut the strips into the same increment to create squares. Cut the squares on the diagonal to produce triangles. For example, if you need a triangle with a 2" finished height, cut the strips 2 7/8" by the width of the fabric. Cut the strips into 2 7/8" squares. Cut each square on the diagonal to produce the correct-size triangle with the grain on the short sides (Figure 20).

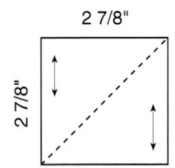

Figure 20
Cut 2" (finished size) triangles from 2 7/8" squares as shown.

Triangles sewn together to make squares are called half-square triangles or triangle/squares. When joined, the triangle/square unit has the straight of grain on all outside edges of the block.

Another method of making triangle/squares is shown in Figure 21. Layer two squares with right sides together; draw a diagonal line through the center.

Stitch 1/4" on both sides of the line. Cut apart on the drawn line to reveal two stitched triangle/squares.

Figure 21
Mark a diagonal line on the square; stitch 1/4" on each side of the line. Cut on line to reveal stitched triangle/squares.

If you need triangles with the straight of grain on the diagonal, such as for fill-in triangles on the outside edges of a diagonal-set quilt, the procedure is a bit different.

To make these triangles, a square is cut on both diagonals; thus, the straight of grain is on the longest or diagonal side (Figure 22). To figure out the size to cut the square, add 1 1/4" to the needed finished size of the longest side of the triangle. For example, if you need a triangle with a 12" finished diagonal, cut a 13 1/4" square.

If templates are given, use their measurements to cut fabric strips to correspond with that measurement. The template may be used on the strip to cut pieces quickly. Strip cutting works best for squares, triangles, rectangles and diamonds. Odd-shaped templates are difficult to cut in multiple layers using a rotary cutter.

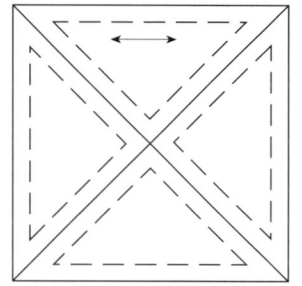

Figure 22
Add 1 1/4" to the finished size of the longest side of the triangle needed and cut on both diagonals to make a quarter-square triangle.

Foundation Piecing

Foundation Piecing. Paper or fabric foundation pieces are used to make very accurate blocks, provide stability for weak fabrics, and add body and weight to the finished quilt.

Temporary foundation materials include paper, tracing paper, freezer paper and removable interfacing. Permanent foundations include utility fabrics, non-woven interfacing, flannel, fleece and batting.

Methods of marking foundations include basting lines, pencils or pens, needlepunching, tracing wheel, hot-iron transfers, copy machine, premarked, stamps or stencils.

Tips & Techniques

If you cannot see the lines on the backside of the paper when paper-piecing, draw over lines with a small felt-tip marker. The lines should now be visible on the backside to help with placement of fabric pieces.

There are two methods of foundation piecing—under-piecing and top-piecing. When under-piecing, the pattern is reversed when tracing. We have not included any patterns for top-piecing. *Note: All patterns for which we recommend paper piecing are already reversed in full-size drawings given.*

To under-piece, place a scrap of fabric larger than the lined space on the unlined side of the paper in the No. 1 position. Place piece 2 right sides together with piece 1; pin on seam line, and fold back to check that the piece will cover space 2 before stitching.

Stitch along line on the lined side of the paper—fabric will not be visible. Sew several stitches beyond the beginning and ending of the line. Backstitching is not required as another fabric seam will cover this seam.

Remove pin; finger-press piece 2 flat. Continue adding all pieces in numerical order in the same manner until all pieces are stitched to paper. Trim excess to outside line (1/4" larger all around than finished size of the block).

Tracing paper can be used as a temporary foundation. It is removed when blocks are complete and stitched together. To paper-piece, copy patterns using a copy machine or trace each block individually. Measure the finished paper foundations to insure accuracy in copying.

Appliqué

Appliqué is the process of applying one piece of fabric on top of another for decorative or functional purposes.

Making Templates. Most appliqué designs given here are shown as full-size drawings for the completed designs. The drawings show dotted lines to indicate where one piece overlaps another. Other marks indicate placement of embroidery stitches for decorative purposes such as eyes, lips, flowers, etc.

For hand appliqué, trace each template onto the right side of the fabric with template right side up. Cut around shape, adding a 1/8"–1/4" seam allowance.

Before the actual appliqué process begins, cut the background block and prepare it for stitching. Most appliqué designs are centered on the

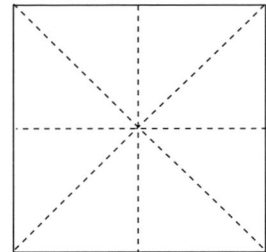

Figure 23
Fold background to mark centers as shown.

block. To find the center of the background square, fold it in half and in half again; crease with your fingers. Now unfold and fold diagonally and crease; repeat for other corners referring to Figure 23. Center-line creases help position the design. If centering the appliqué design is important, an X has been placed on each drawing to mark the center of the design. Match the X with the creased center of the background block when placing pieces.

If you have a full-size drawing of the design, as is given with most appliqué designs in this book, it might help you to draw on the background block to help with placement. Transfer the design to a large piece of tracing paper. Place the paper on top of the design; use masking tape to hold in place. Trace design onto paper.

If you don't have a light box, tape the pattern on a window; center the background block on top and tape in place. Trace the design onto the background block with a water-erasable marker or chalk pencil. This drawing will mark exactly where the fabric pieces should be placed on the background block.

Hand Appliqué. Traditional hand appliqué uses a template made from the desired finished shape without seam allowance added.

After fabric is prepared, trace the desired shape onto the right side of the fabric with a water-erasable marker, light lead or chalk pencil. Leave at least 1/2" between design motifs when tracing to allow for the seam allowance when cutting out the shapes.

When the desired number of shapes needed has been drawn on the fabric pieces, cut out shapes leaving 1/8"–1/4" all around drawn line for turning under.

Turn the shape's edges over on the drawn or stitched line. When turning the edges under, make sharp corners sharp and smooth edges smooth. The fabric patch should retain the shape of the template used to cut it.

When turning in concave curves, clip to seams and baste the seam allowance over as shown in Figure 24.

During the actual appliqué process, you may be layering one shape on top of another.

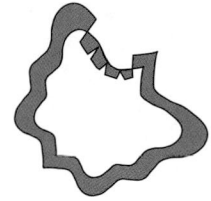

Figure 24
Concave curves should be clipped before turning as shown.

Where two fabrics overlap, the underneath piece does not have to be turned under or stitched down.

If possible, trim away the underneath fabric when the block is finished by carefully cutting away the background from underneath and then cutting away unnecessary layers to reduce bulk and avoid shadows from darker fabrics showing through on light fabrics.

For hand appliqué, position the fabric shapes on the background block and pin or baste them in place. Using a blind stitch or appliqué stitch, sew pieces in place with matching thread and small stitches. Start with background pieces first and work up to foreground pieces. Appliqué the pieces in place on the background in numerical order, if given, layering as necessary.

Machine Appliqué. There are several products available to help make the machine-appliqué process easier and faster.

Fusible transfer web is a commercial product similar to iron-on interfacings except it has two sticky sides. It is used to adhere appliqué shapes to the background with heat. Paper is adhered to one side of the web.

To use, dry-iron the sticky side of the fusible product onto the wrong side of the chosen fabric. Draw desired shapes onto the paper and cut them out. Peel off the paper and dry-iron the shapes in place on the background fabric. The shape will stay in place while you stitch around it. This process adds a little bulk or stiffness to the appliquéd shape and makes hand quilting through the layers difficult.

For successful machine appliqué a tear-off stabilizer is recommended. This product is placed under the background fabric while machine appliqué is being done. It is torn away when the work is finished. This kind of stabilizer keeps the background fabric from pulling during the machine-appliqué process.

During the actual machine-appliqué process, you will be layering one shape on top of another. Where two fabrics overlap, the underneath piece does not have to be turned under or stitched down.

Thread the top of the machine with thread to match the fabric patches or with threads that coordinate or contrast with fabrics. Rayon thread is a good choice when a sheen is desired on the finished appliqué stitches. Do not use rayon thread in the bobbin; use all-purpose thread.

Set your machine to make a zigzag stitch and practice on scraps of similar weight to check the tension. If you can see the bobbin thread on the top of the appliqué, adjust your machine to make a balanced stitch. Different-width stitches are available; choose one that will not overpower the appliqué shapes. In some cases these appliqué stitches will be used as decorative stitches as well and you may want the thread to show.

If using a stabilizer, place this under the background fabric and pin or fuse in place. Place shapes as for hand-appliqué and stitch all around shapes machine.

Tips & Techniques

Before machine-piecing fabric patches together, test your sewing machine for positioning an accurate 1/4" seam allowance. There are several tools to help guarantee this. Some machine needles may be moved to allow the presser-foot edge to be a 1/4" guide.

A special foot may be purchased for your machine that will guarantee an accurate 1/4" seam. A piece of masking tape can be placed on the throat plate of your sewing machine to mark the 1/4" seam. A plastic stick-on ruler may be used instead of tape with the same results.

When all machine work is complete, remove stabilizer from the back referring to the manufacturer's instructions.

Putting It All Together

Many steps are required to prepare a quilt top for quilting, including setting the blocks together, adding borders, choosing and marking quilting designs, layering the top, batting and backing for quilting, quilting or tying the layers and finishing the edges of the quilt.

As you begin the process of finishing your quilt top, strive for a neat, flat quilt with square sides and corners, not for perfection—that will come with time and practice.

Finishing the Top

Settings. Most quilts are made by sewing individual blocks together in rows which, when joined, create a design. There are several other methods used to join blocks. Sometimes the setting choice is determined by the block's design. For example, a house block should be placed upright on a quilt, not sideways or upside down.

Plain blocks can be alternated with pieced or appliquéd blocks in a straight set. Making a quilt using plain blocks saves time; half the number of pieced or appliquéd blocks are needed to make the same-size quilt as shown in Figure 1.

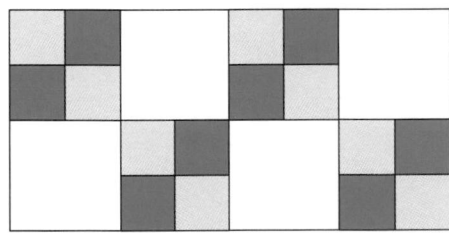

Figure 1
Alternate plain blocks with pieced blocks to save time.

Adding Borders. Borders are an integral part of the quilt and should complement the colors and designs used in the quilt center. Borders frame a quilt just like a mat and frame do a picture.

If fabric strips are added for borders, they may be mitered or butted at the corners as shown in Figures 2 and 3.

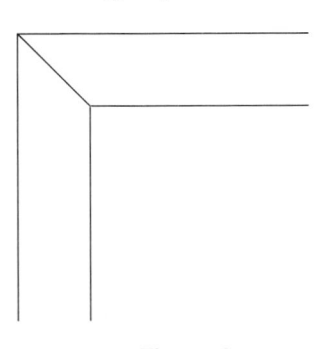

Figure 2
Mitered corners look like this.

To determine the size for butted-border strips, measure across the center of the completed quilt top from one side raw edge to the other side raw edge. This measurement will include a 1/4" seam allowance. Cut two border strips that length by the chosen width of the border. Sew these strips to the top and bottom of the pieced center referring to Figure 4. Press the seam allowance toward the border strips.

Measure across the completed quilt top at the center, from top raw edge to bottom raw edge, including the two border strips already added. Cut two border strips that length by the chosen width of the border. Sew a strip to each of the two remaining sides as shown in Figure 4. Press the seams toward the border strips.

To make mitered corners, measure the quilt as before. To this add twice the width of the border and 1/2" for seam allowances to determine the length of the strips. Repeat for opposite sides. Center and sew on each strip, stopping

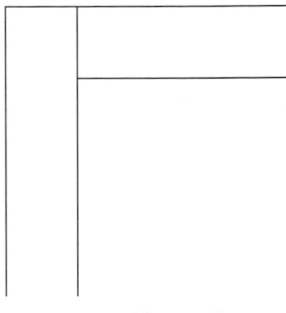

Figure 3
Butted corners look like this.

Figure 4
Sew border strips to opposite sides; sew remaining 2 strips to remaining sides to make butted corners.

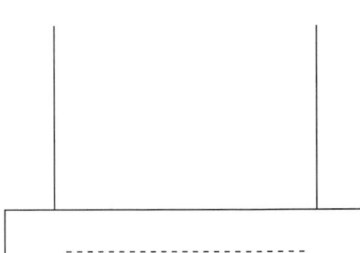

Figure 5
For mitered corner, stitch strip, stopping 1/4" from corner seam.

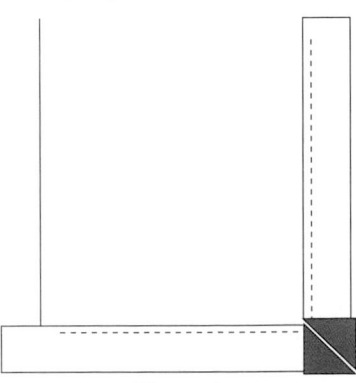

Figure 6
Fold and press corner to make a 45-degree angle.

stitching 1/4" from corner, leaving the remainder of the strip dangling.

Press corners at a 45-degree angle to form a crease. Stitch from the inside quilt corner to the outside on the creased line. Trim excess away after stitching and press mitered seams open (Figures 5–7).

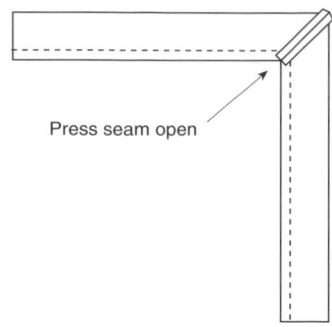
Press seam open

Figure 7
Trim away excess from underneath when stitching is complete. Press seams open.

Carefully press the entire quilt top. Avoid pulling and stretching while pressing, which would distort shapes.

Getting Ready to Quilt

Choosing a Quilting Design. If you choose to hand- or machine-quilt your finished top, you will need to choose a design for quilting.

There are several types of quilting designs, some of which may not have to be marked. The easiest of the unmarked designs is in-the-ditch quilting. Here the quilting stitches are placed in the valley created by the seams joining two pieces together or next to the edge of an appliqué design. There is no

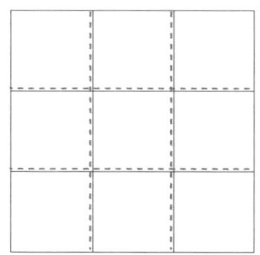

Figure 8
In-the-ditch quilting is done in the seam that joins 2 pieces.

need to mark a top for in-the-ditch quilting. Machine quilters choose this option because the stitches are not as obvious on the finished quilt (Figure 8).

Outline-quilting 1/4" or more away from seams or appliqué shapes is another no-mark alternative (Figure 9) which prevents having to sew through the layers made by seams, thus making stitching easier.

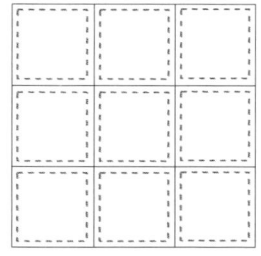

Figure 9
Outline-quilting 1/4" away from seam is a popular choice for quilting.

If you are not comfortable eyeballing the 1/4" (or other distance), masking tape is available in different widths and is helpful to place on straight-edge designs to mark the quilting line. If using masking tape, place the tape right up against the seam and quilt close to the other edge.

Meander or free-motion quilting by machine fills in open spaces and doesn't require marking. It is fun and easy to stitch as shown in Figure 10.

Marking the Top for Quilting or Tying. If you choose a fancy or all-over design for quilting, you will need to transfer the design to

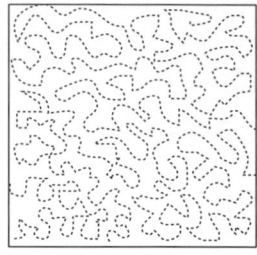

Figure 10
Machine meander quilting fills in large spaces.

your quilt top before layering with the backing and batting. You may use a sharp medium-lead or silver pencil on light background fabrics. Test the pencil marks to guarantee that they will wash out of your quilt top when quilting is complete; or be sure your quilting stitches cover the pencil marks. Mechanical pencils with very fine points may be used successfully to mark quilts.

Manufactured quilt-design templates are available in many designs and sizes and are cut out of a durable plastic template material which is easy to use.

To make a permanent quilt-design template, choose a template material on which to transfer the design. See-through plastic is the best as it will let you place the design while allowing you to see where it is in relation to your quilt design without moving it. Place the design on the quilt top where you want it and trace around it with your marking tool. Pick up the quilting template and place again; repeat marking.

No matter what marking method you use, remember—the marked lines should never show on the finished quilt. When the top is marked, it is ready for layering.

Preparing the Quilt Backing. The quilt backing is a very important feature of your quilt. In most cases, the materials list for each quilt in this book gives the size requirements for the backing, not the yardage needed. Exceptions to this are when the backing fabric is also used on the quilt top and yardage is given for that fabric.

A backing is generally cut at least 4" larger than the quilt top or 2" larger on all sides. For a 64" x 78" finished quilt, the backing would need to be at least 68" x 82".

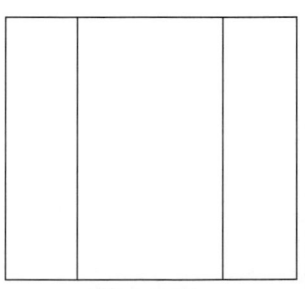

Figure 11
Center 1 backing piece with a piece on each side.

To avoid having the seam across the center of the quilt backing, cut or tear one of the right-length pieces in half and sew half to each side of the second piece as shown in Figure 11.

Quilts that need backing more than 88" wide may be pieced in horizontal pieces as shown in Figure 12.

Layering the Quilt Sandwich. Layering the quilt top with the batting and backing is time-consuming. Open the batting several days before you need it and place over a bed or flat on the floor to help flatten the creases caused from its being folded up in the bag for so long.

Figure 12
Horizontal seams may be used on backing pieces.

Iron the backing piece, folding in half both vertically and horizontally and pressing to mark centers.

If you will not be quilting on a frame, place the backing right side down on a clean floor or table. Start in the center and push any wrinkles or bunches flat. Use masking tape to tape the edges to the floor or large clips to hold the backing to the edges of the table. The backing should be taut.

Place the batting on top of the backing, matching centers using fold lines as guides; flatten out any wrinkles. Trim the batting to the same size as the backing.

Fold the quilt top in half lengthwise and place on top of the batting, wrong side against the batting, matching centers. Unfold quilt and, working from the center to the outside edges, smooth out any wrinkles or lumps.

To hold the quilt layers together for quilting, baste by hand or use safety pins. If basting by hand, thread a long thin needle with a long piece of unknotted white or off-white thread. Starting in the center and leaving a long tail, make 4"–6" stitches toward the outside edge of the quilt top, smoothing as you

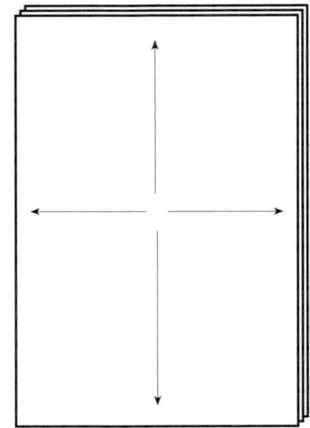

Figure 13
Baste from the center to the outside edges.

baste. Start at the center again and work toward the outside as shown in Figure 13.

If quilting by machine, you may prefer to use safety pins for holding your quilt sandwich together. Start in the center of the quilt and pin to the outside, leaving pins open until all are placed. When you are satisfied that all layers are smooth, close the pins.

Quilting

Hand Quilting. Hand quilting is the process of placing stitches through the quilt top, batting and backing to hold them together. While it is a functional process, it also adds beauty and loft to the finished quilt.

To begin, thread a sharp between needle with an 18" piece of quilting thread. Tie a small knot in the end of the thread. Position the needle about 1/2" to 1" away from the starting

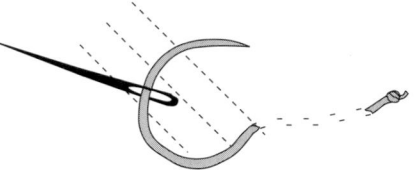

Figure 14
Start the needle through the top layer of fabric 1/2"–1" away from quilting line with knot on top of fabric.

Tips & Techniques

Knots should not show on the quilt top or back. Learn to sink the knot into the batting at the beginning and ending of the quilting thread for successful stitches.

When you have nearly run out of thread, wind the thread around the needle several times to make a small knot and pull it close to the fabric. Insert the needle into the fabric on the quilting line and come out with the needle 1/2" to 1" away, pulling the knot into the fabric layers the same as when you started. Pull and cut thread close to fabric. The end should disappear inside after cutting. Some quilters prefer to take a backstitch with a loop through it for a knot to end.

Making 12–18 stitches per inch is a nice goal, but a more realistic goal is seven to nine stitches per inch. If you cannot accomplish this right away, strive for even stitches—all the same size—that look as good on the back as on the front.

You will perfect your quilting stitches as you gain experience, your stitches will get better with each project and your style will be uniquely your own.

point on quilt top. Sink the needle through the top into the batting layer but not through the backing. Pull the needle up at the starting point of the quilting design. Pull the needle and thread until the knot sinks through the top into the batting (Figure 14).

Some stitchers like to take a backstitch at the beginning while others prefer to begin the first stitch here. Take small, even running stitches along the marked quilting line (Figure 15). Keep one hand positioned underneath to feel the needle go all the way through to the backing.

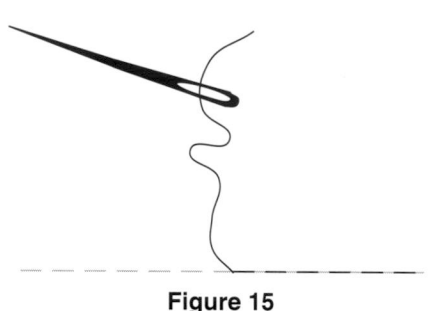

Figure 15
Make small, even running stitches on marked quilting line.

Machine Quilting. Successful machine quilting requires practice and a good relationship with your sewing machine.

Prepare the quilt for machine quilting in the same way as for hand quilting. Use safety pins to hold the layers together instead of basting with thread.

Presser-foot quilting is best used for straight-line quilting because the presser bar lever does not need to be continually lifted.

Set the machine on a longer stitch length (three or eight to 10 stitches to the inch). Too tight a stitch causes puckering and fabric tucks, either on the quilt top or backing. An even-feed or walking foot helps to eliminate the tucks and puckering by feeding the upper and lower layers through the machine evenly. Before you begin, loosen the amount of pressure on the presser foot.

Special machine-quilting needles work best to penetrate the three layers in your quilt.

Decide on a design. Quilting in the ditch is not quite as visible, but if you quilt with the feed dogs engaged, it means turning the quilt frequently. It is not easy to fit a rolled-up quilt through the small opening on the sewing machine head.

Meander quilting is the easiest way to machine-quilt—and it is fun. Meander quilting is done using an appliqué or darning foot with the feed dogs dropped. It is sort of like scribbling. Simply move the quilt top around under the foot and make stitches in a random

pattern to fill the space. The same method may be used to outline a quilt design. The trick is the same as in hand-quilting; you are striving for stitches of uniform size. Your hands are in complete control of the design.

If machine-quilting is of interest to you, there are several very good books available at quilt shops that will help you become a successful machine quilter.

Tied Quilts, or Comforters. Would you rather tie your quilt layers together than quilt them? Tied quilts are often referred to as comforters. The advantage of tying is that it takes so much less time and the required skills can be learned quickly.

If a top will be tied, choose a thick, bonded batting—one that will not separate during washing. For tying, use pearl cotton, embroidery floss, or strong yarn in colors that match or coordinate with the fabrics in your quilt top.

Decide on a pattern for tying. Many quilts are tied at the corners and centers of the blocks and at sashing joints. Try to tie every 4"–6". Special designs can be used for tying, but most quilts are tied in conventional ways. Begin tying in the center and work to the outside edges.

To make the tie, thread a large needle with a long thread (yarn, floss or crochet cotton); do not knot. Push the needle through the quilt top to the back, leaving a 3"–4" length on top. Move the needle to the next position without cutting thread. Take another stitch through the layers; repeat until thread is almost used up.

Cut thread between stitches, leaving an equal amount of thread on each stitch. Tie a knot with the two thread ends. Tie again to make a square knot referring to Figure 16. Trim thread ends to desired length.

Figure 16
Make a square knot as shown.

Finishing the Edges

After your quilt is tied or quilted, the edges need to be finished. Decide how you want the edges of your quilt finished before layering the backing and batting with the quilt top.

Without Binding—Self-Finish. There is one way to eliminate adding an edge finish. This is done before quilting. Place the batting on a flat surface. Place the pieced top right side up on the batting. Place the backing right sides together with the pieced top. Pin and/or baste the layers together to hold flat referring to page 171.

Begin stitching in the center of one side using a 1/4" seam allowance, reversing at the beginning and end of the seam. Continue stitching all around and back to the beginning side. Leave a 12" or larger opening. Clip corners to reduce excess. Turn right side out through the opening. Slipstitch the opening closed by hand. The quilt may now be quilted by hand or machine.

The disadvantage to this method is that once the edges are sewn in, any creases or wrinkles that might form during the quilting process cannot be flattened out. Tying is the preferred method for finishing a quilt constructed using this method.

Bringing the backing fabric to the front is another way to finish the quilt's edge without binding. To accomplish this, complete the quilt as for hand or machine quilting. Trim the batting *only* even with the front. Trim the backing 1" larger than the completed top all around.

Turn the backing edge in 1/2" and then turn over to the front along edge of batting. The folded edge may be machine-stitched close to the edge through all layers, or blind-stitched in place to finish.

The front may be turned to the back. If using this method, a wider front border is needed. The backing and batting are trimmed 1" smaller than the top and the top edge is turned under 1/2" and then turned to the back and stitched in place.

One more method of self-finish may be used. The top and backing may be stitched together by hand at the edge. To accomplish this, all quilting must be stopped 1/2" from the quilt-top edge. The top and backing of the quilt are trimmed even and the batting is trimmed to 1/4"–1/2" smaller. The edges of the top and backing are turned in 1/4"–1/2" and blind-stitched together at the very edge.

These methods do not require the use of extra fabric and save time in preparation of binding strips; they are not as durable as an added binding.

Binding. The technique of adding extra fabric at the edges of the quilt is called binding. The binding encloses the edges and adds an extra layer of fabric for durability.

To prepare the quilt for the addition of the binding, trim the batting and backing layers flush with the top of the quilt using a rotary cutter and ruler or shears. Using a walking-foot attachment (sometimes called an even-feed foot attachment), machine-baste the three layers together all around approximately 1/8" from the cut edge.

The list of materials given with each quilt in this book often includes a number of yards of self-made or purchased binding. Bias binding may be purchased in packages and in many colors. The advantage to self-made binding is that you can use fabrics from your quilt to coordinate colors.

Double-fold, straight-grain binding and double-fold, bias-grain binding are two of the most commonly used types of binding.

Double-fold, straight-grain binding is used on smaller projects with right-angle corners. Double-fold, bias-grain binding is best suited for bed-size quilts or quilts with rounded corners.

To make double-fold, straight-grain binding, cut 2"-wide strips of fabric across the width or down the length of the fabric totaling the perimeter of the quilt plus 10". The strips are joined as shown in Figure 17 and pressed in half wrong sides together along the length using an iron on a cotton setting with no steam.

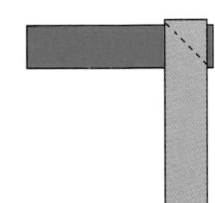

Figure 17
Join binding strips in a diagonal seam to eliminate bulk as shown.

Lining up the raw edges, place the binding on the top of the quilt and begin sewing (again using the walking foot) approximately 6" from the beginning of the binding strip. Stop sewing 1/4" from the first corner, leave the needle in the quilt, turn and sew diagonally to the corner as shown in Figure 18.

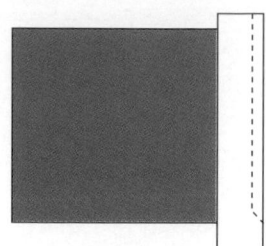

Figure 18
Sew to within 1/4" of corner; leave needle in quilt, turn and stitch diagonally off the corner of the quilt.

Fold the binding at a 45-degree angle up and away from the quilt as shown in Figure 19 and back down flush with the raw edges. Starting at the top raw edge of the quilt, begin sewing the next side as shown in Figure 20. Repeat at the next three corners.

As you approach the beginning of the binding strip, stop stitching and overlap the binding 1/2" from the edge; trim. Join the two ends with a 1/4" seam allowance and press the seam open. Reposition the joined binding along the edge of the quilt and resume stitching to the beginning.

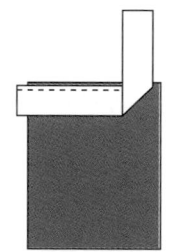

Figure 19
Fold binding at a 45-degree angle up and away from quilt as shown.

To finish, bring the folded edge of the binding over the raw edges and blind-stitch the binding in place over the machine-stitching line on the backside. Hand-miter the corners on the back as shown in Figure 21.

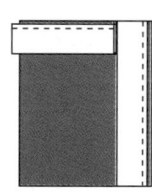

Figure 20
Fold the binding strips back down, flush with the raw edge, and begin sewing.

If you are making a quilt to be used on a bed, you will want to use double-fold, bias-grain bindings because the many threads that cross each other along the fold at the edge of the quilt make it a more durable binding.

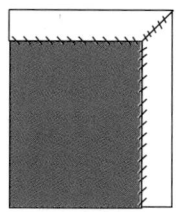

Figure 21
Miter and stitch the corners as shown.

Cut 2"-wide bias strips from a large square of fabric. Join the strips as illustrated in Figure 17 and press the seams open. Fold the beginning end of the bias strip 1/4" from the raw edge and press. Fold the joined

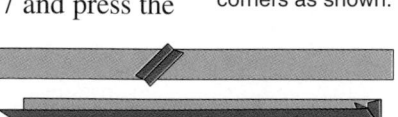

Figure 22
Fold end in and press strip in half.

strips in half along the long side, wrong sides together, and press with no steam (Figure 22).

Follow the same procedures as previously described for preparing the quilt top and sewing the binding to the quilt top. Treat the corners just as you treated them with straight-grain binding.

Since you are using bias-grain binding, you do have the option to just eliminate the corners if this option doesn't interfere with the patchwork in the quilt. Round the corners off by placing one of your dinner plates at the corner and rotary-cutting the gentle curve (Figure 23).

Figure 23
Round corners to eliminate square-corner finishes.

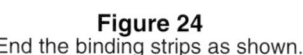

Figure 24
End the binding strips as shown.

As you approach the beginning of the binding strip, stop stitching and lay the end across the beginning so it will slip inside the fold. Cut the end at a 45-degree angle so the raw edges are contained inside the beginning of the strip (Figure 24). Resume stitching to the beginning. Bring the fold to the back of the quilt and hand-stitch as previously described.

Overlapped corners are not quite as easy as rounded ones, but a bit easier than mitering. To make overlapped corners, sew binding strips to opposite sides of the quilt top. Stitch edges down to finish. Trim ends even.

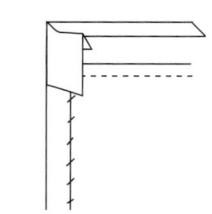

Figure 25
Fold end of binding even with previous edge.

Sew a strip to each remaining side, leaving 1 1/2"–2" excess at each end. Turn quilt over and fold end in even with previous finished edge as shown in Figure 25.

Fold binding in toward quilt and stitch down as before, enclosing the previous bound

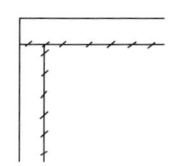

Figure 26
An overlapped corner is not quite as neat as a mitered corner.

edge in the seam as shown in Figure 26. It may be necessary to trim the folded-down section to reduce bulk.

Making Continuous Bias Binding

Instead of cutting individual bias strips and sewing them together, you may make continuous bias binding.

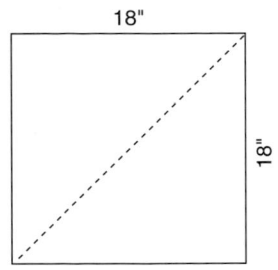

Figure 27
Cut 18" square on the diagonal.

Cut a square 18" x 18" from chosen binding fabric. Cut the square once on the diagonal to make two triangles as shown in Figure 27. With right sides together, sew the two triangles together with a 1/4" seam allowance as shown in Figure 28; press seam open to reduce bulk.

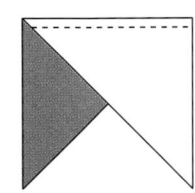

Figure 28
Sew the triangles together.

Mark lines every 2 1/4" on the wrong side of the fabric as shown in Figure 29. Bring the short ends together, right sides together, offsetting one line as shown in Figure 30 to make a tube; stitch. This will seem awkward.

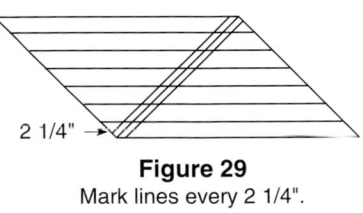

Figure 29
Mark lines every 2 1/4".

Begin cutting at point A as shown in Figure 31; continue cutting along marked line to make one continuous strip. Fold strip in half along length with wrong sides together; press. Sew to quilt edges as instructed previously for bias binding.

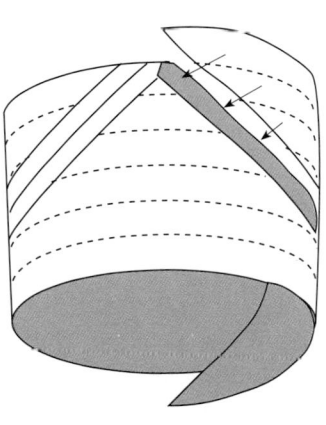

Figure 30
Sew short ends together, offsetting lines to make a tube.

Final Touches

If your quilt will be hung on the wall, a hanging sleeve is required. Other options include purchased plastic rings or fabric tabs. The best choice is a fabric sleeve, which will evenly distribute the weight of the quilt

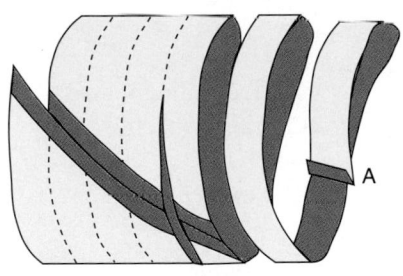

Figure 31
Cut along marked lines, starting at A.

across the top edge, rather than at selected spots where tabs or rings are stitched, keep the quilt hanging straight and not damage the batting.

To make a sleeve, measure across the top of the finished quilt. Cut an 8"-wide piece of muslin equal to that length—you may need to seam several muslin strips together to make the required length.

Fold in 1/4" on each end of the muslin strip and press. Fold again and stitch to hold. Fold the muslin strip lengthwise with right sides together. Sew along the long side to make a tube. Turn the tube right side out; press with seam at bottom or centered on the back.

Hand-stitch the tube along the top of the quilt and the bottom of the tube to the quilt back making sure the quilt lies flat. Stitches should not go through to the front of the quilt and don't need to be too close together as shown in Figure 32.

Slip a wooden dowel or long curtain rod through the sleeve to hang.

When the quilt is finally complete, it should be signed and dated. Use a

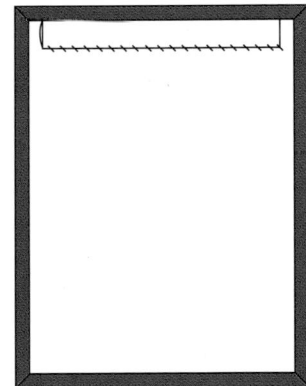

Figure 32
Sew a sleeve to the top back of the quilt

permanent pen on the back of the quilt. Other methods include cross-stitching your name and date on the front or back or making a permanent label which may be stitched to the back.

Special Thanks

We would like to thank the talented quilt designers whose work is featured in this collection.

Vicki Blizzard
Country Garden Quilt, 151

Ann Boyce
Home Sweet Home Cardigan, 20
Reversible Rug, 24
Lazy Log Cabin Bed Quilt, 138

Kathy Brown
Halloween Treat Bag, 104
Jack-o'-Lantern Bib, 106
Ho-Ho Santa Pillow, 109
Bear's Paw Sweatshirt, 34

Christine Carlson
Ohio Bear Paw, 147

Barbara A. Clayton
Grapes Pot Holder, 10
Golden Pearls Album, 30

Holly Daniels
Stationery Holder, 39
Harvest Candle Mat, 100
Garden of Flowers, 135

Phyllis Dobbs
Log Cabin Mantel Cover, 16
Heart in Diamond Chair Back, 80
Forever Stripes Place Mat, 86

Lucy A. Fazely
Flowers for Mother Teresa, 120
Petite Pineapple, 141
Bear Paw Jewels, 144

Sue Kruger
Pete Goes Skating, 60

Joyce Livingston
Autumn Leaves, 92

Janice Loewenthal
Happy Birthday Place Mat, 54
Little Sheriff Vest, 57
Pillowcase Sleep-Over Bag, 68
Happy Easter Coaster Set, 83

Jill Reber
Froggy, Froggy Baby Quilt, 44
Wild Goose Chase, 8

Maple Leaf Table Runner, 89
Sugar Bowl Baskets, 126

Judith Sandstrom
Love of Patchwork, 77
Eight Tiny Reindeer, 112
Holly & Angel Tree Skirt, 115
Love of Patchwork Friendship Quilt, 123
Tantalizing Tulips Bed Quilt, 155

Christine A. Schultz
Autumn Apples Wall Quilt, 97

Carla Schwab
Funny Furry Felines, 13

Charlyne Stewart
Snowflake Duo Ornaments, 74

Norma Storm
Cathedral Window Pincushion, 36
Butterfly Bedroom, 49
Sailboat Bedroom, 63

Ruth M. Swasey
Field of Sunflowers, 129
A Walk in Spring, 132
Square Within a Square, 159

Eileen Westfall
Autumn Hostess Apron, 27

Fabrics & Supplies

Page 13: Funny Furry Felines—Heat 'n Bond fusible transfer web

Page 16: Log Cabin Mantel Cover—Soft & Bright polyester batting from The Warm Company and fabrics from VIP, Division of Cranston Print Works

Page 24: Reversible Rug—Mission Valley fabrics

Page 44: Froggy, Froggy Baby Quilt—Master Piece 45 ruler and Static Stickers

Page 77: Love of Patchwork—Springs Kashmere fabric collection, Hobbs Heirloom Organic cotton batting, Fiskars 45mm rotary cutter, mat and ruler and Sullivans Quilt Basting Spray

Page 80: Heart in Diamond Chair Back—Warm & Natural cotton batting and Steam-A-Seam 2 fusible transfer web from The Warm Company

Page 86: Forever Stripes Place Mat—Soft & Bright polyester batting from The Warm Company

Page 89: Maple Leaf Table Runner—Master Piece 45 ruler and Hobbs Heirloom cotton batting

Page 100: Harvest Candle Mat—Warm and Natural lightweight batting from The Warm Company and Heat 'n Bond Lite fusible transfer web from Therm O Web

Page 112: Eight Tiny Reindeer—Hobbs Heirloom Organic cotton batting, Sullivans Quilt Basting Spray and Fiskars 45mm rotary cutter, mat and ruler

Page 115: Holly & Angel Tree Skirt—Hobbs Heirloom Organic cotton batting, Sullivans Quilt Basting Spray, Pellon WonderUnder fusible transfer web and Pigma pen

Page 120: Flowers for Mother Teresa—Benartex fabrics, Mountain Mist Quilt-Light batting from The Stearns Technical Textiles Co. and Sew/Fit templates

Page 123: Love of Patchwork Friendship Quilt—Springs Industries Bell Fleur and Language of Flowers fabrics, Hobbs Heirloom Organic cotton batting, Pigma pens, Fiskars 45mm rotary cutter, mat and ruler and Sullivans quilt basting spray

Page 126: Sugar Bowl Baskets—Master Piece 45 rulers and Static Stickers

Page 138: Lazy Day Cabin Bed Quilt—Fairfield Processing Polyfil batting

Page 141: Petite Pineapple—Sulky Tear Easy Stabilizer, Sew Easy Snap-Shot Ruler and Mountain Mist batting

Page 144: Bear Paw Jewels—RJR Fashion fabrics, Mountain Mist Quilt-Light batting from The Stearns Techinical Textiles Co. and Sew/Fit rotary-cutting mat and 6 1/2" x 24" Snap-Shot ruler

Page 151: Country Garden Quilt—Springs Industries fabrics, ReadyBias premade bias binding, Hobbs Bonded Fibers quilt batting, Fiskars rotary cutter and cutting mat, Wrights jumbo rickrack, Coastal Buttons red, green, yellow and blue button assortment and Crafty Productions wooden ladybug and bumblebee buttons

Page 155: Tantalizing Tulips Bed Quilt—Tiffany Garden, Belle Fleur and Colors in Motion fabric collections from Springs Industries, Hobbs Heirloom Organic cotton batting, Sullivans Quilt Basting Spray, Pellon WonderUnder and Fiskars 45mm rotary cutter, mat and ruler